Great
Western
Heroes

Great Western Heroes

Seven True Stories of Men
Who Tamed the West

Edited by RAFER BRENT

BARTHOLOMEW HOUSE, INC.
New York

FIRST PRINTING

Library of Congress Catalog Card Number: 57-11978

MANUFACTURED IN THE UNITED STATES OF AMERICA
by Morry M. Gropper Associates, Inc.

Foreword

~~~~~~

There has been a lot of talk lately to the effect that the Western story is making a spectacular comeback. It certainly is true that there is an avid interest these days on the part of the American public in Western movies, television plays, books, and magazine features. But I can't go along with the argument that this proves the Western is making a comeback. As far as I'm concerned, at least, it has never been away.

Along with millions of other people, I have been reading Westerns since I was old enough to understand the words. I have been caught up in the special atmosphere of the Western scene and the special character of the Western hero. If there is anything different about the success of Western stories today, it is, in my opinion, simply that the writers and producers have caught on to the fact that there is no story as good as a true story, no hero as exciting to read about or as easy to identify yourself with as the hero who was a real person. My astonishment at the feats of these heroes, at the adventures they experienced, at the risks they took, and my admiration of their bravery is increased tenfold by the knowledge that these were real men who actually lived real lives.

As if, for that matter, anybody could invent a Buffalo Bill, a Wyatt Earp cleaning up the incredibly lawless town of Tombstone, or a Pat Garrett relentlessly stalking the deadly Billy the Kid. There are no heroes like Western heroes.

ED FITZGERALD
Editor-in-Chief
Saga Magazine

Contents

Rifle for Hire 9
  By John Gregor

The Three Lives of Bat Masterson 25
  By Clair Huffaker

Pat Garrett 50
  By Clair Huffaker

The Saga of Wyatt Earp 81
  By Jack Pearl

The Saga of Sam Bass 115
  By Clair Huffaker

Sheriff Slaughter of Tombstone 141
  By Edwin Johnson

The Saga of Buffalo Bill 162
  By Jack Pearl

Rifle for Hire

By John Gregor

〜〜〜〜〜〜〜〜〜〜〜〜〜〜〜〜〜〜〜〜〜〜〜〜〜〜〜〜〜〜〜〜

Hendry Brown won his reputation taming the toughest town on the border. But he was a born killer and he didn't care on which side of the law he was shooting

No one knew Hendry Brown when he rode into Caldwell, Kansas, on a stifling July afternoon in 1882. Caldwell was the cowboy capital that year, the drinking, gaming, killing, northern terminus of the Chisholm Trail. It was a tough town of violent men and bad women. An hour after he arrived, when they were betting that Brown would be dead by sunup, few even knew what he looked like.

"He's not such a big guy," said the florid-faced barkeep at the Texas House. "Packs two six-shooters and a rifle, but he didn't look so tough to me. Just another tinhorn."

A customer whispered confidentially, "I hear Sandy Jim is offering ten-to-one odds against this new deputy."

"Ten-to-one!" the bartender snorted. "It ought to be fifty-to-one. He'll be killed, just like them four others. Or was it five?"

"I lost track," said the customer. "Well, here's to tomorrow's funeral . . ."

Hizzoner, the mayor of Caldwell, had his fingers crossed about the new deputy marshal too. He probably wouldn't have hired the unimpressive stranger with no reputation except that it was obvious something had to be done if the gun-toters weren't going to shoot Caldwell right off the map. The town had been hardly more than a crossroads saloon, the First and Last Chance, on the edge of Indian Territory (now Oklahoma), until the Santa Fe tracks extended across the Kansas plains and reached it. Then Caldwell boomed. Frontier riff-raff flocked in to pluck the cattlemen who brought the big herds up from Texas for shipment east. Cattle barons and cowhands alike were full of pent-up emotion after the long, arduous, dangerous, trail drives. They wanted fast action and got it. Too much so after a while; gunplay and killings became nightly occurrences.

George W. Flatt was marshal until the strain made him a drunkard, and he was slain from ambush. Deputy Frank Hunt took over. He was waylaid in the Texas House, but took four badmen with him to Boot Hill. Mike Meagher was the third marshal. He lasted longer but was gunned down when the Jim Talbott gang took over the town. George S. Brown put on the star then and wore it until June 22, 1882, when two gunmen left him dead on the floor of the Red Light Dance Hall.

Bat Carr was marshal when Hendry Brown rode in that July. Unhappily, Carr spent his time drinking with the wild bunch, rather than trying to control them. Carr was willing to leave any law enforcement to his deputy, but that job had been long vacant until Brown braced the mayor. "I hear you're lookin' for a deputy," said Brown. "I know a man who'll take the job." ·

"Yeah?" The mayor was interested. "Who?"

"Me," said Brown.

"You!" Hizzoner was incredulous. It had to be a joke. This mild-looking young fellow was asking for the toughest law job on the border . . . The mayor almost laughed, but Brown tensed, and Hizzoner saw something deadly in the stranger's mirthless blue eyes. The mayor took a good long look at Hendry then. No great figure of a man, the mayor decided, but he sure had a jaw, like that of a pit bulldog. Besides the short-barreled .44 Winchester cradled over his left arm, Brown wore a revolver on each hip. Not many men packed two guns. Those who did were of two types—showoff punks headed for early graves or expert gunfighters. Brown didn't look like a showoff, but you never could tell. "We've had half a dozen lawmen killed," the mayor said.

"So I heard," said Brown.

"And you still want the job?"

"Yeah," Hendry said.

"What's your name?"

"Brown." Hendry hesitated. He was pretty sure no one in Caldwell knew him by sight. But in some places in the Southwest the name of Hendry Brown was too well-known. He decided to drop the "d." "Henry Brown," he said.

"All right." The mayor shrugged. Maybe this guy was tougher than he looked. Anyway, they'd soon find out. "You're hired. Report to Bat Carr. He's the marshal. But remember, it's your funeral."

"Maybe," Brown said, pinning on the five-pointed deputy's badge.

Hendry left the mayor and walked back to the Texas House. As he pushed through the swinging doors, a faro dealer glanced up and saw the star. A small sneer showed under his full mustache. He said something to the case-keeper and nodded toward Brown. By the time Brown reached the bar, every man in the sweltering room knew Caldwell had a new deputy—or a new target. The barkeep automatically plunked down a glass and reached for a bottle. But Brown shook his head. "I'm lookin' for the marshal," he said.

"He's over there in the corner," the bartender told him.

Marshal Bat Carr sat with a few barflies. He was well-oiled and had trouble focusing his red-rimmed eyes.

"Your name Carr?" Hendry asked.

"That's me. Marshal Bat Carr. What do you want?"

Hendry tapped the star on his vest. "I'm your new deputy."

"Huh?" squeaked Bat. "The hell you say! Who hired you?"

"The mayor," Hendry said. "Okay?"

"I guess so," Carr grunted. "You can go on duty at six o'clock tonight. But don't you come bothering me if you get in trouble. You're on your own."

"Okay," Hendry said.

"Well then, how about a drink?"

"Not me," Brown said. He turned a rude back on Carr and walked away. Some gunmen drank heavily to keep up their nerve; others, like Wyatt Earp, drank lightly or not at all. But not Hendry. A sober trigger-finger sometimes was all the edge a man had in a gunfight.

Brown rented a room and took in his gear—saddlebags, worn blanket roll and Winchester. He washed off the trail dust and sat down to clean his guns, waiting for his first night on the job. Meanwhile, the word that Caldwell had a new deputy flashed through the saloons and gambling houses, the honky-tonks and cribs. Sandy Jim, boss gunman and gambler, called some kindred killers together in the Golden Wedding Saloon. There were three of them, hardcases with notched gun-butts.

"Any of you ever hear of this new deputy?" Sandy Jim asked. "I'm laying bets against him. Life insurance in reverse, you might say." They all laughed. "Now, I don't want him around by tomorrow morning," Sandy Jim said. "Here's what I want you to do—"

Brown probably was the only man in Caldwell who didn't know of the betting against him. And if he had known, he wouldn't have given a damn.

The time and place of Brown's birth is unknown. He is generally believed to have been a Texan. In his early twenties he hunted buffalo with such men as Wyatt Earp, Bat Masterson, Jack Gallagher, Billy Dixon, Cheyenne Jack, Bermuda Carlisle, Old Man Keeler, Curly Walker, John W. Poe, Billy Tilghman, and Dutch Henry. These men owed their legendary skill with firearms to constant practice. On an average day, they killed twenty-five buffalo. Modern hunters seldom kill that many deer in a lifetime. The hide-men often shot 100 or more buffalo in a few hours from a good "stand." They learned to live by the gun—and most of them died by it.

Brown was one of the twenty-seven buffalo hunters at the Adobe Walls fight in 1874. Quanah Parker, half-breed Comanche war chief, led some 400—some say 1,000 —warriors against them. The hide-men had hard fighting for three days and were besieged for two weeks. But they won.

By the time the buffalo were gone, Brown was a man who killed to live—and who lived to kill. He rode with Billy the Kid in New Mexico's Lincoln County war. They were paid gunhands of the McSween-Chisum faction in the bloody struggle with the Murphy-Dolan gunmen for control of the Pecos River ranges. Brown savored danger as an exhilarating companion. He fought in all the little skirmishes and in the last big battle when seventy Murphy-Dolan gunfighters pinned his gang in the Mc-Sween home for three days. Brown and Billy the Kid were among the few who shot their way out after the house had been set on fire.

Everything had been legal, for those days, until they lost that fight. After that, the Kid's remaining men were "on the dodge." Brown liked it. Outlawry had a dark attraction for him. He still lived by his rifle. But as time went on he began to want steady pay as well and the power that a marshal like Wild Bill Hickok had in Abilene.

Brown cut loose from the Kid's wild bunch late in 1878 when they drove a herd of stolen horses into Tascosa in the Texas Panhandle. When the Kid rode back to New Mexico and death, Brown stayed behind—as Tascosa's first constable.

Hiring a killer to ride herd on killers was a common practice in the early West. Brown was a good constable, but he was so feared that no Panhandle gunslinger would tangle with him. Brown got bored. When he heard about hell-roaring Caldwell, Brown headed north.

At six on the dot, Hendry strolled out of the Texas House. He left the Winchester behind, regretfully, because the rifle was his favorite weapon. But frontier protocol demanded that he rely this night on the two Colt peacemakers in their tied-down holsters. Whisky Row blazed with lights. Cowpunchers, bluecoated cavalrymen, bull-whackers, mule-skinners, railroaders, gawking tenderfeet, tinhorns, and gunmen elbowed their way in and out of bars where no-limit games operated twenty-four hours daily. As Hendry started down Main Street, a lookout posted by Sandy Jim passed the word along to the Golden Wedding: "He's coming."

"Good," said Sandy Jim. He would make a killing this night in more ways than one. He turned to his three gunhands: "All right. Let's give this guy a welcome he won't forget."

Brown walked by "Lengthy John's" blacksmith shop and Hubble's General Store. He ignored the obscene invitations of the bare-shouldered sporting girls leaning out of the second-story windows of the Red Light Dance Hall. He heard the professor switch from a dance tune to a derisive, honky-tonk piano version of *O Bury Me Not on the Lone Prairie*. Then he was opposite the Golden Wedding. Inside, one gunhand started yelling as if he was just a drunken cowhand. "Yoweee!" The gunhand sent three shots crashing into the smoke-shrouded ceiling. It was an old ruse, and other lawmen, now dead, had rushed in to arrest fake drunks, leaving their backs exposed to deadly crossfire.

Brown went in fast, but not with the bullheaded rush of a stampeding buffalo. He had his back against the wall before the batwing doors stopped swinging. The fake drunk fired three more shots into the ceiling to draw him on. But Brown's quick glance saw how the crowd was jammed against the bar and along the far wall, leaving clear lanes of fire. And he saw two other toughs going for their guns. He beat them to it. His peacemakers were out and firing first. When the shooting stopped, the two men lay dead in the grimy sawdust. Brown stepped up and pistolwhipped the first gunhand, whose gun was empty, and then stared at Sandy Jim. "That'll be all now," Brown said. "But I'll be around."

Instead of one funeral, with Hendry Brown as the guest of honor, Caldwell had two the next day. Then Sandy Jim summoned Marshal Bat Carr to the Golden Wedding, gave him a free drink, and got down to cases. "Bat," Sandy Jim said, "I want you to fire Brown."

"Uh-uh," squeaked Carr. "Not me."

"You'd better," Sandy Jim said, "unless you want to make that ride up to Boot Hill yourself. Brown's got to go before he ruins the whole setup."

"I'll try," Carr said. He downed another drink with a shaky hand and shambled down the street to the jail office. Brown was happily cleaning his guns and humming a tune about "Billy, Billy the Kid . . ."

Well fortified by whisky, Carr summoned the last of his courage. "Brown," he squeaked, "you're fired."

"You got that wrong, Bat," Brown said. "You're the one that's fired." He reached across the desk and yanked off the marshal's star. "Okay?" he asked, toying with one of his six-guns.

"I guess so," Carr mumbled. "I was thinking of leavin' town anyway."

"So long," Hendry said.

The mayor and the town council quickly approved Brown's self-promotion from deputy to marshal. Caldwell knew an unaccustomed but uneasy peace for several days while Hendry made his rounds, as confident as a sawed-off shotgun loaded with buckshot.

Then a traveling minstrel show arrived on the Santa Fe. The performers were scheduled to parade to the Opera House before their first show, each performer wearing a tall silk hat.

"We'll have a regular shooting match," Sandy Jim decided happily. "Every gent chip in five bucks, and the pot goes to the one who hits the most hats."

The mayor didn't like the idea at all. All that lead zinging around Main Street . . . the windows that would be broken, not to mention innocent bystanders . . . Hizzoner buttonholed the manager of the show. "You'll have to call off the parade," he said and explained the forthcoming jamboree.

"You're right," the sweating manager agreed. "I'll call it off."

"No you won't." Marshal Hendry Brown brushed Hizzoner aside and addressed the manager. "Get that parade going," he commanded. "Lots of folks want to see it and they're going to."

"But, Brown, we can't let this go on," the mayor protested.

"Forget it," Brown said. "I'll handle it."

Horns blared, drums boomed, and the minstrel men marched. Marshal Brown cut through an alley to the Golden Wedding. All eyes were on the street in anticipation. No one noticed Hendry as he took a position near Sandy Jim. The first plug hat came bobbing by. Sandy Jim fired his gun and the hat sailed off. At the same time, Brown drew his gun and fired. The slug spattered dust over Sandy Jim's polished boots. "Dance," Hendry said.

Sandy Jim started prancing. "You call that dancing?" Brown demanded coldly. "Faster."

Sandy Jim danced until the sweat ran down his pale face. "You're lousy," Brown decided. "Try running."

Sandy Jim ran. Brown's gun roared, and the gambler sprawled dead in the street. Brown had a gun in each hand now, threatening Sandy Jim's dumbfounded pals. "He was resisting arrest," Hendry said.

Brown got away with it. The mayor and the town council were pleased. Now they had a tough town-tamer for marshal. If he fractured the law while enforcing it, they didn't care just as long as he was shooting it out with known badmen, and no peace-loving citizens got hurt in the process.

Then one of Brown's friends from New Mexico, Ben Wheeler, drifted into Caldwell. Brown convinced the council that he needed a deputy and Wheeler was hired. Wheeler was a huge man, with a body as large as his brain was small. He made the perfect foil for the hair-trigger Hendry.

Caldwell had an anti-gun ordinance. All weapons were supposed to be checked while a man was in town. Brown and Wheeler started enforcing it rigidly. Several gunmen were killed in the process, but they should have known better than to argue with Marshal Hendry Brown.

Morton Boyce, a faro dealer, was one who should have known better, for instance. He had been a drinking companion of the late Sandy Jim. Boyce went on a spree one night, and Deputy Ben Wheeler had to cuff him about and lock him up. Boyce was too full of 40-rod for his own good. He cussed out Caldwell, the town council, the mayor, and especially Hendry Brown. Wheeler told Brown about it, and the next morning Boyce was dead, five rifle slugs in his body. "He tried to escape," Brown said.

The coroner accepted the explanation, but there was a lot of angry talk around the Golden Wedding, the Texas House, the Red Light, and other Whisky Row joints. Gamblers and dance hall girls claimed that Hendry had told Wheeler to turn Boyce loose. Brown had waited in the shadows with his Winchester. When Boyce stepped out of the cell, Hendry shot him down.

The talk didn't faze Brown. He was fast making a reputation as one of the great marshals of the West. For proof, he had a gold-mounted Winchester, the gift of a grateful town council. The rifle was the finest ever seen in Caldwell, and Brown spent hours cleaning and fondling it.

But there was sour talk in the barrooms about that, too. Some soreheads insisted that the council had been bulldozed into presenting the rifle to the marshal in appreciation of his services. Their story was that the city fathers finally were beginning to fear Marshal Brown, with his shoot-first, talk-later methods. The council met to consider how Brown and Wheeler could be fired—safely. But the pair got wind of the meeting and stalked in. "Heard you wanted to fire me," Brown said.

"Oh, no!" the mayor protested. He had a sudden inspiration as he looked at Brown's guns. "No, indeed. We were just thinking we'd give you a new rifle."

"That'd be mighty nice," Brown said.

"I so move," said Hizzoner. The "ayes" from the rest of the councilmen came faster than bullets from a Gatling gun.

When Hendry put the lid on Caldwell, though, it stayed on. No more killings occurred after his first month as marshal. Caldwell became known as the "Queen City of the Border." After a while, the town was too tame for Brown. He became surly, harder to get along with than ever. With his split personality, he supported the law when doing so gave him the shooting satisfaction his nature craved. But essentially the only law he recognized was that of the fast gun. When he couldn't satisfy his murderous instinct lawfully, he was willing to move to the other side.

One day late in April, 1884, Brown and Wheeler sat in the marshal's office swapping yarns about the good old days in New Mexico. Hendry, as usual, was cleaning his gold-mounted Winchester. "Ben," he said, "how'd you like to make a little trip to Medicine Lodge?"

"What for, Hendry?"

"There's a bank there. We're going to bust it."

"Aw, Hendry, we're sitting pretty here. What do you want to go robbin' a bank for?"

Brown couldn't have told him the real reason, even if he had known it himself—that he was just spoiling for excitement. But he knew how to arouse Wheeler's interest. "That bank's bulging with money," he said. "We can take it easy. Once we're back here, who's going to suspect us? We're the law, aren't we?"

"Sure, Hendry. I could use some dough. But two of us ain't enough for a bank job."

"I already thought of that," Brown snapped. "There's a couple of good boys working for the T5 Ranch over on the Eagle Chief. We'll get them."

Brown and Wheeler, fully armed, rode south out of Caldwell on April 30, 1884. Hendry had his gold-mounted Winchester in a scabbard on his saddle.

"Where you going, Marshal?" asked a saloon lounger.

"Down to the Cherokee Outlet to scout for horse thieves," replied Brown.

Once out of sight, they circled over to the T5 range. Brown made his proposition to Billie Smith and John Wesley. Smith was just a youth, but Wesley had ridden outlaw trails before. "Sure," they said. "Glad to go along."

Brown led his three men into Medicine Lodge, a cow-town about sixty miles west of Caldwell, early on May 1, 1884. They rode through a drizzling rain that gave no signs of easing. Hendry was pleased. Rain kept people off the streets. It did, all right. Some fifty cowmen were in the livery barn. A roundup was scheduled for that

morning on Antelope Flat. The cowmen had their horses
saddled and were ready to ride as soon as the rain cleared.
But what Hendry couldn't know didn't bother him. There
was the Medicine Lodge Bank up ahead now. They'd be
in and out as slick as a whistle. He and Wheeler and
Wesley dismounted and tossed their reins to Billie Smith.

"Keep them horses quiet now, kid," said Brown.

He loosened his Colts in their holsters and headed for
the bank. A few strides in the muddy street and then up
on the plank sidewalk. Hendry drew his revolvers and
pushed through the door. Wheeler and Wesley were right
at his heels with drawn guns. There were only two men
in the bank. "Stick 'em up!" Brown commanded. He had
the drop on E. Wylie Payne, the bank president.

Wheeler leveled his gun at George Geppert, the
cashier, whose hands rose quickly into the air. Wesley
backed up Wheeler and kept a wary eye on the door.

Payne was a square-jawed man who had started from
nothing and fought his way up to become a big cattleman
as well as the bank president. He was no coward, and
no man ever buffaloed him. Payne had a revolver in his
open desk drawer. He grabbed for it. Brown shot. The
.45-caliber bullet drilled through Payne, breaking his
spine. He sagged back in his chair.

Hulking Ben Wheeler lost his head and shot the
cashier. The dying Geppert staggered to the vault, twisted
the knob that locked it, and then slumped to the floor
dead.

Barney O'Connor was the marshal of Medicine Lodge.
He was new on the job and had never been in a gunfight.
But he came running when he heard the shooting. He
fired at Smith. The kid shot back. But the horses were
bucking, and Smith scored no hits. Neither did O'Connor.

Inside the bank, Wheeler held a sack while Brown
and Wesley filled it with loose coin. Wheeler panicked
again when he heard the shooting outside. He dropped

the sack and his gun and ran out. Wesley followed him. Hendry cursed. "Come back here, you chicken-livered bastards!"

It was no use, and he couldn't stay in the bank alone. He ran out, too.

Smith still held the horses. Bullets crackled down the street now as the cowmen piled out of the livery stable and started shooting. Brown, Wheeler, and Wesley mounted their rearing horses. Brown yanked the Winchester out of its scabbard. Fast shots drove O'Connor to cover and temporarily cleared the street of the cattlemen. "Let's go!" Hendry shouted.

They galloped out of town. O'Connor and the cowmen were riding hard after them in minutes. The steady rain was no longer a friend for Brown, but a foe. Mud slowed their horses, and they couldn't shake the posse. Wheeler's horse bogged down in quicksand at the Medicine River ford. He abandoned the animal and mounted behind Billie Smith. That slowed them up still more. The horse with the double load struggled heavily through the mud. From the posse behind came occasional long-range shots that plunked wild. They were in the Gypsum Hills now, strange country. Hendry led them into a likely looking canyon. Their horses were blown when they discovered the canyon ended in precipitous cliffs, impassable for horse and man.

Rifle in hand, Brown swung off his jaded mount and faced the canyon entrance as the first horsemen of the posse came pounding into sight. They were dim figures in the streaming rain. Brown fired, scoring no hits but halting their advance. "Get off them horses," he told his three pals. "We'll fort up behind these rocks and hold 'em off."

He bellied down behind a boulder. Wesley and Smith got on either side, while Wheeler hung back with the horses. Rain poured down on their backs, and a regular waterfall cascaded down the canyon walls. The possemen dismounted too and began working their way up the canyon, dodging from cover to cover. Bullets whistled overhead or ricocheted from the rocks. Brown and Smith shot slowly and coolly. Wesley banged away excitedly. Neither side hit anything. The rain cut down visibility too much for good shooting. "If you can't see 'em, you can't hit 'em," Brown thought sourly.

"We'll never get out of this," Wesley whimpered. His teeth chattered from cold and fear.

"Take it easy," Brown said. "I've got out of worse spots than this one."

"Yeah. We'll make it," Smith said. Brown thought the kid was the best man he had with him.

The possemen kept closing in. It was like a noose tightening slowly around their necks. They gave ground, retreating farther back in the box canyon. By mid-afternoon, they had been forced back to the end of the canyon. There was a slight depression in the ground there. It filled with icy water until they were standing in it up to their hips.

"I'm out of cartridges," Wesley said. "We better quit before they kill us."

"Yeah, Hendry," Wheeler said. "We'll drown here if we don't."

Brown had only a few cartridges left. Smith was almost out of ammunition too. Brown looked at the kid shivering from the cold. "How about it?" Brown asked.

"Let's quit," Smith said. He wasn't as frightened as Wheeler and Wesley, but there was no more fight left in him.

Brown drew a sodden handkerchief from his hip pocket. With numb fingers, he tied it to the muzzle of his gold-mounted Winchester. He stuck it up in the air and waved it slowly.

The shackled gunmen were brought into Medicine Lodge at sundown and locked in a cottonwood shack that served as a jail. Payne, the bank president, still was alive, but he was sinking. He didn't complain about himself, but he said he was sorry his actions had caused the death of his cashier.

Knots of angry but ominously quiet men gathered in the street. Hendry knew what that meant—a lynch mob. The county attorney entered the crackerbox jail. He wanted statements from the prisoners. "I'll give you $1,000," Brown said, "if you keep us alive until daybreak."

"It's my duty to protect you from any mob," the attorney said. "But if Payne dies, nothing can save you."

And Payne died during the first hours of dark. The mob grew larger, more excited, and at ten o'clock it filled the street and closed in on the flimsy jail. One grim vigilante busily tied a hangman's noose in each of four ropes. The county sheriff and a few deputies gathered before the jail door.

Brown, Wheeler, Wesley, and Smith struggled with their shackles. Somehow they got loose as guns sounded in the street. Hendry could see from the flashes that all the shots were going in the air. The sheriff and his men were making just token resistance. The mob surged forward and shoved the lawmen aside. Two husky cowmen crashed against the door. It burst from its hinges and fell inward as Brown shouted to Wheeler: "Get 'em, Ben! Fight!"

Big Ben Wheeler rushed the first vigilantes at the door. His huge, desperate hands knocked them aside. Brown dashed through the opening. He ran almost a block before a farmer got him in the sights of a shotgun. Two loads of buckshot left Hendry dead in the mud.

Wheeler followed his idol through the door. A vigilante shot the big man in the arm. He was so close that the muzzle blast from the .45 set Wheeler's shirt on fire. More guns roared, but the wounded Wheeler still managed to run a full 300 yards before he was recaptured.

Wesley and Smith made no resistance. The mob took the three to the bottomlands near Medicine Lodge. Three ropes were thrown over the stout limb of a large elm tree. Wheeler and Wesley pleaded to be spared. But young Billie Smith said, "Go ahead and pull when you're ready."

The coroner held an inquest the next day. After brief deliberation, the jury decided that Hendry Brown, Ben Wheeler, John Wesley, and William Smith met their deaths at the hands of persons unknown. Several days later, the Caldwell town council, donor of Hendry's gold-mounted Winchester, unanimously approved a resolution commending the Medicine Lodge vigilantes for, among other things, shooting the man whose rifle Caldwell had hired.

The Three Lives of Bat Masterson

By Clair Huffaker

~~~~~~

Bat was the kind of a man who could do most anything he set his mind to—gunning down buffalo or outlaws, gambling, fighting, or writing a column for a newspaper.

It was summer in Dodge City, Kansas, biggest boom town and railroad junction in the Far West. Into the shouting, teeming crowds swarming along Front Street, one June morning in 1872, rode young Bill Masterson, an ancient muzzle-loading long-gun crossed on the saddle before him. A handsome six-footer with a high forehead and large alert eyes, he attracted more attention than most strangers in town. Josiah Wright Mooar, an old-time buffalo hunter, was particularly impressed with the way he sat his horse and held his gun. Mooar, who was trying to fill out a buffalo-hunting crew, walked over to the kid as he swung down from the saddle. "Son, you lookin' for a job?"

"What kind of a job?"

"Buffalo crew. Skinnin' or stackin'. Top pay. You can make maybe $100 a month."

"I'm your man. My name's Bill Masterson."

"I'm Joe Mooar."

They shook hands on the deal and two days later moved out of Dodge with fresh supplies and a full crew.

Bill soon learned the buffalo-hunting business. He

worked a short while as a stacker, spreading the hides
taken from the day's kill out flat over an acre or two of
prairie. The hides weighed about 300 pounds apiece, and
they had to be dried a full day on each side under the
blazing sun. When the sun had done its work, the hides
weighed about one-third of their original weight and were
almost as hard and stiff as cast iron. They were then ready
to be stacked into carts and hauled back to the railroad
station at Dodge for shipment to the East.

Masterson quickly moved from stacking to skinning,
and, eventually, when someone in camp discovered he
was a dead shot, to the top of the trade, which was
hunting.

Most men consider themselves lucky if they can make
a go of one career. Bat Masterson took on three and was
successful in all of them; he was a buffalo hunter, a gunman and gambler, and, finally, an editor on a famous
New York newspaper. He was unbelievably fast and accurate with a gun, he was intelligent, and he was cou-
rageous. He was one of those rare people who can do
most anything they set their minds to, and do it well.

His full name was William Barclay Masterson. The
nickname "Bat" came along later when he served as a
deputy under Wyatt Earp in Dodge City. As a boy, he
helped work the family farm in Iroquois County, Illinois,
along with his father and his brothers Ed, Jim, and Tom.
Then at sixteen, he decided that farming was not for him.
He wanted excitement. Always appreciative of a good
editorial phrase, he followed Horace Greeley's dictum:
"Go West, young man . . ."

With his Sharps "Big 50," Masterson soon made a
name for himself as top hunter in Joe Mooar's crew.
"There was absolutely no danger," he later wrote of his
buffalo-hunting experiences. "It was on a par with shooting cows in a pasture, except on occasion, when an injured
bull would charge a hunter. You did have to know some-

thing about buffalo, though, to do the job right. A good hunter shot to hit the buffalo's brain. Hit properly in the head, the animal would fall within a few feet of where he was shot. If you hit him in the heart, he could run four or five hundred feet before going down, and that might set the rest of the herd running too."

Joe Mooar liked a rough, tough crew under him. It was his one sure way of protecting himself from the bully-boys who made a profession of stealing hides from the honest hunters. Indeed, many of Mooar's men were convicts themselves. These assorted murderers and thieves were, for the most part, belligerently loyal to Joe. But once, a fellow named Jason Cook tried to sell Joe and his friends out. Jason wandered out of camp one night, just before the crew was about to head back to Dodge with the buffalo hides. Most of the boys, exhausted from a grinding week's work, were sleeping soundly, but Bill Masterson, a light sleeper, woke up as Jason was moving out of the light of the campfire. He became suspicious and pulled on his boots and followed the man.

Half a mile out of camp, Jason joined a gang of waiting confederates who had carts all ready to pick up the valuable skins. Ten minutes later, as they were starting their highjacking operation, Bill Masterson's clear voice came firmly through the night. "We've got you surrounded. First man that moves, dies."

It's likely he would have kept them surrounded too, all by himself, except that Jason panicked and made a break through the silver moonlight playing down on the scene. When he ran, the others scattered too. Masterson fired his "Big 50" just once. A few minutes later Mooar and the others joined him. The only trace of the crooks was a stream of Jason's blood trailing off to the east. They all got away, but Mooar was satisfied; his hides were safe.

"Any man who can surround a whole gang with a

single-shot rifle is a good man to have next to you in a gun fight," he said.

The truth of that statement was demonstrated when Masterson and eight other people held off some 300 Arapahoe and Cheyenne Indians for twenty-one days at the Battle of Adobe Walls.

Adobe Walls was a trading depot consisting of several small buildings and corrals. Joe and his brother, John Mooar, left Masterson and the rest of the crew there while they went back to Dodge for supplies.

Among those staying at Adobe Walls were: Jim Hanrahan, the owner of Hanrahan's Saloon; Tom O'Keefe, a blacksmith; Bill Olds and his wife, who ran the small restaurant there; and completing the list, Bill Masterson, Billy Tyler, and a few more buffalo hunters.

The big Indian war party that swooped down upon the buffalo range was as well organized as it was swift. Two camps of hunters were wiped out before they could fire a defending shot.

Adobe Walls was sleeping peacefully at two o'clock in the morning, unaware of the onrushing redskin juggernaut. Then something happened that has not been explained to this day. There was a loud, cracking noise from the ridgepole supporting the roof in Hanrahan's Saloon, the largest and most solid building in Adobe Walls. Instantly, the men sleeping there woke up. Masterson lit a lamp, and they examined the ridgepole, a thick beam about two feet in diameter. To their surprise, they found it was as solid as ever. They could think of no reason why it should have snapped.

The men scratched their heads, and Hanrahan poured a drink around as they started talking it over. It was getting on toward morning anyway, and there was no real point in their going back to bed.

Whatever the noise was, it saved their lives. They were

wide awake half an hour later, when the Indians silently surrounded the camp and prepared to take it by surprise. Masterson's keen ears picked up the sound of unshod horses moving over rock, and he went outside to investigate. He saw the savages advancing over the crest of a nearby hill and ran back into Hanrahan's to give the alarm. "Get your guns," he said. "Trouble coming."

When the Indians swarmed into Adobe Walls, they found they had grabbed a mountain lion by the tail. Masterson assembled everyone in the saloon, and under his leadership the handful of men made a formidable fighting force.

The whites had every available gun loaded and ready for action; the trading post had practically unlimited guns and ammunition. Each man would fire one gun, drop it, and pick up another, repeating the maneuver about ten times.

The warriors screamed past Hanrahan's, pouring arrows and lead slugs into the building. With Masterson's "Big 50" setting the beat, a mighty chorus of firearms answered them. Thinking that there were at least 100 men inside the building, the redskins retired to think the whole thing over.

Masterson knew that a war party as large as this one must have attracted considerable attention on its way to Adobe Walls. "All we have to do," he told the others, "is sit tight until help comes. It's bound to get here sooner or later."

"Maybe not," Billy Tyler grumbled. "Maybe nobody knows the spot we're in."

At daylight the Indians made another rush upon the small, determined saloon-fortress. Hanrahan was a miserable marksman, so he made himself useful by serving up drinks to the others as they blasted gaping holes in the enemy lines.

Masterson kept the consumption of alcohol down to a point where the men could feel a glow, but their eyes and trigger fingers were as steady as ever. Probably no warriors were ever jollier at the height of a battle. In attack after attack, 300 crazed savages charged, only to be repulsed each time. Everybody was feeling pretty good, except Tyler. The liquor wasn't helping him.

As evening came, he complained, "I'm not goin' to stay here and get myself killed! I'm gonna make a break for it!"

"Calm down," Masterson said. "Joe Mooar will be coming back this way soon, even if no one else does. And Joe'll head back for Dodge to get help."

"Joe may walk right into 'em! He may be dead already!"

"You don't know Joe," Masterson grinned.

Tyler couldn't let well enough alone. A few minutes later when no one was watching him, he pulled down a barricade and leaped through a window. He'd gone about fifty feet when a slug from an Indian rifle went through his neck and dropped him. A couple of braves crept up through the evening shadows to collect his scalp. At the same time, Bill Masterson charged through the saloon door.

Masterson and the Indians reached Tyler at the same time. In the saloon, they were afraid to shoot for fear of hitting Bill, but as it turned out, he didn't need their help anyway. Shooting his "Big 50" from the hip, at a dead run, he cut one Cheyenne nearly in half. As the other warrior started to raise his gun, Masterson was on him, swinging the "Big 50's" cannon-sized barrel. It collided with the redskin's head, and he went down as though his legs had been blown out from under him. Masterson tossed Tyler over his shoulder and ran for Hanrahan's as half a dozen Cheyennes on horseback thundered over the hill to run him down. He plunged through the door to safety as his friends picked off three of his pursuers. But after all this trouble, poor little Billy Tyler was dead. He was the only one who was killed in the siege.

It was three weeks before government troops arrived to rescue the men trapped at Adobe Walls. At the rate the fighting was going, if the U.S. army had delayed much longer, the Indians would have been completely wiped out.

From the troops who frightened the war party back into the hills Masterson learned that the marauding Indians had been responsible for several raw atrocities in the neighborhood. Five women had been taken captive by a band of braves after their men had been killed. They had all been assaulted, and two of them had been roasted over a slow fire. One of the women had all of her hair pulled out, handful by handful.

While the rest of his friends went back to Dodge, Masterson joined General Nelson A. Miles as an Army scout under Lieutenant Baldwin.

During the period that he served as a scout, he picked up an interest in books from the officers with whom he associated. He read everything they could supply him with: drilling manuals, the Bible, the biographies of Julius Caesar, and the plays of William Shakespeare. His schooling on the farm back in Illinois had been limited, but now he found a new teacher in every book he came across. Lieutenant Baldwin recognized that his unusual young scout had an alert and intelligent mind and encouraged his appreciation of reading and writing. It was his help and encouragement that shaped Bill's future career.

Masterson served with distinction at the Battle of Red River. From then on, the Indian threat in the territory became less and less through the years.

About this time, Masterson met a young man he'd known briefly as a buffalo hunter; a slim fellow with sandy-blond hair, piercing eyes, and a firm, quiet voice.

His name was Wyatt Earp. They liked each other right
away. Earp was just making his mark in the territory as
a lawman. He'd been sheriffing at Newton with considerable success, and he told Masterson that a job as
deputy was waiting for him any time he wanted to quit
scouting.

Later that year, Masterson moved on to Sweetwater,
Texas, still serving as a civilian scout. Here he met the
one girl he truly loved, and, through his whole career in
the West, he never loved another.

Bill was having a drink with some army friends in
the Blue Ox Dance Hall in Sweetwater when he saw a
pretty blonde across the room. He looked at her and she
looked at him, and things looked pretty good to both of
them. She didn't have the familiar come-hither commer-
cial gleam in her eyes.

They got to talking. Her name was Alice, and she was
a dance-hall girl; no more, no less. She didn't frequent
the rooms on the second floor at the drop of a dollar. She
dressed prettily, came to the hall and danced with the
boys, drank with them sometimes, and then went home
alone. Within a few days Bill and Alice were in love.

If everything had gone right, Masterson might have
disappeared from the history books. He might have married, settled down, and lived quietly ever after. But fate
was as fickle and cruel those days as it is now, and things
didn't go right. A cavalry sergeant named King had his
heart set on Alice.

One night Bill and his sweetheart were dancing together when King plunged into the room, a six-gun in
each hand.

Alice, looking over Bill's shoulder, saw King come in.
"Look out, Bill!" she screamed and whirled so that her
body was shielding Masterson.

King cut loose with both .45's as Alice spun into the
line of fire. Masterson shoved her aside and whipped his
revolver out of its holster. His first slug killed King. In-

stantly he dropped to his knees beside Alice. She was dead. King had got off one well-aimed shot.

"Say, Masterson," someone whispered after a moment. "You better look to yourself or you'll bleed to death."

The bullet that had killed Alice had been deflected and had hit him high up in the thigh. It was only a flesh wound, but it was bleeding badly.

It had all happened so fast, Bill couldn't quite believe it for a while. When full realization of the tragedy struck him, he stood and limped out the door.

A few days later, Masterson rode into Dodge City and looked up his brother Jim, who had moved there a few months earlier. His leg wound was healing, but it still caused him to limp, and he had to walk with a cane.

"What are you going to do now?" Jim asked.

"I don't know. Haven't thought much about it."

"Wyatt Earp just took over as marshal," Jim said. "He's offered me a deputy badge. I know damned well he'd give you a job."

Bill shook his head. "Not with a game leg."

As soon as Jim told Wyatt that Bill was in town, Wyatt hurried over to see him. "Even crippled I'd rather have you for a deputy than anyone else I know," Earp growled. He hauled a badge out of his pocket. "Pin this on. You're enforcing the law in Dodge City with me as of now."

Before the day was out, two cowboys saw Bill Masterson limping down Front Street, his new badge pinned onto his shirt.

"Dodge must be hard up for policemen," the first one remarked loudly. "Now they're hiring 'em with one leg."

"You know why that is," the other said. "If they had two legs, they could run away and hide."

"That ain't it at all," the first laughed. "Truth is, if they're half dead in the first place, the city don't lose so much when they're killed." He drew his gun and fired at the ground near Bill.

"Are you two gentlemen finished?" Masterson asked

quietly. "Because if you are, I'm running you in for disturbing the peace."

The two cowboys had just started to roar with laughter when Bill flattened them with his cane.

A third puncher rushed out of the adjacent saloon to revenge his fallen pals by shooting the new deputy sheriff "between the eyes." His six-gun had not cleared leather when Bill Masterson's cane creased the side of his head.

"Holy jumpin' hell!" an old bullwhacker mumbled. "Did you see the way he wuz battin' them around?"

"Yeah," his drinking partner agreed in a properly subdued voice. "He's better with that bat than most men are with a revolver."

Thus did Bill Masterson become "Bat" Masterson. By the time his leg had healed and he'd thrown away his cane, the honorary title had caught on, and he was never known as anything else for the rest of his life. Roughly three dozen craniums were thoroughly dented by Bat's cane in his debut as a peace officer. Indeed, there are those who claim Dodge City heaved a sigh of relief when he tossed away his bat and moved through the streets of Dodge with only his Colts at his hips.

Dodge City passed the most peaceful and law-abiding summer in its short, hectic life that year of '76. Wyatt and Bat knew that it was impossible to stop all the rough stuff. Dodge was the terminal of the cattle drives, where the Texas cowhands were paid off after being on the range for as long as six months at a stretch; it was the headquarters of the buffalo hunters; it was the nearest town the soldiers from Fort Dodge could come to for excitement and high times. There were bound to be ruckuses. So they set a deadline at the railroad. South of the deadline, where the redlight district and the tough dives were located, a man could raise hell pretty much as he pleased. North of the deadline, no man could carry a weapon, and even disturbing the peace with a loud warwhoop might mean

a night in jail. It was a sensible arrangement, but the wild
element in Dodge resented it. The Texans, in particular,
felt they needed more elbow room to carry on, come payday. But since none of them wanted to tackle Bat or
Wyatt personally, a few well-to-do ranchers kicked in to
import Clay Allison for the job.

The morning Clay rode into town, he already had some
eighteen or twenty killings behind him. Wyatt got the
news of his arrival just before breakfast. He and Bat discussed it in the hotel restaurant over their coffee.

"You need some backing," Bat said.

"No. I'll have to see Allison alone," Wyatt disagreed
as he lit a cigar.

"I don't mean that. I mean he's going to have friends
backing his play. I'll just even things up."

Bat crossed Front Street a few minutes later and wandered up toward Second Avenue.

Wyatt came onto the street straightening his big black
hat. He was about half-way to the Second Avenue inter-
section when Clay Allison stepped out of a doorway and
approached him. Within five seconds, the street was
cleared of traffic.

"You Wyatt Earp?" the hired gunman demanded.

"I'm Wyatt Earp."

At this point Allison seemed to have very little left to
say. He glanced nervously up and down the street, trying
to keep his eyes on Wyatt at the same time. Finally he
muttered something about Earp's having killed a soldier
who was a friend of his. Although this was not true, Wyatt
said simply, "What business is it of yours if I did?"

Allison, at last, backed down completely, aware that
from his point of view the whole affair was a miserable
fiasco. He got on his horse and rode slowly toward the
outskirts of town. He turned once and rode back toward

Earp. Then he brought his pony to a sliding halt in front
of Wright & Beverly's store. "You dirty bastards were
supposed to back me up!" he yelled. He wheeled his horse
and galloped out of Dodge.

A group of Texans gathered behind the window of
Wright & Beverly's hung their heads sheepishly. Across
the street, leaning casually against a wall, was Bat Masterson.

After an interlude of several relatively peaceful
months, Bat, his brother Jim, and Wyatt decided that
being peace officers in Dodge was becoming a bit of a
bore. Wyatt went to Texas, and Bat and Jim stayed on in
Dodge as gamblers. In the meantime, Bat's older brother
Ed had moved west and wanted to try his hand at wearing
a badge. By June of '77, Bat was a highly successful gambler and had maneuvered his brother Ed into the post
of assistant marshal. The marshal, a giant of a man named
Larry Deger, was all muscle and no brain, and Dodge had
deteriorated into as tough a town as it had ever been.

One morning, a little fellow named Bobby Gilmore
was standing in front of Fred Zimmerman's General Store
and telling a few friends how he wished the good old days
of peace and quiet would come back. Marshal Deger over-
heard Bobby's remarks and told him to shut up.

"I will not," Bobby said. "I'm an American. I can say
what I want."

Bat wandered up as Deger grabbed Gilmore by the
neck and threw him into the dusty street. The marshal
kicked the little man when he tried to get to his feet and
vowed that he was going to put him in jail after he had
roughed him up.

"You aren't going to rough him up or put him in jail,"
Bat said. "Leave him alone."

"Who's gonna make me?" Deger bellowed. He was
drawing back his right foot for another kick at the pros-
trate Gilmore when Bat kicked his left leg out from

under him. The big man was up again instantly, roaring with rage. Bat knocked him down twice before a bunch of Deger's friends piled onto him. Seven men had to fight every inch of the way to get Bat to jail, but they finally succeeded.

Bat was fined $25 and costs. When the City Council next convened, however, it remitted Bat's fine and apologized to him publicly for the miscarriage of justice.

In any case, Bat decided it was time to start wearing a badge again. He promptly ran for sheriff of Ford County and won handily. Since Dodge was the county seat of Ford County, Bat spent most of his time there. Deger, who had more prudence than valor, spent the rest of his term in office as marshal of Dodge City muttering quietly into his shot glass at his favorite bar.

It is to Bat's credit that he almost always made arrests without having to resort to gunplay. But the time was coming when he would have to use his guns in the most famous—and infamous—gun battle in Dodge City's history.

Ed Masterson's first shooting scrape as assistant marshal of Dodge City led indirectly to the later and deadlier gunplay. His first call to pull a gun came one night when Texas Dick Moore and Bob Shaw got into an argument at the Lone Star. Bob yelled loud and clear that Texas Dick had cheated him of $40.

"Talk like that'll get you a slug in the guts," Dick warned.

"I'll say it again," Bob shouted. "You cheated me out of $40!"

Ed entered the Lone Star just as Bob Shaw had pulled his hogleg and was about to bombard poor Texas Dick.

"Put up that gun!" Ed commanded sharply.

"Keep out of this!" Bob snarled.

Shaw then began blasting at Dick, who was heading toward an exit.

At this point, Ed clouted Bob behind the ear with the barrel of his Colt, as was fitting and proper. But he clouted Bob too tenderly. Instead of flooring the badman, it merely irritated him. He turned and shot Ed in the chest. Ed dropped, flipping his gun from right to left hand as he fell, and shot Bob through the arm and leg. Wounded as he was, Ed held out until help came. They found him covering Shaw and several of the gunman's friends. As soon as his fellow officers arrived to take over, Ed passed out cold from shock and loss of blood.

When he came to, Bat was leaning over him. "You'll be all right, Ed," he said softly. "And you did a fine job. But damn it, when the time comes to buffalo a man, buffalo him! Sometimes you have to be as mean as a wolf in this job. Otherwise you'll get yourself killed."

In a few months Ed was up and around once more, as well as ever. But unfortunately he didn't take his brother's advice.

On April 9, 1878, a little after nine o'clock at night, Ed and his assistant deputy, Nathaniel Haywood, heard several pistol shots from south of the deadline. They hurried across the tracks and found a rugged gang of Texans in the Lady Gay Dance Hall who were bent upon having a wild old time of it.

One of the punchers, Jack Wagner, had made a good start at drinking Dodge dry. He was still sober enough though to be plenty dangerous, and he was packing a gun. Ed asked Wagner for the revolver, and the cowpoke grumbled a little but handed it over. Ed then located the ramrod of the outfit, Al Walker, and gave him the gun, suggesting that Walker check it with the bartender as required by law south of the deadline. Walker said he would, and Ed and Nat left the Lady Gay.

Within two minutes, the lawmen made a quick turn of the block and were passing the Lady Gay once again on their way back to the north side of the deadline.

Wagner and Walker were leaving the dance hall at that moment, and Ed saw that Wagner was still wearing his gun.

Ed stepped over to the puncher and said, "I'll take that gun."

"Like hell you will!" Wagner growled. "I'd just like to see you try to take it!"

The other cowmen in the Texas outfit started out the door at the sound of Wagner's angry voice. Nat said that one of them poked a gun in his face and pulled the trigger, but the gun misfired. At this point, Nat took off up the street for help, leaving Ed to face the cattlemen single-handedly.

In the meantime, Bat heard a few scattered shots and walked across the tracks to investigate. There were more shots, shouts, and the sound of a scuffle. He broke into a run. He was in time to see Ed, ringed by armed Texans, stagger back under the impact of a heavy-caliber gun, fired so close to him that his clothes caught fire.

Seeing Bat, the Texans cut loose on him. Bat's guns bucked furiously in his fists, roaring and coughing fire. His first volley cut Wagner, literally, to pieces. Then he turned his fire on Walker, who ran a short distance and collapsed. The other Texans were now in full retreat, dodging into narrow alleys, diving through windows, crawling under porches, and doing anything to get out of Bat's withering, deadly fire.

Suddenly there was nothing more to shoot at. There was a moment of intense silence, then a roar of voices, as people flooded out onto the street from every direction.

"Hey Bat!" someone called. "Ed's over here. In Hoover's Saloon!"

Bat went into Hoover's and found his brother stretched out on a table. Ed looked up and tried to speak, but he couldn't get the words out. He gave Bat a good-natured grin. Then he died.

This was the second time someone Bat loved had been the victim of vicious, stupid gunfire. And each time he had been powerless to save them. The fact that he had avenged both murders was small consolation. Bat walked aimlessly through the lonely streets of Dodge the rest of that black night, talking to no one and thinking his own dark thoughts.

Charlie Tinkam, a friend of Bat's, said later: "From talking to Bat after the death of his brother Ed, I got the idea he'd decided all killing was senseless and useless and that he was going to do his best to do right by his badge without ever shooting to kill again. He ordered two new .45's from Colt's Manufacturing Company that same week. He wanted them 'easy on the trigger,' and he wanted them nickel-plated with gutta-percha handles. He wanted the front sights a little higher and wider than usual, with barrels about the length of the ejector rods. Same time he sent for them, he ordered the complete works of Shakespeare and a volume on Eighteenth Century English poets. I know he was looking forward to getting those books a whole lot more than he was looking forward to getting the guns."

The killing of a lawman—despite the immediate and drastic revenge it received—encouraged the cowboys, drifters, and assorted badmen of Dodge to regain some of their confidence. As sheriff of Ford County, Bat couldn't spend all of his time at the county seat, and while he was away, the town went wild. Horsemen galloped through the streets, blasting away recklessly at the stars or the sun, depending on the time of day. Tinhorn gamblers cropped up at all the gambling halls. Two young cowboys devised an interesting contest one night. Trying to imitate William Tell, they shot each other's hat off two or three times, until one got to laughing too hard and accidentally blew his friend's head off.

The City Council finally brought Wyatt Earp back

from Texas to serve as city marshal again. Masterson and Earp were together in Dodge City when Dora Hand was murdered.

The shooting of Dora Hand was as tragic and sensational a case as Kansas had ever seen. Dora Hand was the most beautiful girl in Dodge City. While she was, admittedly, a successful prostitute in Dodge's busy redlight district, she had many qualities that set her above and apart from her professional sisters. She had played the role of frontier Florence Nightingale on numerous occasions, nursing the hurt or sick with tender devotion. She was kind and generous to a fault in everything she did. Any man who insulted Dora in Dodge City most likely would have been raised on a rope in short order.

Her killing was a fearful blunder.

A Texan named Kennedy had fallen out with Mayor Kelley. Kelley had taken exception to something Kennedy said and punched him in the nose. Kennedy, a habitual troublemaker, rode out of town nursing his nose and a grudge.

That very day Mayor Kelley left for Fort Dodge and turned his home over to Dora Hand and one of her girl friends for the night.

Not knowing this, Kennedy came back to town in the middle of the night. Walking his horse quietly, he crept up to Kelley's home and emptied his pistol through the thin outside bedroom wall. Dora was hit by one of the slugs and killed instantly. Without realizing his mistake, Kennedy raced out of Dodge at full speed.

Earp, Masterson, and a young deputy named Bill Tilghman headed for Wagon Bed Springs on the hunch that the killer would try to escape into the desolate Indian territory. They rode all night and all the next day. Finally, certain that they had bypassed him, they laid an ambush in a small valley through which their quarry would have to pass, if their idea was correct.

A short time later, Kennedy came riding along the trail. He did not see them until he was within shooting range. Then Bat rode out and called, "You're under arrest, Kennedy!"

The Texan spun his horse around and galloped back in the direction he had come from. Bat took careful aim with one of his new Colts and pulled the trigger. Kennedy was knocked sprawling from his horse, his arm shattered.

On the way back to Dodge, the prisoner asked if he had succeeded in killing Kelley. When Wyatt Earp told him what had happened, Kennedy cursed Bat furiously for not killing him. "Dora Hand once grubstaked me when I was down and out," he cried. "I deserve to die!"

Bat killed no one else during the remainder of his term in office. He shot a lengthy list of unscrupulous characters, from crooked poker dealers to horsethieves, but he always drilled them neatly in an arm, a leg, or a shoulder.

On one memorable occasion, the celebrated comedian Eddie Foy was almost certain that Bat Masterson was going to kill him. Eddie was playing Dodge for the first time. The day after his debut a group of quiet but determined men called for him at his hotel. The handsome, smartly dressed young man who was the leader of the crowd introduced himself as Bat Masterson. The comedian was a bit surprised; he expected Bat to be at least eight feet tall, with a killer's vicious, narrowed eyes, and half-a-dozen huge revolvers dangling from his hips.

Foy was even more surprised when Bat said in a cultured, well-modulated voice, "We're terribly sorry to disturb you, Mr. Foy. But as you are aware, most of the town saw your opening act at Ham Bell's Varieties last night. Consequently, the citizens of Dodge City have formed a committee to carry out the town's decision in regard to you."

"Decision?" Foy looked puzzled.

Bat nodded slowly. "After seeing you on stage, the

people of Dodge have decided the only thing to do is hang you."

Several men standing behind Bat who, Foy observed, looked like alarmingly desperate types surged forward and led the unhappy comedian into the street.

At first Foy tried bravado. But the unsmiling men went quietly about the business of leading him to a large tree and bringing up a horse for him to sit on. As they tied his hands behind his back, with Masterson supervising all the details carefully, a large crowd began to gather.

For the first time, it occurred to Foy that they actually might be going to hang him. His heart pounded nervously as someone threw a rope over the branch above him and pulled it until the noose hung level with Eddie's head.

Masterson at last broke the long silence. "Mr. Foy," he asked, "before we go ahead, is there any last word you'd like to say?"

Foy gulped down his panic and wet his lips. "Yes," he said.

"What is it?"

"Could I buy all you boys a drink?"

The crowd roared with laughter and approval at Foy's last words. Slapping him on the back, they untied him and helped him from the horse. Everyone retired to the Long Branch, where the hanging was conceded to be one of the most successful of the year.

By the time 1880 rolled around, Bat was losing interest in his position as sheriff of Ford County. The adventurous, glorious day of Dodge City were declining. Buffalo hunting, along with the buffalo, had died out. The Texas cowboys, who had once stormed the town, were dwindling in number as farming pushed farther west and other cattle markets came into existence. Also, there was more money in professional gambling.

Early in '80, when Wyatt Earp moved on to Tombstone to take the job of federal deputy marshal there, Bat resigned too. About that time Jim Masterson, against Bat's advice, went into partnership with Al Peacock in a gambling house and dance hall. Peacock was a sharp, hard-faced dealer who had an unsavory background and who moved in tough circles. Jim, the perennial little brother, took Bat's advice as a personal offence and promptly threw in with Peacock.

Bat was ripe for a deal that Dave Rickabaugh offered him. "I own the Oriental, the finest place in Tombstone," Dave told him. "Certain parties are trying to take it over. I want men with a gunslinging reputation to work for me to discourage 'em. If you take me up, I'll make it worth your while."

After due consideration, Masterson moved to the Oriental in Tombstone, along with Luke Short, who also had a name as a good man in a fight.

There was plenty of action in Tombstone. Luke got into a gunfight with a mean gunman named Charlie Storms shortly after their arrival and put several holes in poor Charlie before Bat broke it up.

A few weeks later, two ungracious visitors visited the Oriental when Bat was on duty alone. They amused themselves by tossing yellow chips into the air and trying to shoot them in midflight.

"I'll have to ask you gentlemen not to carry on like that," Bat said politely. "Rules of the house."

One made the mistake of swiveling his gun in Bat's direction and found his arm dangling helplessly at his side in no time at all. Bat shot the other in the shoulder as he tried to finish what his friend had started.

"Now you two boys just move along and don't be so rough next time you're in the Oriental," Bat admonished them. The truth of the matter is that they avoided the Oriental altogether from that time on.

Bat served as a deputy to Wyatt once or twice and was just getting to enjoy Tombstone when he got a letter from a friend in Dodge City. The letter said that his brother Jim was in trouble up to his eyebrows. It seemed that Al Peacock and Jim had a falling out. Peacock and the tough bartender who worked for the two partners were out to kill Jim.

Bat took the first stage out of Tombstone to Deming. At Deming he caught the train to Dodge. One thought was uppermost in his mind. He had lost his girl in the fight at Sweetwater and one brother in Dodge. It wasn't going to happen again if he could help it.

The train pulled into Dodge at noon on April 16th; it was half an hour late. The engine slowly chugged to a halt, and Bat hopped off the passenger car, his bag in one hand. As he looked up and down the platform, he saw Peacock and Updegraff, the bartender, standing near the station. They turned away as Bat approached them and started to walk rapidly toward Front Street.

"Wait a minute, you two," Bat called. "I want to talk to you!"

They bolted and took cover behind the nearby caboose, pulling their guns as they ran. Both opened fire from their protected position, and Bat dropped quickly behind the railroad grading. Shooting wildly, the two men raked the street behind Bat with lead. Shells plowed into Hoover's Liquor Store, the Long Branch Saloon, and McCarty's Drugstore.

Bat finally had a clean shot at Updegraff. From the way the two men had reacted when they saw him, he thought they might have already killed Jim. So when he pulled the trigger, he wasn't interested in simply winging Updegraff. He shot to kill. With Updegraff out of the fight, Peacock threw down his gun.

As soon as the shooting was over, Bat allowed himself to be arrested and taken to jail. He was only held briefly. To his relief, he learned upon his release that Jim was still alive.

Updegraff lived a few days, then died. Most of the citizens of Dodge were relieved that it was he, rather than Masterson, who had died. But there was a new reform element in town, led by the new mayor a pious crook named Webster. Out of petty spite, Webster insisted that Bat be fined $8.00 for "unlawfully and feloniously discharging a pistol upon the streets of said city."

A crusading newspaper, the Walnut City *Blade*, which was spearheading Webster's drive for a town completely under the mayor's thumb, editorialized: "It costs $8.00 to shoot a man through the lung in Dodge City. Such was Bat Masterson's fine." It didn't go into the proper etiquette one should observe when two other men start using you for target practice.

Dodge City had changed. It was no longer honestly dishonest. Its one time healthy, hell-for-leather deviltry had given way to stealthy, sneaky corruption. Disgusted with Dodge, both Bat and Jim left town a few months after the Updegraff shooting. Bat moved on to Trinidad, Colorado, where he leased a gambling concession.

One morning he got a telegram from his old friend Luke Short. Luke was in trouble. He had moved back to Dodge from Tombstone and taken over the Long Branch. Always a good businessman, Luke hired a cute girl to play the piano and sing for his customers. Consequently, the Alamo, next door to the Long Branch, began to lose business. Luke returned to his place one evening to find the doors locked by order of the sheriff. His silver-voiced songstress, being automatically out of a job, had instantly accepted an offer to sing for the owner of the Alamo.

Bat was not particularly surprised at these events, since the owner of the Alamo was none other than the Honorable Mayor Webster. To add to Luke's woes, the mayor had run him out of town.

Bat sent word to Wyatt Earp, who promptly gathered some of their old friends together: Charlie Bassett, Frank

McLane, Neal Brown, and Billy Potillion—all champion gunslingers.

Bat, Wyatt, and Luke's other friends arrived in Dodge, set up a semi-legal "peace commission" consisting of themselves, and took the town over. A chastened Mayor Webster changed his high-handed views overnight, and Luke Short's raw deal was miraculously turned into a square deal for all concerned.

With that score settled, Bat Masterson next tried his luck in Deadwood, Leadville, Ogallala, Tombstone, and Cimarron, looking for excitement and adventure.

When the Santa Fe and the Rio Grande railroads were having a small war over a track right-of-way, a Santa Fe agent came looking for Bat.

"This is the story," he said nervously. "Man named Palmer has a whole army aboard a train. They've killed a couple of men at Cucharas, and they're heading to Pueblo to take over the Santa Fe's railroad property. We've already started making a fort out of the old Pueblo roundhouse, but we need someone to take over when it comes to actual fighting."

Bat accepted the assignment.

When General Palmer and his army arrived at Pueblo, they found the doors of the roundhouse barred with heavy timbers. Inside, with a smaller army and a couple of Gatling guns, was Bat Masterson.

There was a tense moment as Palmer weighed the possibilities of storming the fortress. Usually a determined man, he couldn't quite bring himself to give the order to attack. He had heard too many stories about Bat Masterson. Palmer's treasurer, realizing that both armies were composed of mercenaries, suggested talking to the men in the fortress under a flag of truce. He figured they could buy off the opposing army by offering them more money than the Santa Fe was paying them.

Bat wanted to remain loyal to the Santa Fe, but his

men didn't see it that way. They couldn't see any sense
in fighting if they could get more money by surrendering.
At last Bat was outvoted, and the fight was averted.

On another occasion, an eccentric millionaire named
Soule wanted to move the county seat of Gray County,
Kansas, from Cimarron to Ingalls. He hired Bat and
another veteran gunfighter, Jim Marshall, to take a gang
of fighters to Cimarron. They were to raid the county
courthouse, swipe all official county papers and the county
seal, and take them to Ingalls. Soule was convinced that if
he could get all official county documents to Ingalls, he
could succeed in making Ingalls the new county seat.

This sounded like good fun to Bat. He and Marshall
got to Cimarron with a platoon of hired scrappers. Leaving their men outside, the two of them rushed into the
courthouse and began gathering up the documents.

In the meantime, word had spread through Cimarron
of what was going on. A mob of irate citizens marched
on the courthouse, many of them armed. In the face of
howling criticism and whining bullets, the mercenaries
outside fled, leaving Bat and Jim inside to face the music.

It is a tribute to the gunslingers' marksmanship that
they managed to hold the enraged mob at bay for several
hours without killing off half the population of Cimarron.
With all the flying lead, an innocent bystander two blocks
away was the only fatality. It is highly unlikely that either
Bat or Jim shot the fellow, but when they surrendered
after several hours of siege, they were tried for murder.

Their defense was unique. They claimed they couldn't
have murdered the man because they didn't even know
him. And if one of their bullets had accidentally hit the
poor fellow, it was only because they were deliberately
firing over the heads of the mob—and, incidentally, firing
to protect their own lives.

Eventually they were released, with a warning that if they ever showed up in Cimarron again, they would be immediately hanged.

Bat's love of good books, reading, and writing shaped his final destiny. Following the turn of the century, he realized that the West as he had known it was dead. He moved to New York and managed to get a job as a writer with the *Morning Telegraph*. He wrote well, and his byline soon became common. Bat developed a tremendous interest in sports, especially boxing. He felt that a man, if he is a man, is bound to have fight in him and that he should have some way of getting that fight out of him. Boxing was the most civilized way of accomplishing this, Bat thought.

In time, Bat became a well-known and respected sports writer. Later, he became an editor with the *Telegraph*.

On October 25, 1921, Bat died of a heart attack at his desk. He was sixty-seven years old.

The boom of six-guns is far removed from the clatter of typewriters; yet, somehow, they both seemed right for Bat. His sophisticated editor and writer friends probably would have agreed that the simple prayer Bat's western friends said over him was just about right.

"Lord. Take care of this man."

Pat Garrett

The Man Who Killed Billy the Kid

By Clair Huffaker

~~~~~~

The cocky little badman and the easygoing sheriff kicked off a legend that made the Kid famous and, unjustly, cast the lawman as the biggest traitor since Brutus

There once was a cocky, tough little undersized cowboy who turned to horse stealing and was for a while a resounding success in that hazardous occupation. At the same time and in the same locality, there was a long-legged, soft-spoken, oversized cowboy who turned to sheriffing and was for a while conspicuously successful in that dangerous calling. Between the two of them, they kicked off a legend that made the short cowpoke more famous than most Presidents of the United States. His name was William H. Bonney, but he is better known in song and story as Billy the Kid.

The law-enforcing wrangler, who was six feet, four inches tall and was named Patrick Floyd Garrett, got the short end of the legend, despite his exceptional length. While Billy has come down through the years as a clear-eyed, hot-tempered, adventuresome little scrapper, Pat usually has been described as a Judas, a coward, or a snake-eyed, battle-wise gunslinger, who killed Billy by taking advantage of the Kid's personal regard for him. But the truth is that Pat never betrayed anybody and was every bit as brave as Billy, even though he had done only about one-twentieth as much gunfighting as the Kid when they finally went for each other.

Furthermore, in tracking down and killing Billy, Pat was only doing his sworn duty—and a mighty painful duty it was too, since he and the Kid had spent many happy hours together, playing cards, punishing the jug, swapping yarns, and swaggering around town side by side, if not shoulder to shoulder. It was a curious friendship, this one between the law-abiding citizen and the trigger-happy outlaw. When you take everything into account, about the only explanation you can find for the strong attachment between them is that each must have seen in the other the kind of man he sometimes wished he could be. It wasn't an altogether unique bond though. Another celebrated case that comes to mind was the close friendship of Wyatt Earp and Doc Holliday. But Wyatt got a better break than Pat Garrett. He wasn't forced to kill Doc Holliday.

Pat's life commenced one warm night in June of 1850. On the Alabama farm where he was born, and, later in Louisiana, he spent a pleasant, generally peaceful boyhood with his family. They do say, though, that at ten he tracked a thirteeen-year-old bully through five miles of snow to give him a punch in the nose. Just what the older boy had done to merit the punishment is not clear—but the incident is significant. When Pat Garrett took on a job, he saw it through.

At nineteen, Pat decided to go out into the world to make his fortune. He said, "So long," to his mother and father and struck out for the magic, golden land called Texas. The Lone Star State turned out to be neither magic nor golden, and Pat didn't make his fortune the way he had planned. But he had a lot of good times, and he learned considerable about riding, roping, and shooting. For six carefree years he worked as a cowpuncher around Lancaster and as far north as the Red River.

Then, wanting a change of pace, Pat ranged the southern plains of Texas hunting for buffalo. In the winter of '76, toward the beginning of his hunting career, Pat joined a civilian expedition aimed at cracking down on warring Comanches who had been shooting buffalo hunters with disturbing regularity. He distinguished himself as a fighting man in skirmishes with the Indians. He also built a reputation as a man who thought some about the thing called Justice. As one member of the expedition said, "Pat had the softest, slowest drawl ever you heard. And he was one of the youngest men in the outfit, something under twenty-six. But for all his quiet manners and his youth, when he said something, everybody listened. And once he started out to accomplish something, it got done come hell or high water. But I remember Pat best because he was one of the few men who regretted fighting the Indians. He figured it wasn't fair, that actually they had first call on the buffalo, and naturally they were peeved that white men were shooting them. If the Comanches hadn't been a threat to the families in the section, I doubt if Pat would have gone along with us."

Garrett didn't go hog-wild killing buffalo the way most of the hunters did, and consequently he didn't make any money to speak of. In 1878 he felt the urge to move on farther to the west, and, with a few dollars from the sale of hides in his pocket, he rode toward New Mexico.

Late in the fall the tall young rider was in the Pecos Valley. Near Fort Sumner he rode up to Pete Maxwell's big ranch. Pete himself was sitting on the porch of the ranch house. His practiced eye swept over the threadbare stranger as they exchanged brief salutations. "You lookin' for work?"

"I wouldn't mind a job," Pat admitted.

"It so happens there's a rack in the bunkhouse that'll accommodate that long frame of yours. Step down. Cooky just started out back to ring the dinner bell."

On his first payday Pat finished branding a few calves in the early evening, went to Maxwell to draw his roll, and saddled up to go into Fort Sumner. Another cowhand on the Maxwell spread, Charlie Bowdre, called from the barn, "Ridin' to town?"

"Yes."

"Hold on. I'll go along with you."

On the way Charlie said, "Bill Bonney'll be in Sumner. He's a friend of mine. Maybe you can meet him."

"Fine. Who's he?"

"You don't know?" Charlie was part amazed and part indignant. "He's had a lot of write-ups in the papers around here. They call him Billy the Kid. He rustles steers and mules and horses for a livin'. I've worked on a couple of ranches with him when he wasn't nothin' but a cowboy," Charlie said proudly. And, in a conspiratorial tone, he added, "I still take a ride with Billy sometimes."

Then he filled Pat in on some of the Kid's gunslinging exploits and wound up by saying: "He's like lightning on the draw. I sure would hate to have to face him myself."

At Fort Sumner they swung down at the hitching rail before a saloon and went through the batwing door, taking themselves a table in the back of the barroom. They were polishing off their second shot when five men came pushing through the door and took possession of the bar.

"There he is now," Charlie said, and, raising his voice, he called out: "Hey there, Billy! Come over here. I want you to meet a friend of mine, Pat Garrett."

Billy tossed off his drink, wiped his mouth on the back of his hand, and grinned. "Sure," he said, swaggering toward the table. "Why not? I got nothing to lose by it."

They were a typical bunch of cowboys, Pat figured, living recklessly from day to day. This Billy Bonney,

heading toward the table, was evidently the acknowl-
edged leader, in spite of his youth, since he had been in
the most trouble and the largest number of shooting
scrapes. Without changing expression, Pat took in Billy
from top to bottom. No great shakes of a man at first
glance, he was small and slender. His most prominent
feature was his buck teeth, which gave him a kind of
perpetual smile that set well with his aggressive air of
self-confidence.

Acknowledging Bowdre's introduction with a wave of
his hand, the Kid swung a chair around and plunked himself down. "Mind if I take the load off my feet?"

"Proud to have you with us," Pat replied in his slow
Southern drawl.

Billy eyed him closely. "Where you from?" he asked.

"Alabama, to start with."

"That's a long ways off," Billy said. "Well, seeing as
I'm from a long ways off too—me and you, we might just
as well be friendly."

"Always better to start out being friendly," Pat smiled.
"Today being payday, I'm good for a setup."

Bonney laughed, although there didn't seem to be anything particular to laugh about. Then he winked at Bowdre and said: "I just got back with the boys from taking
in some mules and horses. So I'm good for a few rounds,
too."

That's the way it started, with easy-going, law-abiding
Pat and the lawless Kid hitting it off right from the start,
each evidently catching a glimpse of something in the
other to admire. There's no doubt that the Kid suffered
from a nagging, desperate need to be admired by men
like Pat. He wanted to be held in high esteem as a fear-
less man with an iron will who always had a good excuse
for being quicker on the draw than the other guy. Just
the same, he was continually plagued by the thought that
some of his gunslinging wasn't entirely justifiable, even by

the liberal code of the tolerant frontier. Time after time, when he was mulling over the details of his various gun fights, he would keep on insisting: "I had to kill him. There wasn't any way out of it. Can't you see that? He had it coming to him. He was asking for it."

As he sat there now, sizing up Pat Garrett's steel-steady, conscience-free manner, he wondered how much Pat had heard about some of those killings and how he would have behaved under similar circumstances. As for Pat, there was something about Billy that put him in a speculative mood too. Chuckling at this bantam rooster's cocky, comical way of expressing himself, and at the same time calmly taking the Kid's measure, Pat wondered how he himself would behave if something forced him to unleash all the wild impulses he kept so tightly bound up deep inside himself.

Brushing aside that disturbing thought, Pat called for another round of drinks. He and this edgy half-pint were going to like each other more than a little. That was clear enough. It was in the cards. They were going to be friends.

The next payday it was Pat who suggested to Bowdre that they go to town together, and this time they found Billy and his three favorite henchmen—Tom Foliard, Tom Pickett, and Billy Wilson—in the back of the saloon warming up to what looked like the beginnings of a marathon poker session.

"Well," Billy said, looking up from his tightly held cards, "if it ain't the tall drink of good old well water! How 'bout you? You know anything about poker?"

"Enough to get by," Pat said, pulling up a chair. "You just playing table stakes, or no limit?"

"Now here's a man after my own heart," Billy kidded. "Kind of man my daddy must of had in mind when he got down to business."

Five hours later it was obvious enough that Pat did

know something about poker; more, in fact, than anybody else sitting at the table. At any rate, when the long, fierce session finally ended, he had cleaned them all out, raking in the last sweet pot with a pair of measly tens, back to back. "You can't make money out of poker," he said, "unless you know how to coax the bum hands into paying off as well as the good ones."

Billy drummed his agile fingers on the table. But he wasn't sore. Far from it.

"There's plenty more where that came from," he said, as he watched Pat pocket his winnings. "I've got to hand it to you, Pat. When you set out to pull something off, you don't let up until you settle it once and for all. You do everything the same way you play poker?"

"Could be," Pat conceded. "Like to try me out on blackjack or faro?"

"Not right away," Billy replied. "You'll have to hold your horses until I put over a little deal I got in mind."

Billy shot a quick glance around the table, winding up with Bowdre. "Charlie," he asked, "how good is this here pardner of yours in a saddle?"

"None better," Bowdre said.

"Think he might like to take a little ride with us down the Pecos?"

"Why don't you ask him?"

"Hell fire, that's what I'm doing." Billy looked straight at Pat. "We're going to bring back some disgruntled cows that feel the need of a change. Big boodle in it. Want to go along with us?"

Pat shook his head. "No thanks."

"How come? Don't tell me you're feather-legged?"

"I wouldn't say that. It's just that I like the job I'm doing."

"You're passing up a good bet."

"I don't think so."

Instead of turning Billy against him though, this flat

refusal to join the gang only made the Kid like Pat more
than ever. They began to spend more and more time together, gambling, drinking, and sitting around. When one
of them ran out of money, the other would loan him some
cash to recoup. Folks in the town even made up a little
joke about them. When Pat and the Kid were seen approaching, they would say, "Well, here comes the long
and the short of it." They were careful never to say it
so Billy would hear because, after all, Bonney had the
reputation of being the meanest badman around.

From Pat Garrett's point of view, he found a number
of things about the Kid that he liked. In the book he later
wrote about him, he described Billy as "bold, daring, and
reckless, but open-handed, generous-hearted, and frank."
And Pat saw even deeper into the Kid's personality. "He
had a lurking devil in him. It was a good-humored, jovial
imp, or a cruel and bloodthirsty fiend, as circumstances
prompted."

For two years Pat worked up and down the Pecos
River as a cowhand while Billy went from bad to considerably worse. Eventually, as the Kid's name as a rustler
and gunman became better known, folks forgot that he
ever had been a cowboy at all.

In the meantime, Pat was getting to know most of
the people in that part of the Southwest. He made friends
with John Chisum, top cattleman in the territory, whose
Long Rail and Jingle Bob brand often included as many
as 80,000 head of prime beef ranging from Fort Sumner
clear down over the Texas border. Garrett made hundreds
of friends among the poorer people and the newcomers to
the country who were just getting started. One of his
closest comrades was a young blacksmith named Jim Carlyle, a powerfully built, happy-go-lucky newcomer to New
Mexico. In his own easygoing fashion, Pat managed to
be on good terms with just about everyone he met.

Early during Pat's first couple of years in the territory,

one tragedy marred his life. At Fort Sumner, where he and
his friends spent most of their free time, he met a beautiful
girl named Juanita Martinez. He escorted her to a few
Mexican dances and in no time fell in love with her. They
were married in the church at Sumner. Then, only a few
weeks after their wedding, Juanita became suddenly ill.
Pat got the best medical help available for his bride, but it
was no use. She died within a few days.

Pat was lonely and unhappy for many months. Finally,
nearly two years later, Pat married for the second time.
His new wife was Polinaria Gutierrez, a girlhood friend
of Juanita. That year, 1880, was a high spot in Pat's life.
Polly was a fine woman. Garrett, now in his thirtieth year,
began to think of buying his own ranch and raising a
family. But then, later in the year, John Chisum and
George Curry, who was later to become governor, paid
him an unexpected visit. "Pat," John told him, "George and
me represent damn near every decent person in the territory. We've been talking this over between ourselves and
with everybody we know for a long time now."

"Talking what over?"

"Short and simple, we'd like you to run for sheriff of
Lincoln County. We'll all back you to the hilt."

"Why me?" Pat asked. "I wouldn't know how to run
a sheriff's office. Never even been inside one."

"You can learn," Curry said.

Chisum, in his brusque way, said, "Damn it, Garrett,
the number one problem around here, as you well know,
is Billy the Kid and his gang. They're stealing us all
blind. And as long as the Kid keeps at it there's a hundred
other punks willing to take a try at imitating him.

"There's been no law in the land for more than two
years, not since Brady was murdered. Kimbreel, Peppin—
as sheriffs they would have made fair bartenders. But
you're different. Besides, Billy respects you. Chances are
you could handle him."

The thought of being a law officer had never occurred to Pat. "I don't know. I'll have to think it over."

"That's right," John agreed. "You ought to think it over. No one wants to rawhide you into a job like that. Everybody knows it'll be a tough nut to crack."

"While you're thinking of it," Curry said, "remember one thing, Pat. You'll be bringing up a bunch of kids in this territory like the rest of us. You have to decide what kind of a place you want them to grow up in. Now, we think you're the man to bring in the law for once and for all. If you think you're up to it, you let us know."

Two months later, in October, Pat Garrett was elected sheriff of Lincoln County on a reform ticket by an overwhelming majority. During his first days in office, he paid a purely social call on Billy the Kid. "Billy," Pat told him, "I'm still a friend of yours as of right now. But I'm going to do my level best to stop the stealing and killing in the county. I hope you don't cross me. But if you do, I'll be looking for you."

"If it comes to that, don't try to take me alive," the Kid said. And he meant it, and Pat knew it.

Early in November, Billy stole a herd of fine horses from the Grzelachowski ranch. Within a few days he was raiding near White Oaks. On the night of November 23, which was the Kid's birthday, he and the gang celebrated by riding into White Oaks and making a drunken, senseless attempt to kill Jim Redmond, who happened to be the only man in sight. Pat got word that the Kid was in Bosque Grande. Quickly forming a posse, he rode to Roswell, then up the Rio Pecos to Bosque Grande in a vain attempt to catch his quarry.

The posse did manage to round up one member of the gang, but since there was no sign of Billy, Pat finally decided to turn back. The tired riders finally arrived in Fort Sumner on November 27, 1880. There Pat got word that Billy had been back at White Oaks. A posse led by

Deputy J. W. Bell had closed in on the gang, and, after
a sizable gun battle, the outlaws had split up, some of them
taking refuge in a nearby ranch house. Carrying a flag of
truce, Pat's young blacksmith friend, Jim Carlyle, went
to the ranch house and told Billy the place was surrounded, and he had better surrender if he knew what was
good for him. That kind of talk didn't sit well with
the Kid, and he refused to let Jim return to the posse,
apparently intending to hold him as a hostage. At any
rate, after some wrangling back and forth, Carlyle suddenly decided to make a break for it and jumped out of
a window, taking the sash and the pane with him. Billy
must have had his eye on Jim all the time because he
managed to whip his gun out quick enough to shoot the
blacksmith in the back before he hit the ground.

When Pat heard that Billy had killed Jim Carlyle,
he didn't say anything for a long time. He just sat in his
chair, gripping the arms with both hands, tapping one
foot on the floor and staring into space. Pat had a lot
of friends. Pretty nearly everybody in Lincoln County
was his friend by now. But sometimes a man who has a
raft of friends hates to lose one worse than a man who
doesn't have very many. Shooting Jim Carlyle like that
just didn't make any sense. Jim never harmed anybody.
However you looked at it, it was ugly. No matter what
the Kid had to say now, no matter how much he argued,
he never would be able to come up with an honest-to-
God excuse this time. Jim was gone, and Billy was going
to have to go too.

Pat summoned the members of his posse and hit the
trail again. When last seen after making their escape from
the ranch house near White Oaks, Billy's gang had been
headed south toward a ranch called Las Canaditas. The
only members left in the gang now were Billy himself,
Tom Foliard, Dave Rudabaugh, Billy Wilson, Tom Pick-

ett, and Charlie Bowdre. Many a night Pat had spent playing cards and drinking red liquor with those fellows, every one of them, and it was no pleasure to be out gunning for them now.

After stoking up on all the grub they could hold, Pat and his posse left Fort Sumner and moved along at an easy lope toward Las Canaditas. Half-way to their destination they caught sight of a man on horseback, stock still on a ridge and silhouetted against the sky, evidently surveying the countryside. He was too far away to be recognized with the naked eye, but Pat managed to identify him through a pair of strong field glasses. "It's Tom Foliard," he announced, a note of excitement in his usually calm voice. "He's on that bay stallion of his—one of the fastest horses around these parts. He's got field glasses too, and he's looking this way."

Before Pat finished speaking, Tom had recognized the posse. The next instant he spurred his big bay around and lunged into a mad gallop, quickly dropping out of sight beyond the horizon.

"We haven't got a Chinaman's chance of catching up to him, not with him on that horse," Pat said. "But come on, let's see how good we can do."

They thundered up the rise toward the ridge—but their mounts weren't quite fast enough. By the time they reached the ridge, Tom had passed on over the next hill, and they never got a glimpse of him again—not on that wild ride. When they got to Las Canaditas, Billy and his gang had vanished. "He tipped 'em off all right," Pat said, as he dismounted to make a close scrutiny of the fresh hoofprints around the ranch house. "I'd say he beat us here by close on to half an hour."

After a few minutes, Pat remounted and pointed toward the higher hills in the distance. "That's the way they went. They're heading for Los Portales."

Los Portales was Billy's hide-out, deep in the hills. The newspapers had been referring to the place as "Billy the Kid's Castle," but when Pat and his men got there they soon saw that "castle" was nothing but a highfaluting newspaper exaggeration. What the place turned out to be was nothing more than a cave dug into a rocky hillside with a post sunk into the ground beside the entrance. The cave was empty and there was no sign anywhere around of Billy and his henchmen.

It was obvious, though, that the Kid was feeling Pat's breath hot on the back of his neck. On their way back to Fort Sumner, the posse stopped off at the Wilcox ranch, about twelve miles from town. While they were there, Wilcox's partner, an easygoing fellow named Brazil, showed up and said he had some interesting news for Pat. "Charlie Bowdre got in touch with me," he said, "and he wants to know if you're willing to have a little personal talk with him, just for old times' sake."

"Sure," Pat said. "I'm game. But no monkey business. I ain't aiming to let those mavericks dry-gulch me."

"Oh, no—none of that!" Brazil hastened to explain. "Charlie's on the level, far as I can figure, and he's plenty scared. He wants to meet you tomorrow afternoon at that spot where the road forks off about two miles outside of Sumner. I'll ride along with him a piece of the way and then pull up before he gets there, so you can have your confab without anybody listening to you."

"Okay," Pat agreed. "But keep your eyes peeled while I'm talking to him."

The next afternoon Pat rode up the dusty route alone and saw Charlie sitting on his horse where the path branched out in two directions. "Howdy, Charlie," he said. "What's on your mind?"

Bowdre was nervous and frightened. "What'll you do for me, Pat, if I come in and give myself up?"

"I can't promise you anything, Charlie. But I'll tell you this. If you come in on your own, I'll do everything I can to get you released on bail and to help you get started back on the inside of the law."

Charlie couldn't make up his mind. He kept glancing at the hills as though he thought he was being watched. At last he said, "I don't know. How 'bout if I promise I won't ride with the Kid no more?"

"You're in too deep to get off that easy. You were with the gang when they were rustling up at White Oaks. You were in on the shooting of Carlyle. I wish you'd surrender to me, Charlie. If you don't, chances are you'll be captured or killed."

Bowdre said he would think about it. Then he turned his horse and rode on back to rejoin Brazil.

Soon after that, bad weather set in, and trying to find the Kid turned from difficult to downright impossible. Billy still had enough friends to confuse his whereabouts with lies, and he knew nearly every hiding place in New Mexico. Frank Stewart, an agent hired by some Panhandle stockmen who had been missing considerable livestock, joined Pat in the search. But there was no break in the manhunt until mid-December when a message came that the Kid was again hanging around Fort Sumner.

Pat arrived at the Fort during the night with thirteen men. He left Frank Stewart and eleven men in hiding when morning came and went out onto the streets with only one man. Soon he met Iginio Garcia, a relative of Billy's friend, Manuel Garcia.

"I hear Billy's around here," Pat said.

"I haven't seen him," Garcia muttered.

"No matter. I don't care to meet Billy and his gang with only one man. I'm leaving town as soon as I take care of a few things."

Within a few minutes Pat saw Garcia galloping out

of Sumner. Billy would soon be hearing from Garcia that Pat was in town with one lone deputy, which was just what Pat wanted.

It began to snow heavily. Darkness came early as a thickening blanket of white covered the ground. Pat and his men waited patiently for the Kid and his bunch to show up. About eight o'clock they were just starting a game of blackjack to pass the time when a guard came to the door and whispered, "Pat! Some riders are coming!"

"Get your guns, boys!" Pat said. "Nobody but the men we're looking for would be out on this kind of night."

Billy the Kid, with Tom Foliard on his right, was moving into Fort Sumner at the head of his gang. As the riders came closer to the lights of the town that could be seen dimly through the falling snow, Billy had a premonition that something was wrong. Turning to Foliard, the Kid said, "I want a good chew of tobacco, Tom. Wilson's got some." He swung his horse out of line until Wilson, bringing up the rear of the group, was abreast of him. With Billy riding at the tail end of the line now, the gang entered Sumner.

Pat recognized Foliard as the lead horse came up to the building where the posse was waiting. "Halt!" the sheriff commanded. Foliard made the fatal mistake of going for his gun; a bullet from Pat's Winchester crashed through him. The rest of the outlaws, taking advantage of the confusion and the heavy snow, whirled and galloped away as the guns of the posse roared and bullets sang around their ears. Pat tried for a shot at Pickett, next in line, but the man standing beside him threw up his gun for a wild shot that knocked Pat's aim off.

Foliard had managed to escape with the others, but, after he had gone a few yards into the protecting snow, he wheeled his horse around and rode slowly back toward the lawmen now grouped in the street. "Don't shoot me, Pat!" he called out. "I'm killed."

"Put up your hands, Tom!"

"I—I can't."

They carried Tom inside out of the cold, and very soon he was dead.

Pat took out after the Kid as soon as Tom had died. But the trail was covered with fresh snow and the posse finally returned to Sumner.

The next morning Brazil showed up in Fort Sumner with some more news for Pat—news that was more to the point this time. "Billy and his bunch moved in on me and Wilcox last night," he said. "The Kid put the bite on me to ride over here and sniff out the lay of the land for him." He hesitated a second as he looked Pat straight in the eye. "But when it comes to a showdown, you know which side I'm on."

"Sure I do," Pat said.

"That's what I figured. That's how come I'm laying it on the line. You got 'em guessing, Pat. The way you suckered 'em in to Sumner and got Tom Foliard, they can't dope out what you'll be up to next. They're all of them as jumpy as jackrabbits and fighting among themselves. All of 'em, that is, except the Kid. He's as cool as a morning breeze. All he wants for a Christmas present is a chance to blow your brains out. That's how he feels about you now."

"Can't say as I blame him," Pat said. "That's understandable."

"He's got it up his sleeve to come riding in on you here in Sumner from some other direction and either polish you off or drive you down the Pecos."

"Look," Pat said, "here's what you do. You go right on back to your place and tell the Kid you found me here in Sumner with only Mason and three Mexicans. Maybe that will sucker him in again."

It didn't though, and when the night passed without the Kid and his gang riding into Sumner from any direction, Pat and his posse rode out to the Wilcox ranch, deploying when they got in sight of it so as to make a cautious approach while keeping the place surrounded. But when Pat got to the house, he found that the Kid and his men had pulled out during the night without anybody getting a chance to see which way they went. Pat studied the situation a while and then announced that, sure as shooting, they had headed for Stinking Springs. "There's an old deserted cabin up there," he said, slapping his lanky thigh, "and that's where I'm going to bring this thing to a head. That's the only cover anywhere around, and even the Kid ain't staying outdoors this kind of weather any longer than he has to."

Pausing just long enough at the Wilcox ranch to stow away a good hot meal, the posse took to the saddle again and reached the vicinity of Stinking Springs an hour or so before sun-up. Sure now that they were moving in for the kill, they stopped about half a mile from the old adobe shack and sat for a long time listening and looking around in every direction. It was bitter cold, in fact, just a little short of unbearably cold. There was no moon, but the sky had cleared and was brilliant with stars. "All right," Pat said, "we'll hobble the horses here. Don't want any of them giving us away by snorting. And remember, I want all you men to keep your lips buttoned up tight. This is for keeps."

When they were about 400 yards from the shack, Pat stopped the posse again and divided it into two parties. There were thirteen men in all, and he kept six of them with him. He put Stewart in charge of the other five men and sent them circling around one side of the cabin while he led his party around the other way. Pat hadn't gone far before he came upon a dry arroyo, which was just right for his purpose. Leading his men down the bed of the arroyo, he was able to get around close to the front of the house under perfect protection. When he was about fifty feet from the front of the shack, he came to a stop. In the dim light that preceded dawn, they could see the shack clearly. It didn't have any windows and it had only one doorway, which was wide open to the elements now, the wooden door and most of the frame having rotted away long ago. There were three horses in front of the doorway, tethered to the projecting rafters.

Counting Billy, there must have been five men in that cabin. So it figured they must have taken two of their horses inside to help keep themselves warm. After studying the three tethered horses, Pat speculated in a soft whisper that one of the horses inside the cabin was undoubtedly Billy's famous gray mare, a splendid animal later described by Pat in his book about the Kid as being "celebrated for her speed, bottom, and beauty." The fact that Billy had that fine, fast horse inside the cabin with him put an entirely different complexion on the situation. If the Kid once got wind of the posse's presence, it was a cinch he would come riding out of there like a bat out of hell and maybe give them the slip again.

After a whispered conference, Pat sent a man around to tell Stewart to bring his men to the arroyo, so they could all sneak up together to the doorway and flush out the gang. But Stewart sent back word that he was against such a plan and insisted they wait until dawn.

Pat made no comment when he got Stewart's message. He just nodded and twisted himself around so that he could lie flat against the sloping bank of the arroyo, with his head up above the rim just high enough to keep his eyes fixed on the cabin doorway. For quite a while he lay there like that, silently brooding. This was it. This was what it had come to. He and the Kid would be shooting it out now, as soon as there was light enough to get going.

Just when the other men in Pat's party were beginning to wonder if the sheriff had fallen off to sleep, he stirred slightly and wriggled around until he was in the midst of

his men. "Look," he whispered, "I don't know what you
fellows been thinking, lying here freezing like this. You
all know how I used to feel about the Kid. But if you
figure I'm liable to let that make me cave in when we
get down to business, you're dead wrong. I'm here to get
the Kid. I know exactly how he's dressed. I got Brazil to
give it to me down to the last detail. The second he comes
through that doorway, I'm letting him have it. I'm going
to get in the first shot. You keep your eyes on me, all of
you, from now on. Get yourself in position and keep
your eyes on me. When you see me raise my rifle to my
shoulder, you bring up your guns too, and fire away. But
remember! The first shot is mine!"

He stopped all of a sudden and caught his breath, as
if somebody had kicked him in the groin, and he didn't
want to let on how much it hurt. Then he twisted himself
back around into his previous position and riveted his
eyes on the doorway again.

After a while a shadowy figure appeared in the doorway carrying a feed bag. With Billy's gray mare inside
that cabin, it didn't seem likely that the Kid himself would
be coming outside to feed the other fellows' horses. But
Pat must have been too keyed-up to waste any time cogi-
tating over a point like that. The instant he saw the figure
in the doorway there flashed through his mind a clear-cut
image of the Kid, and for a second he was tricked into
thinking this was the Kid. He raised his Winchester to his
shoulder and fired. A second later, six other shots rang
out, and the figure in the doorway spun around and reeled
back into the cabin.

A tumultuous commotion broke out in the cabin. For
a second all that Pat and his men could hear was a lot of
loud and spectacular cursing, the sum and substance of it
being a full and bitter expression of the outlaws' fury over
the discovery that they were trapped for fair. Then Billy's
voice cracked out over the general tumult like a sudden

clap of summer thunder, slashing across a windstorm: "You goddamn bastards, you got Charlie Bowdre! He's done for!"

Charle Bowdre! Out of the corner of their eyes, the men closest to Pat saw him stiffen a second, then sort of loosen up as he raised one foot a little and gave the wall of the arroyo a vicious kick. He had hoped it was the Kid.

"Garrett!" It was Rudabaugh's voice now, rising above the confusion. "Bowdre's bad hit. He wants to come out and surrender."

"Okay," Pat shouted. "Tell him to ,come ahead, but with his hands up!"

What went on in the cabin right after that was carried out with such stealth that the men on the outside didn't catch on to it. But when Pat heard about it later, it made him feel a little better about how everything finally turned out.

"Here," Billy had said in a grim whisper as he jerked Bowdre around toward the door and shifted the mortally wounded man's gun belt so his revolver was in front of him and in easy reach of his gun hand. "You're done for, Charlie. Go out there and kill some of those sons-of-bitches before you die." Then he gave Charlie a rough shove toward the door. But as Bowdre came staggering out toward Pat, he kept his hands up, making no attempt to pull his gun. Maybe he didn't want to. Maybe he was too far gone to give a damn. At any rate, he just stood there a few seconds, teetering on the edge of the arroyo, as he looked down at the man he used to pal around with. Choking from the blood that was welling up inside of him, he waved his arm back toward the cabin and mumbled: "I wish—I wish—"

No one will ever know what Charlie wished with his last breath. He died on his feet and toppled over into the arroyo beside Pat Garrett. *Another old friend gone.* Pat drew in a deep, long breath and let it blow back through

his clenched teeth, turning into a little white cloud as it
hit the freezing air. Then he pulled poor Charlie's body
over and stretched it out on his own blanket, folding the
blanket over to cover him up. It was a good thing to do,
any way you looked at it, for Charlie surely wasn't a
pleasant sight right then, not after what those seven slugs
had done to him, point-blank at fifty feet.

It was broad daylight shortly after that, and pretty
soon Pat noticed a slight movement of the rope on which
one of the horses outside the cabin was tethered. He
figured the men inside the cabin wanted to get their
horses inside so they could make a run for it, and he was
right. His first notion was to shoot the rope in two, but
it was shaking so much he was afraid he might miss it.
He waited until the horse was in front of the doorway
and then killed it instantly. The dead animal lying there
would, he reflected grimly, make it hard for the horses
inside to get out. Just to be on the safe side, he shot away
the ropes holding the other mounts and they trotted
quickly away from the disagreeable noise of gunfire.

It looked now as if the men in the arroyo were going
to have to settle down for a good long siege, so to while
away the time, Pat decided to open up a conversation
with the Kid.

"How you fellows fixed in there?" he called out.

"Pretty well," the Kid shouted back, in his usual
bantering tone of voice. "But there's no wood to cook
breakfast."

"Come on out and get some. Might as well be a little
sociable."

"Can't do it, Pat," Billy replied. "Business is too con-
fining. No time to run around."

Things being the way they were, Pat figured this was a
good time to twit the Kid a little about sending Brazil into
Sumner to spy on him. "Say," he said, "didn't you fellows
forget your program yesterday. The way I got it, you were

supposed to come sneaking in on us at Sumner from some other direction, give us a square fight, set us afoot, and drive us down the Pecos."

When he heard that, Billy knew that he had been betrayed by Brazil. He clammed up tight, and nothing the men in the arroyo said to him could get another word out of him.

Pat and his men hadn't had anything to eat now for quite a spell, so he divided the posse into two sections so they could take turns going back to the Wilcox ranch for breakfast. While Pat himself was at the ranch, looking exceedingly solemn and not joining in the conversation to any extent, Brazil came over to him.

"I see you're taking the Bowdre thing right hard," he said.

"Can't help it," Pat said tiredly. "I killed the very man I didn't want to."

"Look, Pat," Brazil said. "You shouldn't feel that way about it. You know what Charlie said to me when we were riding away from the crossroads that day I brought him to see you? He said to me, 'I wish you'd get that long-legged sonofabitch out to meet me just once more. I'd kill him and end all this trouble for good.'"

Just the same, Pat didn't seem to be any more cheerful when he got back to the arroyo and took up his part in the siege again. Nobody had any idea how long the outlaws would be able to hold out, so as the day wore on, Pat sent some of his men to the Wilcox ranch to bring a load of firewood, forage, and grub. About two o'clock in the afternoon, Billy turned loose the two horses in the cabin and drove them out, but he had a little trouble doing it because the horses didn't like passing the dead carcass at the doorway. About four o'clock, the wagon from the ranch showed up with the supplies.

When the men started to build a fire to cook the grub, Pat told them to wait a minute while he studied the direction the wind was blowing. Then he had them start the fire in a spot where the smell of the cooking food would be carried straight through the cabin door. "That'll fix 'em," he said, and it did.

Over a roaring fire, Pat's men roasted several sides of prime beef. The delicious smell of the beef, reinforced by the aroma of hot coffee, was too much for the starving men inside the cabin. Their bellies rebelled. A long stick came poking out of the doorway with a white rag tied to it. After the stick had been shaken around for a minute or so to attract attention, Dave Rudabaugh came stepping out gingerly, carrying the stick with its flag of truce in front of him. Halfway to the arroyo, he stopped and said: "If we surrender, will you guarantee that no one'll shoot us, Pat?"

"I'll guarantee none of us here shoots you. But I got no control over what might happen further on."

"I know that," Rudabaugh growled, "but will you agree to do your best to get us into some safe place where we can be sure of a fair trial?"

"Look, Dave," Pat replied, a trifle impatiently. "I'm the sheriff. That's my business. That's what I'm here for. Now, if you fellows really aim to surrender, all right, come on out, one at a time, with your hands up. But no monkey business. And I want Billy to come out first. Go on back and tell him that."

Rudabaugh went back into the cabin, and while the conference between him and Billy was going on in there, every man in the arroyo kept his gun trained on the doorway. There was one thing about Billy you had to remember if you knew what was good for you. In any situation, he was utterly unpredictable. So while Pat and his men waited, the tension got so thick you could stir it with a longhandled spoon. Then Billy finally came swaggering out, as cocky as ever, his hands shoulder-high. Pat raised himself up out of the arroyo in a crouched position, steadying himself on one knee, his Winchester trained straight at Billy.

"Stewart," he said, "you step over and get his gun."

After Billy had been disarmed, Rudabaugh, Pickett, and Wilson came out, one by one, and were also relieved of their weapons. Then the four outlaws were allowed to come in close to the hot fire and warm themselves, while they tore into chunks of rare beef. "Best Christmas dinner I ever et," Billy said, as cheerful as you please. And what he said made some sense at that, because the day was December 25, 1880. Then he grinned at Pat and announced: "You know, Pat, if we had got the horses inside, we'd have made a break for it. Matter of fact, I had my mare saddled and set for a try all by myself when you killed the horse in front of the door. I knew my mare wouldn't try to pass a dead horse like that. Or, if she did, soon as she saw it she was liable to rear up and knock my head clean off on top of the doorway."

On the way back from Stinking Springs, Pat had his hands full keeping his word that he would do his best to prevent his prisoners from getting hurt. He dropped Pickett off at Las Vegas, where the man was wanted on several charges. Then he took the other three to Deputy United States Marshall Conklin at Santa Fe, making the last leg of the journey by train. At several points, mobs of hostile citizens had the idea they would like to string Billy up personally. Usually a mild word of warning from the tall sheriff was enough to discourage direct action. Once when a crowd was particularly stubborn, Pat told them he would sure hate to do it, but if they pushed in any closer he would hand a six-shooter to Billy. That sent the crowds scattering in every direction remarkably fast.

At Santa Fe, Rudabaugh was convicted of robbery. Bill Wilson was arraigned twice for passing counterfeit money. The Kid was taken to Mesilla, where he was tried before Judge Ira Leonard and found guilty of the murder of Sheriff William Brady. The judge sentenced Billy to hang on the thirteenth day of May, 1881, at Lincoln, the county seat of Lincoln County.

Lincoln had no jail capable of holding a halfway healthy calf, let alone a dangerous bandit like Billy. With the Kid once more on his hands, Pat locked him in a room on the second floor of a building the county had recently bought and placed two guards on duty to keep him from straying. Since Billy was in irons, it looked as though he ought to stay put.

But on the evening of April 28, when Pat was in White Oaks, one of the most famous jailbreaks in the history of the West took place. On the 29th, Pat got a message from John Delaney in Lincoln. It said that Billy had escaped and that both of the guards, Bob Olinger and J. W. Bell, had been murdered. Later in the day, Deputy Bill Nickey arrived in White Oaks on a sweating horse to give Pat the details—at least what few details were known.

During the normal course of events, Olinger had left Billy with Bell on the second floor while he went across the street to have dinner. No one knew exactly what happened next, but suddenly there had been a shot from the county building. Olinger jumped up and hurried out of the restaurant to find out what was wrong. Larry Clements, who was also eating in the restaurant, got outside in time to see Olinger stop just inside the gate across the street that led up to the door of the county building. An old man named Geiss shouted from the corral gate beyond the corner of the building, "Bob, the Kid has killed Bell!"

At the same time a pleasant voice came down from the second-floor balcony above. "Hello, old boy." The Kid was leaning casually out over the railing looking down at Olinger. What stopped Olinger cold in his tracks was the fact that Billy was pointing the deputy's own double-barreled shotgun at him. Olinger had loaded it only that morning, and he knew there were eighteen buckshot in each barrel. He had remarked as he loaded the gun that the man who got hit with that would never be the same again. Olinger had but a split second to appreciate the irony of it all. The scattergun went off with a sound like two locomotives ramming head-on, and the deputy's body was thrown hard against the ground.

Still the Kid wasn't satisfied. He hated Olinger, a sadistically inclined man who had taken great pleasure in taunting the manacled, chained Kid. He pulled the other trigger, and the guard's lifeless body bounced under the impact of the second charge. Then Billy broke the gun over the railing and threw the pieces down at the mangled corpse. "Take it, God damn you," he yelled and then added this classic understatement: "You'll never follow me again with that gun!"

Billy filed off his chains and rode out of Lincoln armed with a rifle and two revolvers. Nobody stopped him.

After the Kid's spectacular escape, Pat played a waiting game for a while. He hoped Billy would gain confidence and show himself. The plan worked. In a short time Pat got word from the rancher Brazil that Billy had been seen around Pete Maxwell's place near Sumner. To confuse Billy's friends, who acted as spies for the Kid, Pat and two of his men headed toward Roswell as though they were intent on going south. At Roswell, under the cover of darkness, they swung back up north along the Pecos River. For three days they stuck to the hills, following unused trails and traveling as much as they could by night. Finally, on the third night, they arrived at the mouth of the Tayban Arroyo, five miles south of Fort Sumner.

Pat decided the best thing to do would be to go and have a talk with his old boss, Pete Maxwell. Pete was known and liked by almost everyone, and he would know, if anyone did, whether the Kid was hiding out nearby.

The three men set up a temporary camp a short distance from Pete's ranch. Then, in the darkness, they made their way quietly to an orchard which led to Pete's main house. When they reached the orchard, they heard voices in the night only a few yards away. The voices, speaking in Spanish, carried to them in low tones. Then, by the dim light of the stars, they saw a figure rise up from the ground. The man moved to a fence that bordered the orchard, jumped over it, and disappeared into the night.

Pat could not know that the dim figure he had seen was Billy the Kid. Billy, who spoke fluent Spanish, had been talking to some friends. Now he went to the shack of a Mexican companion who worked for Maxwell. He pulled off his hat and his boots and flopped onto the bed alongside his sleeping friend to read a newspaper. A little later, Billy slapped his friend on the rump to wake him up. "Start some coffee and get me a butcher knife," he said. "I'm hungry. I'll go up to Pete's house and get some beef."

In a few seconds Billy was headed toward Pete's place up the hill, with a knife in his hand and only his stockings on his feet.

Pat Garrett was approaching the house at the same time, but he had a slight head start. When he and his two friends arrived at the corner of Pete's long front porch, Pat whispered, "Wait for me here. I'll go in and have a powwow with Maxwell."

Almost tripping over a porch stair in the black shadows, Pat made his way into Pete's large, one-room house. He had been there many times, and he knew exactly where Pete's bed was. Walking across the floor to the bed, he said, "How are you, Pete? I'm looking for the Kid. Have you seen him around here?"

"Yes. He's been around for awhile," Pete answered as Pat sat on the edge of the bed. "I don't know if he's here right now or not."

At that moment Pat looked up and saw someone come to the doorway. The visitor glanced through the shadows to where Pat's two deputies stood outside the house and said in Spanish, "Who comes there?" There was no reply from the men near the corner of the building, and the man came on in. Pat thought he recognized Billy's voice, but he could not be sure. As the man entered through the doorway, Pat could make out that he held a knife in one hand and a revolver in the other.

As the dark figure started across the room, silent as a phantom, Pat leaned toward Pete and whispered, "Who is it?"

Maxwell didn't reply, and Pat wondered fleetingly if it might be Pete's brother-in-law. The unrecognizable figure that was in fact Billy the Kid came directly to where Pat was sitting on the edge of the bed. Billy leaned down so close that the knife in his hand brushed Pat's knee. "Who're those men out there, Pete?" he demanded in a low tone.

At last Pete got enough breath in his tight chest to talk. He had a choice of two loyalties, and he chose Pat. He whispered brokenly to Garrett, "That's him!"

The Kid raised his revolver within a foot of Pat's chest, realizing for the first time that there was another man with Maxwell. He demanded, *"Quien es? Quien es?"* as he backed swiftly across the room.

Maxwell rolled off one side of the bed, taking his blankets with him, as Pat sprang from the other side, drawing his gun and firing about a fifth of a second before the Kid got off his own shot. Pat fired at the Kid once more, but the second shot was a waste of time. His first bullet had gone straight into Billy's heart. Billy never spoke again. He was dead before his body fell on the floor.

Exactly where the last bullet Billy ever fired went was never discovered. The hammer of his .41 self-cocker was resting on a spent shell. Every man present heard three shots fired, but no one could find where the Kid's slug went. From the sharp angle it was fired, it was inconceivable that it could have gone out one of the two small windows in the room. It seemed to have disappeared into thin air.

After the Kid's death, Pat went back to sheriffing. But within a few months he figured he had a final job to do on Billy. At least eight "yellowbacks"—sensational magazines of the time—had made up their own histories of the Kid, and their stories were for the most part pure fiction. Some of them made Billy a fourteen-karat, sugar-coated Robin Hood of the plains, who did nothing but pay off mortgages for helpless old ladies and dispose of black-hearted villains. Others made him out to be the most cold-blooded killer the world had ever known.

To squelch all such absurdities, and to put the true story—as he knew it—on the record, Garrett wrote *The Authentic Life Of Billy The Kid, The Noted Desperado Of The Southwest,* which was first published in 1882, and is the source of a great deal of what is known about the Kid.

Pat put in his book all the things the Kid had told him back in the old days when they had tipped the bottle and played cards together—and the Kid seems to have had a fine imagination. For example, he told Pat that as a boy of twelve he had killed a drunken loafer who had insulted his mother. Although this sounds like whisky talk, it was included prominently in Pat's story of the Kid. More than that, it served as the inspiring cornerstone upon which the entire Billy the Kid legend was based—the legend that made him into a western Robin Hood.

Pat Garrett went on to become a rancher after he finished his term as sheriff of Lincoln County. Later on, in the 1880's, he put on a star once more as a captain in the Texas Rangers. He was in charge of a company of Rangers in the Panhandle working at putting down rustling there. Although he saw no more notable action in defending the law, he went on to serve one final term as sheriff in New Mexico after his stint with the Rangers.

The years wore on, and pretty soon Pat had five grown kids and a gray-haired wife, and it was the turn of the century.

Over these later years of his life, Pat was well known and respected by people in high places. He loved to ride and gamble and hunt, and among his friends were John Nance Garner, who became Vice-President in 1932, the author Emerson Hough, and even President Teddy Roosevelt. In 1901, it was Roosevelt who appointed Pat the Collector of Customs in El Paso, and, in 1905, when the Rough Riders had their reunion in San Antonio, Pat was invited as a special guest of the President.

After serving as Collector of Customs for a few years, Pat retired to his ranch in the Mesilla Valley and led a quiet life raising horses for a living.

On February 29, 1908, Pat left his ranch to drive through the Organ Mountains to Las Cruces. He was driving a wagon, and a friend, Carl Adamson, was sitting beside him on the seat. Pat never made it to Las Cruces. Somewhere along the lonely route, somebody held a gun behind Pat's head and pulled the trigger. Pat obviously never had a chance. His gun hand was gloved. His revolver had never left its holster.

Pat Garrett's murderer was never discovered. There was a lot of hard feeling over the killing because Pat was one of the best-liked men in New Mexico. But, for all the hullabaloo, no one was ever convicted of the crime. Carl Adamson said he and Pat had stopped the buckboard to take a stretch. That's when Pat was shot. But from there on, his testimony was meaningless. Wayne Brazil, a tenant on Pat's ranch, later confessed to the killing and was brought to trial, but was found not guilty. Still later, a hired gunman by the name of Jim Miller talked freely about how he had killed Pat Garrett, but he was never arrested. Many people were convinced that Carl Adamson was the murderer. They were sure that only someone Pat trusted could have sneaked behind him and put a bullet in him without warning.

All that is really known is one thing: Pat left his ranch driving a wagon and came back to the ranch lying dead in the back of the rig with a bullet hole through his head.

Even more perplexing than the question of who killed Pat is the question, why? One thought that comes to the romantic mind is that the fingers of Billy the Kid somehow stretched up out of the grave, after twenty-seven long years, and brought a vengeful death to Pat. This fanciful theory argues that some friend or relative of Billy waited patiently for more than a quarter of a century to pull the trigger that would send a lead slug crashing into Pat's brain and even the old, old score.

That seems highly unlikely. But, of course, both Pat Garrett and Billy the Kid lived highly unlikely lives.

The Saga of Wyatt Earp

By Jack Pearl

For ten years he outgunned the worst killers in the Old West and tamed the wildest cowtowns on the Chisholm Trail, but he never used bullets when his fists or a bluff could do the job

Sprawled on a bench beneath the wooden awning of Beebe's general store in Ellsworth, Kansas, Wyatt Earp was reading a newspaper. He was a slender man in his early twenties, with long legs, broad shoulders, and handsome features distinguished by unblinking blue eyes. Thick brown hair curled down the back of his neck, and he had a sweeping, well-groomed mustache. Except for him, the town square was deserted this blistering August day; the only signs of life were occasional shouts and gusts of laughter from the several saloons.

The story in the paper that held Wyatt's rapt attention started off by saying: "As we go to press, Hell is still in session in Ellsworth." It went on to tell how the community was enjoying an unexpected boom because a drought had burned off the grazing range around Dodge City, Abilene, Wichita, and the other cowtowns from which Texas ranchers usually sent their cattle and horses to the Eastern markets. By some freak of weather, the long dry spell of 1873 had skipped Ellsworth, where the grass was still growing thick and green. As a result, the

town was serving as the shipping terminal of the Chisholm
Trail, and about 1,700 cowobys had been raising hell all
summer in the thirty saloons and gambling houses that
constituted one of Ellsworth's principal industries.

Just as Wyatt turned the page, the stillness in the
square was broken by angry shouting coming from a
saloon a few doors away from Beebe's store. Two cowboys
burst through the swinging doors and stalked away with
a determination that could mean only one thing—trouble.
Staring at their retreating backs, Wyatt identified them
as Texas men by their Mexican sombreros and tight doe-
skin trousers. He put down the paper, took up his high-
peaked, black Stetson from the bench, and got to his feet.
He saw Sheriff Whitney, a short, heavy-set man in his
forties, come hurrying across the plaza from his store.
Perspiring and red-faced, the sheriff was strapping on his
gun belt, the two heavy Colts dragging low on his hips.
He stopped in front of Beebe's and looked up anxiously
at the man under the awning.

"Hello, Wyatt. Is it trouble?"

Earp mopped his sweaty palms on the chest of his
loose white shirt and shrugged. "I don't know."

Attracted by the commotion, faces began to appear in
the doorways of the stores and windows of the buildings
that faced the plaza. A bystander, drifting up to Beebe's
from the saloon, answered Whitney's question. "It started
out to be a friendly game. They all checked their guns at
the hotel to make sure there wouldn't be any trouble.
Then this hassle got started between Bill Thompson and
John Sterling. John slapped Bill and now the Thompsons
have gone after their guns."

"Oh, Lord!" the sheriff groaned. "It would have to be
the Thompsons!" Shaking his head, he hurried along and
pushed into the saloon where the fight had started.

Ben and Bill Thompson were the proprietors of a
traveling faro game that preyed on the cow circuit. They

were two of the most notorious gunslingers in the West and were reputed to have sent twenty-six men to Boot Hill. Wyatt Earp could appreciate the sheriff's concern over the Thompson's flareup.

A few minutes later, Whitney, looking vastly relieved, rejoined the growing group of spectators under Beebe's awning. "Sterling's friends have him in tow. If I can distract the Thompson boys for a spell, they'll get him out of town." He walked back and planted himself in front of the saloon.

Wyatt Earp turned curiously to the man at his elbow. "Where's Marshall Norton and his deputies? And where's Hogue?"

The man grinned. "Soon as Brocky Jack and the boys heard the name Thompson, they set about lookin' for some nice safe gopher holes to crawl into."

A hush settled over the plaza as the Thompsons reappeared. Each had a pair of six-guns swinging from his cartridge belt, and in addition Ben was armed with a shotgun and Bill with a rifle. When they reached the spot where Whitney was posted, they stopped and engaged the sheriff in a heated argument. Finally they appeared to relax a little and allowed Whitney to herd them into Brennan's saloon next door to Beebe's. Later, Whitney came out alone, mopping his face with a red bandanna.

"Whew!" he breathed. "That was close."

"Did you get their guns?" Wyatt demanded.

"Well, no." Whitney colored slightly. "But they've cooled off now, and, anyway, Sterling's gone. His friends got him out the back way."

"Hey you, Whitney!" Unexpectedly, Bill Thompson, ugly with drink, came charging out of Brennan's carrying Ben's shotgun. "That was a dirty trick you pulled, lettin' that bastard sneak out." He raised the shotgun. "This is what I think of double-crossers." He fired both barrels into Whitney's chest and ran back into Brennan's.

Before the echo of the shots had died out, the plaza was teeming with Texas men, their rifles and six-guns cocked for action. While his followers kept the town at bay, Bill Thompson strolled leisurely out of Brennan's and swaggered around the square. Wyatt Earp watched in disgust as the local peace officers, who had finally put in an appearance, peeped furtively from doorways without making any attempt to stop him.

With all of Ellsworth tucked neatly in his hip pocket, Ben Thompson decided to indulge himself a little. With 100 Texas men backing his play, he began to parade up and down in front of the Grand Central Hotel flourishing his shotgun, inviting the citizens of Ellsworth to make a fight of it and, in particular, reviling the ancestry and courage of the peace officers. In this last respect, he was unanimously supported by the townspeople.

"I'll pay a thousand dollars to any man who kills another marshal!" Cad Pierce, a rich cattleman, roared. The Texans cheered lustily.

Mayor Miller had arrived on the scene and was trying unsuccessfully to goad his peace officers into action. At this point, Wyatt Earp commented dryly, "You got some brave men working for you, Mayor."

In exasperation, Miller turned and looked him up and down. "*Who* are you?"

"Wyatt Earp."

"Well, mind your own business, Mr. Earp," the mayor grumbled. "I notice that you ain't even packin' a gun."

"I know," Wyatt said, "but if it was my business, I'd settle Ben Thompson's hash."

"All right," Miller said in sudden desperation, "I'll make it your business." He unpinned the marshal's badge from Brocky Jack's vest. "You're the new marshal of Ellsworth. Arrest Ben Thompson. You can get some guns in Beebe's."

A cowboy who had overhead the exchange between

Wyatt and the mayor skirted the plaza to report to Thompson. The Texans were delighted. "The kid's been out in the sun too long," one of them laughed. "Or maybe he's just tired of livin'. Wyatt Earp? Never heard of him. Did you, Ben?"

Thompson scratched a bushy eyebrow. "I've seen him around."

"Can't have any reputation as a gunfighter," Cad Pierce offered.

"No," Ben said slowly. "The only shootin' I ever seen him do was at a target. But he always took the money. He's a dead shot."

Pierce snorted. "Targets don't shoot back. Boot Hill's filled with sharpshooters."

"It's a funny thing about this Earp," Ben went on. "He's a shy, quiet kid. Usually steers clear of trouble. But he ain't scared. I saw him get riled just once. It was in a poker game. These two gamblers were working together and stacking the deck 'til Wyatt got on to them. He looks at these boys and says, just as cool as you please, 'Leave your money on the table and get out of here. This is an honest game.' And he sits there, nice and relaxed, with both hands on the table. Before you could wink an eye, them crooks was on their feet reachin' for their guns, and, goddam, you wouldn't believe it unless you seen it, but they didn't get them half out of their holsters when they found themselves starin' down the barrel of Wyatt's Colt. It was like magic or somethin'. Nobody had even seen him draw." Ben squinted anxiously toward Beebe's store. "He's sure fast."

"You ain't scared of him, are you, Ben?" a Texan needled him.

Thompson growled, "Naw, but I sort of like the kid."

In Beebe's store, Wyatt was making a leisurely inspection of a pile of secondhand .45-caliber Colts on a display table. "We just got a shipment of new ones in from the East," the clerk suggested. "They're real beauties. And since the town's payin' for 'em . . ." He winked.

Wyatt shook his head. "New guns and holsters slow you up." He picked up a gun that had the trigger wire back tight against the guard and grinned. "Bet the former owner of this little trick is resting peacefully. I never saw a fanner who could hit the side of a barn." He simulated a draw, and, with the gun held close to his hip, fanned the hammer back five times with his left hand. "Bang! bang! bang! bang! bang!" Still smiling, he tossed it back on the pile. He discarded several others like it—a few had their triggers removed entirely—and finally settled on a pair of well-worn 45-caliber Colts with fine hair triggers. With the cartridge belts adjusted to give just the right amount of drag, he slipped the guns into their holsters and made a few practice draws to see that they slid smoothly out of the leather. Then he loaded five shells into each gun, leaving one chamber empty for the hammer to rest on. The experienced Western gunman had far too much respect for his weapons to risk the loss of a kneecap or a foot through an accidental discharge. Finally, he let the guns fall easily into their holsters and adjusted them so that they rested slightly forward on his thighs.

As Wyatt stepped through the door of Beebe's into the street, the clamor in the plaza died as abruptly as if someone had given a signal. Without a word to anyone, he started across the square toward the Grand Central, his hands swinging easily at his sides, his hat pulled down low to shade his eyes. Every eye in the plaza followed him hypnotically. In more than a few minds, there must have flashed the analogy of David and Goliath: Wyatt, his boyishness emphasized by the tight, black denim trousers tucked in close around his ankles, in half-boots; Thompson, squat, beefy and muscled, the sense of his invincibility heightened by the 100 armed Texans at his back.

Ben was holding his shotgun at an informal port-arms stance, across his stomach. Ignoring the mob behind him, Wyatt kept his eyes fixed on Thompson's trigger hand gripping the shotgun at belly height. At the first twitch of a muscle or tendon in that hand, he knew he had to go for his gun—but not before. He was fairly certain that unless he drew their fire, the Texans would abide by the code of the West; the privilege of making the kill would be Thompson's.

When Wyatt was halfway across the plaza, Cad Pierce growled, "Let him have it, Ben."

"Shut up, Cad," Ben said absently. He seemed as much fascinated by the figure advancing relentlessly upon him as any of the bystanders. "He sure has guts," he muttered between clenched teeth, more to himself than to anyone else. Wyatt was only about forty yards away now. Ben licked his lips and suddenly spoke. "What do you want, Wyatt?"

"You, Ben," was the calm answer. Earp never broke his step.

It was at this point that the audience in the plaza first became aware that Bold Ben Thompson no longer looked so bold. "Wyatt," he called unexpectedly, "let's you and I talk. I don't want to fight you." The Texans gaped incredulously at him.

"I'm taking you in, Ben. Dead or alive, whichever way you want it."

With only fifteen yards separating them now, Ben was becoming frantic. "Listen, wait a minute. I want to talk to you."

"Throw your shotgun down or fight." Earp's eyes bored hard into Ben's belly.

"All right . . . All right, you win." Smiling nervously, Thompson let the shotgun drop into the dust and raised his hands. Wyatt stopped, and for the first time his hand went to his holster. The cold blue eyes raked the ranks of the Texas men. "You fellows . . . move! Fast!" There was no sound except the rustle of metal against leather as 100 six-guns slid docilely back into their holsters.

A half hour later, Ben Thompson was a free man, drinking with his cronies in Brennan's saloon, once more in possession of his shotgun. He had paid a $25 fine for disturbing the peace.

As soon as the decision was handed down, Wyatt turned in his guns and his badge.

The mayor looked disappointed. "We figured you'd stay on as marshal."

"Not when Ellsworth values sheriffs at $25 a head," Wyatt said evenly. "I think I'll be moving on to Wichita."

Wyatt Earp was born on March 19, 1848. He was one of six boys, three of whom were to become famous as the "fighting triumvirate," Wyatt, Morgan, and Virgil. Nicholas Earp, their father, was a Scotch emigrant who settled in Iowa and became a successful farmer.

Nicholas Earp was a curious product of an early training in the law, a love of the soil, and an unbounded admiration for the harmonious workings of law in nature. He was aware that man-made law was not always just, but he felt that it did express, for the most part, the will of the decent people in a society. And it was his conviction that it was the duty of every man to help enforce the law. Although he played a strong role in shaping the destinies and characters of his sons, Nicholas Earp believed firmly that a man had to do his own thinking. So he encouraged his sons to read and form their own opinions, even when those opinions clashed with his own—as they often did.

In 1864, the Earp family migrated to California, and there Wyatt had his first experience with "the code of the frontier." He was sixteen years old when he saw his first gunfight and saw the loser carried away to Boot Hill. A sensitive and intelligent youth, he was shocked by such brutal disregard for human life and all the civilized values his father had taught him to hold in respect. "I never want to shoot another gun as long as I live," he told his father with a white face.

"That won't be easy, Wyatt," the older Earp explained gently. "This is a new country, and things are a lot different from what we've been used to. Some day your life may depend on how well you can shoot a gun."

Wyatt stared at his father. "You'd never want me to kill a man like that, would you?"

"I'd expect you to give a man the benefit of the doubt every time. But if you were convinced that he was downright vicious, then it would be your duty to stop him any way you could, even if you had to kill him. If you saw a rattlesnake crawling into a neighbor's house, you wouldn't turn your back and walk away, would you?"

Wyatt was sick and confused. "Pa, why did we ever come out here to live?"

"It's not so bad, son. Wherever you go, you'll find out that the majority of folks feel like we do about law and order. Outlaws and killers are the exception. They just talk and act bigger than anybody else." He grasped Wyatt's shoulder and pulled him around so that their eyes met. "I don't hold that a man should go around looking for trouble. You know that, Wyatt. But when a society of decent men lets a few bad apples run the show, they're inviting all kinds of trouble. There's a responsibility that goes with being a decent man. He's got to be prepared to defend the things he believes in. Don't fight unless you have to, but when you have to, hit first and hit hard!"

"But I don't like to fight, Pa," Wyatt protested.

"All the more reason why you've got to be ready. A bully's a bluff, and he won't fight a man he can't buffalo."

In the years that followed, Wyatt Earp put this advice to good use. Born with a keen eye and remarkable reflexes, he practiced tirelessly with the rifle and six-gun and gained the reputation of being one of the best marksmen in California. His gunplay, however, was limited to local shooting matches; until he was over twenty-five years old, Wyatt never squeezed a trigger on a human target. Quiet, aloof, going about everything he did with cool confidence, he commanded the respect and liking of everyone with whom he associated, and those whose company he rejected were too perplexed by his icy contempt to take open offense.

Because he was a crack shot, Wyatt was offered a job as shotgun guard on the Banning Stage Line. Later, he went into business for himself, hauling supplies for the construction camps of the Union Pacific Railroad. Prizefighting was a popular sport in these camps, and bouts between the champions of the various camps were held weekly. As an outsider, Wyatt was often elected to hold bets and to referee. Soon he began to box himself, with considerable success. In 1868, at the suggestion of his parents, he went to live with his grandparents in Illinois and took up the study of law. There he fell in love with a neighborhood girl; within a few months, they were married. But less than a year later, his bride died of typhus. Bitter and grief-stricken, Wyatt gave up the law and headed west again.

It may well be that the death of his young wife offers a significant clue to the character of the man who became the greatest gunfighter in the West. For the tragedy left him with a rare contempt for death, which he knew couldn't hurt him any more than it had done already.

From 1869 until the memorable day in Ellsworth that proved to be the turning point of his life, Wyatt Earp drifted aimlessly from one job to another on the frontier. He served a hitch as a hunter with a government surveying party in Indian territory and made himself a good stake hunting buffalo. In 1871, he gravitated to Kansas City, where he learned a valuable lesson about gunfighting from old-timers like Wild Bill Hickok, Jack Morton, Billy Dixon, and Marshal Tom Speers. The winner of a gunfight, he discovered, was always the man who took his time.

Another lesson he learned was that a sober man always had the edge on a drunken foe. Although his duties and his love of gambling led him to spend a lot of time in saloons and gambling houses, Wyatt never drank or smoked until near the end of his career as a peace officer, and even then he would allow himself only the luxury of an occasional cigar or glass of beer. But, in his prime, you could always single out Wyatt Earp in a crowded barroom by the mug of coffee he held in his hand.

Wyatt's introduction to Wichita was an unusual one. On his first day in town, he blackened the eyes of a saloon-keeper who was whipping a small choreboy. Wyatt was promptly arrested. While he was waiting to see the judge in the courthouse, Mayor Jim Hope came up to him and asked for his name. "Wyatt Earp," he answered curtly. Hope's eyes widened. "You the fellow who arrested Ben Thompson in Ellsworth?" When Wyatt admitted he was, the mayor thrust out his hand. "How would you like to be deputy marshal of Wichita?"

"That might be all right," Wyatt accepted graciously.

To a large extent, Wyatt owed the reputation that had preceded him to Wichita to Ben Thompson. It was an admirable quirk in the outlaw's character that he bore Earp no grudge over the Ellsworth incident. In fact, Ben's highly melodramatic version of their encounter discouraged many a gunman who was tempted to make a play against the young marshal during his early days in Wichita.

Wyatt Earp was an enigma to the lawless element

whose experience had been limited to two types of peace
officers—professional killers, no better than themselves,
who shot first and asked questions later, and jelly-fish
whose motto was "peace at any price." Neither type could
be expected to command much respect. But with Earp,
they were unsure of their ground. He had the knack of
smelling out trouble even before it started and of taking
quick and efficient steps to see that it didn't get started.
It had always been an established custom in the cowtowns for a man to wear his guns wherever he went, and
if a cowhand wanted to indulge in a little innocent gunplay, like shooting up storefronts and plate-glass windows
to celebrate payday, well, that was a prerogative to which
every hard-working Texan was entitled. Furthermore, it
was awkward for even the most law-abiding citizens to
kick up a fuss about such innocent diversion inasmuch as
the cowboy trade was their bread and butter. Wyatt Earp
was the first marshal of Wichita to enforce the ordinance
requiring visitors to check their weapons when they came
to town. Violators were politely requested to comply with
the law, and anybody who chose to argue was apt to
wake up behind bars with a walnut-sized lump on his
head.

Scornful of odds and of the dire threats leveled against
him, the new marshal went about his business with an
attitude of bored detachment that both belittled and frustrated the toughest cowboys. They hated him as they had
never hated any other marshal. When rumors reached him
that the cattlemen were set to run him out of town, Wyatt
requisitioned two dozen shotguns and stashed them away
in strategic spots behind the counters of various stores and
barrooms along the route he patrolled.

The showdown came in the person of Shanghai Pierce.
Shanghai was a millionaire Texas cattle baron, popular
with his men and accustomed to be treated with deference in every cowtown on the Chisholm Trail. The historic

meeting between Wyatt and Shanghai occurred in front of Billy Collins' saloon on Main Street. The cattle king, a hulking brute who stood well over six feet and weighed about 250 pounds, was seated in a chair in the middle of the street, roaring drunk, waving his six-gun and loudly defying one of Wyatt's deputies to take it away from him. Dead-pan, Wyatt marched up to Pierce, disarmed him with a wrist lock, hauled him to his feet, and booted him head first through the swinging doors of Collins'. Turning to Pierce's friends who were shaken to their boot tops by the spectacle, Wyatt grunted, "Better sober him up. Next time, I'll run him in."

An hour later, his patrol brought him past Collins' again. As he came abreast of the doorway, an army of drunken cowboys, guns drawn, burst out into Main Street and dispersed to form a cordon around the staggering figure of Shanghai Pierce. "Lesh see you arrest me, you smart guy!" Shanghai hiccoughed.

As Wyatt turned toward them, Ed Morrison, a highly-rated gun-slinger who was leading the mob, snarled, "If he makes a move, let him have it, boys." With the marshal helpless under their guns, they backed off and disappeared around the corner into Douglas Avenue.

"We got him hog-tied," Shanghai chortled merrily, "Lesh celebrate." He pumped two shots into the air. A chorus of forty-odd six-guns roared their defiance, and the cowboys started down Douglas to shoot up Wichita in earnest. A symphony of gunfire, shattering glass, splintered wood, and high-pitched yells exploded across the city. In Judge Jewett's office a timid clerk, convinced that a wholesale massacre was under way, performed a rash act. Hanging outside the door was a big brass triangle. It had been placed there by the founding fathers who decreed that if the town was ever under attack, it would be rung to summon the citizens to arms. The clerk grabbed a hammer and struck the triangle.

A lump formed in Wyatt's belly as he listened to the ominous clang-clang-clang carry across the rooftops. It was simple to envision what would happen once an army of aroused citizens clashed head-on with an army of drunken cowboys. There would be mass murder on both sides. Jamming his hat down on his head, Wyatt sprinted through an alley, cut into the rear entrance of a store where he had cached one of his shotguns, and peered through the plate glass window at the rioting cowboys who were advancing along Douglas Street. Timing his play to coincide with a lull in the firing when most of them were busy reloading, he leaped out of the store entrance and threw up the shotgun. He singled out the ringleader, Ed Morrison, and addressed him gruffly. "Drop your guns, Morrison, and put up your hands." Wyatt had a shrewd grasp of mass behavior. His observations had convinced him that a mob was like an arch—knock out the keystone and it would crumble.

Staring down the twin barrels of the shotgun, all the heart went out of Ed Morrison. "Throw 'em up or I'll kill you!" Wyatt repeated. Morrison let go of his six-guns and reached for air. Wyatt fanned the shotgun back and forth across the front ranks of the Texans. "The rest of you too. Drop those guns or you'll be all dead men." As the cowboys hesitated, Shanghai displayed some of the common sense that had made him a rich man. "Do as he says, boys," he commanded. "Drop your guns."

Minutes later, a citizen's posse arrived on the scene to find the Texans lined up docilely at the curb, looking like a bunch of shamefaced schoolboys before a schoolmaster. Later, after each of them had been arraigned before Judge Jewett and fined $100 apiece, Wyatt whispered to the judge. "So help me, if I ever catch anyone ringing that triangle again, I'll run him in."

Earp was fast becoming an obsession with the Texans. Wherever the cattlemen gathered, they could talk of nothing else. Something had to be done about him. It was no longer merely a matter of personal esteem—the honor of Texas itself was at stake.

It would have been relatively simple to shoot him in the back or to gang up on him, but at this stage they were unwilling to settle for so humiliating a solution. The only way they could redeem themselves in their own eyes was to find a Texas champion who would stand up to Earp in a fair fight. Or, at least, a reasonably fair one. But no one was eager to claim the honor.

One Saturday night, an eighteen-year-old greenhorn, whose estimate of his skill with a six-gun had been swollen by bad whisky, fell victim to an ambition for glory. "There ain't nothing to it," George Peshaur, a cattle rustler, assured him. "You got your gun on him before you make your play. Then all you got to do is get him to draw on you, and bang! It's all over."

The kid was impressed. According to plan, he loitered in the shadows of a Douglas Avenue saloon until Wyatt came by on his patrol. As the marshal passed him, he slipped his .45 out of its holster and cried, "Hey you, Earp!" Wyatt turned to find himself covered. "Go ahead and draw, Earp," the Texan ordered. " 'Cause I'm going to kill you anyway."

"What do you want to do that for?" Wyatt inquired with deceptive unconcern. His hands hung loosely at his side.

The cowboy blinked as he considered the question. This wasn't the way he had rehearsed it. Instead of making a lunge for his gun, the marshal was apparently giving up. Confronted with the prospect of a completely colorless victory, the young Texan felt obliged to play out the drama. For the benefit of all within earshot, he unleashed a tirade of insults at Wyatt. Then, with the weakness of a true ham actor, he couldn't resist the temptation to see how his audience was reacting. His eyes only left Wyatt for a fraction of a second, but it was just long enough. The blur of the hand and the flash were almost simultaneous. The big Colt leaped out of the Texan's grasp like something alive, and, with a yelp of pain, he clutched at his gun arm.

"Shut up!" Wyatt said disgustedly. "You ain't hurt. I just nicked your hand." Whimpering like a puppy with a sore paw, the disillusioned gunman allowed himself to be led away to the jailhouse.

Convinced that the marshal had cast some kind of spell over them, the Texans finally decided to import a professional assassin to do their dirty work for them. Sergeant King was their man. A veteran of the Civil War, he had one of the most fearsome reputations in the West. He was fast on the draw and quick on the trigger, and he had killed twenty-one men before he was summoned to Wichita. The Texans gave King a warm reception. He was wined and dined and fawned over and encouraged to brag endlessly about his past successes. The only one who had any reservations about King's qualifications for the job was Ben Thompson. As the party was moving from one saloon to another on Douglas Avenue, Ben seized the opportunity to take King aside. "I've been trying to get you alone all day," he whispered, "to warn you not to be dumb enough to make any play for Wyatt Earp. He'll kill you for sure!"

Sergeant King stared at Ben in drunken indignation, sorely grieved by this appalling lack of confidence. "For weeks, all I've been thinkin' about is gettin' that son of a bitch in my sights," he said. He drew his six-gun and squinted along the barrel at an imaginary Wyatt Earp, like a small boy playing cops and robbers. "Bang! Bang!" he said. "You're dead, Earp!"

And then, while 200 spectators looked on tensely, Wyatt Earp materialized from around the corner of Main Street. He headed down Douglas straight toward Sergeant

King. All the tales of Earp's supernatural prowess, which King had laughed at so hard and so long, must have come back to haunt him at this moment. Paralyzed in a half-crouch with his gun still pointing down the street, he waited. Wyatt came marching up with long, confident strides, his arms swinging loosely at his sides. Showing no respect at all for the gun that covered him, he went straight to King, snatched the weapon away with his left hand, and slapped him across the face with his right. Then he grasped the thoroughly demoralized gunman by the scruff of the neck and led him away.

In his career as a marshal, Wyatt was sometimes faced with a problem that required more subtle handling. The incident of Ida May's piano was just such a case. On the outskirts of Wichita there was a popular brothel operated by a buxom madam known as Ida May. A resourceful businesswoman, Ida May was constantly seeking ways to enhance the character of her establishment. Plush furniture, expensive draperies, the finest liquors—nothing was too good for her patrons. One day she read an advertisement for a piano in a Kansas City paper and promptly decided that mood music would add a final touch of distinction to her parlor. She plunked down a twenty-five per cent deposit, with a promise to pay the balance on delivery, and in due course received her piano. However, once the instrument was set up in her parlor, Ida May brazenly informed the delivery man that she had no intention of paying the additional $750. She dared him to do something about it. He took one look at the mob of mean-looking Texans that was hovering around her protectively and left. After numerous other collectors—including the piano dealer himself—had been manhandled by Ida May's patrons, the affair wound up in the marshal's lap.

After some deliberation, Wyatt hit on a diplomatic approach to the case. He arrived at Ida May's early one

Saturday afternoon at the beginning of the weekend
festivities. Four unarmed piano movers stood quaking in
back of him. When he told Ida May that he intended to
repossess her piano, the madam gave a signal and a
dozen burly cowboys began to close in on him. Pretending
not to notice what was happening, Wyatt began to talk.
"I sure hate to do it, Ida May, because I know what this
piano means to you and I know you'd pay for it if you
could." He shook his head solemnly. "There's just one
thing surprises me. I've heard a lot of things said about
Texas men, but I never yet heard them accused of being
cheap. You'd think with all the friends you're supposed to
have, that they'd find it in their hearts to help you out of
this jam. Hell, it wouldn't set them back more than a few
dollars apiece. Well, now you know just what kind of
friends you've got, Ida May."

Ida May, like so many disreputable people, had a
secret yearning for respectability. She was tormented by
the suspicion that behind her back her customers thought
of her as just another cheap woman. The marshal's insinu-
ation confirmed this suspicion. She began to cry, and to
the astonishment of the cowboys, she shifted her attack
from Earp to them, blubbering about fair-weather friends
and stingy Texans. It was more than they could take. A
spokesman took it upon himself to step forward.

"Just a minute, Earp!" he said humbly and put a com-
forting arm across Ida May's shoulders. "No need to upset
the little lady like that. Why didn't you come to us in the
first place? Why, if we had any idea . . ." He trailed off
and looked around at the other cowboys. "Dig in men,
we're going to pass the hat." Wyatt left with the piano
seller's $750.

In the spring of 1876, Wyatt received a telegram from
Dodge City's Mayor Hoover, offering him the job of chief
deputy marshal of the toughest cowtown of them all.
Located in the heart of the Buffalo Range and the furthest

outpost of the railroad on the prairie, Dodge was a head-quarters for hunters, cattlemen, mule skinners, and soldiers from the frontier outposts. Its streets teemed with wagons, horses, and cattle. At the edge of town, blanket camps stretched away on all sides. Saloons, hotels, and gambling houses turned away customers by the hundreds. Tempers were short and gun fights were hourly occurrences. When Wyatt reached Dodge, the Boot Hill score for the year was eighty. His first move was to appoint three new deputies, Jim and Bat Masterson and Joe Mason.

"We get $2.50 for every arrest we make," he told them. "We'll put it into a pool and divide it at the end of the month. But remember one thing: The bounty applies only to live prisoners. If you have to bend a six-gun over a man's head to end an argument, all right. If you have to shoot, wing 'em. Our job is to stop the killings in Dodge, not to increase them."

The success of Earp's campaign against outlawry in Dodge can best be judged by statistics. It was a rare month that the marshal and his deputies averaged less than $800 apiece in bounties. As time went on, Wyatt added to his force such men as Charlie Bassett, Bill Tilghman, and Neal Brown. The exploits of this coterie provided the inspiration for hundreds of frontier yarns by the famous pulp writer, Ned Buntline. In fact, as a token of his appreciation of the peace officers of Dodge City, Buntline had the Colt factory design five special .45-caliber six-guns with 12-inch barrels—four inches longer than standard—which he presented to Earp, Bassett, Bat Masterson, Tilghman, and Brown.

Wyatt stayed on top of the badmen of Dodge relentlessly, never missing a chance to demonstrate his superiority over them. His object was to belittle them at every opportunity. One of his favorite devices was to crash the daily target matches which were a ritual with the professional gunmen. The regularity with which he bested them

in six-gun practice served as a subtle reminder to the
badmen that they stood small chance against him in any
real gun play.

Of this period, Bat Masterson later wrote: "A hundred
men, more or less, with reputations as killers, whom I
have known, have started gunplays against him only to
look into the muzzle of Wyatt's Colt before they could get
their own guns half-drawn. In such a call, if a gunman
thought particularly well of himself or had any record as
a fighting man, Wyatt would bend the long barrel of his
Buntline around the gunman's head.

"In the old days, to buffalo a guntoter was to inflict
more than physical injury; it heaped greater calumny upon
him than any other form of insult could convey. A man
for whom a camp had any respect was entitled to be shot
at. . . .

"When circumstances made it necessary for Wyatt to
shoot, he preferred to disable men rather than to kill
them. I could list at least fifty gun fights in which Wyatt
put a slug through the arm or shoulder of some man who
was shooting at him, when he might as certainly have shot
him in the belly or through the heart . . ."

Stymied where gunplay was concerned, the lawless
element of Dodge tried to get at the marshal from another
direction. A giant of a man who was a champion of rough-
and-tumble fighting back in Texas was chosen to put the
plan into action. His job was to pick a fight with Earp
and beat him to death. One Saturday afternoon he ac-
costed Wyatt outside of a South Side dance hall and
loudly offered the opinion that the marshal's courage was
strictly of the gunslinging variety.

"Let him rave, Wyatt," Bat Masterson advised. "He's
a bad one. I've seen him in action. You wouldn't stand a
chance."

"If I don't fight him," Wyatt said simply, "none of us

will stand a chance. If I back down, it'll be a signal for every cowboy in Dodge to make a play for me."

Grimly, he peeled off his cartridge belts and his Colts, threw them on the ground near Masterson's feet, and turned to face the Texas champion.

The two men squared off, Wyatt looking hopelessly inadequate compared with the cowboy who topped him in height and reach by several inches and outweighed him by at least fifty pounds. In the opening minutes of the battle, a roundhouse right clubbed Wyatt to his knees. His head cleared barely in time for him to roll away from a murderous kick aimed at his ribs. He tumbled to one side and bounced back on his feet like a rubber ball. The Texan charged after him, reaching for him like a big grizzly. Wyatt stopped his rush with a left jab to the nose, then sank his right wrist deep into the Texan's midsection. As the big man doubled up, Wyatt felled him with a rabbit punch. He backed off as the Texan lumbered to his feet with murder in his eye.

Over a hundred people were in the crowd watching the fight, but the audience was predominantly pro-Texan. The two men battled back and forth across the street, plastered with mud and their own blood. Although he looked frail beside the cowboy, Wyatt had the lithe muscularity of a panther. Both men could punch hard and could take it as well. When the fight passed the half-hour mark, each had been down three or four times, and the Texan was gasping for breath. Wyatt moved in cautiously, hooked a left and right to the head, and, as his opponent brought up his arms, drove a short right into the solar plexus. This time the giant went down for good.

Bruised and bloody, his shirt hanging in tatters, Wyatt glared savagely into the ring of faces around him. "Who's next?" he panted. And to the horror of Bat Masterson, who was just beginning to relax, another Texan, even bigger than the first, stepped forward. Most men would have disdained to take advantage of such a challenge, but to this particular Texan, it must have seemed like too good an opportunity to pass up. He swaggered in, confident that he could put the finishing touches on a fight that he figured was three-quarters won for him already. No one was ever able to figure out what hidden reserves Wyatt called upon, but inside of five minutes he had the second cowboy on the ground blubbering for mercy. That was enough for the rest. They slunk back into the saloons and dance halls.

Late in 1876 rumors reached Dodge City that gold had been discovered around Deadwood, South Dakota. Bat Masterson joined the trek north, and Wyatt invited his brother Morgan to replace his ace deputy. His regime was less than four months old, but already things had quieted down to the extent that sometimes a whole day went by without an arrest. In September, Wyatt decided that law enforcement in the cowtown capital was becoming too routine for his talents. He and Morgan handed in their resignations and set out for Deadwood City. It took not quite a year for the gold fever to burn itself out of their systems. In July of 1877 they headed south again, convinced that although they might never grow rich jailing cowboys at $2.50 a head, it was a better living than the average prospector could ever hope for.

When Wyatt arrived back in Dodge he was shocked. In ten months law and order had suffered a critical setback because of bitter political controversy raging between newly-elected mayor "Dog" Kelly and certain powerful interests in the city. Kelly believed in enforcing the law to the letter, while the businessmen who stood to get rich from the cattle traffic had taken advantage of Earp's departure to pressure the law officers into coddling the Texas men. The mayor practically got down on his knees and begged Wyatt to take back his old job again.

He had been installed as marshal only twenty-four hours when the word went out that men in "high places" had guaranteed immunity to any gunman who could kill him and escape beyond the city limits. Wyatt's reaction to this threat was to crack down even harder on the gun-toting cowmen. As his deputies he appointed Neal Brown, Jim Masterson, Ed Masterson, and Bill Tilghman.

In July of 1877 there were 200,000 head of cattle grazing on the prairies around Dodge City and 2,000 cowboys with one idea in mind after the long, dull weeks on the trail—to paint the town red. Once again the jail overflowed with prisoners; bounty payments averaged over $1,000 a month.

But there was no real crisis until Wyatt Earp wrapped the foot-long barrel of his Buntline Special around the head of Tobe Driskill. Driskill was one of the wealthiest cattle men in Texas, and with a single sale he could put half a million dollars into circulation in Dodge. He considered himself to be a privileged character and refused to admit that the ban on gun-toting within the city limits could possibly apply to him. When he took violent exception to Wyatt's polite suggestion that he check his guns at the hotel, the marshal had to pistol-whip him and lug him off to jail.

Soon afterward it was rumored that Driskill had posted a standing offer of $1,000 payable to the killer of Wyatt Earp. A few nervous gunmen made feeble attempts to ambush the marshal, and, when their schemes aborted, they fled town.

In the closing days of the cattle-shipping season, Wyatt rode to Texas in the capacity of deputy U. S. marshal to round up a notorious gang of cattle thieves for the Santa Fe Railroad. In Griffin, Texas, he got some unexpected help from the notorious Doc Holliday—the tubercular dentist who went west to die and lingered twenty years to become one of the most famous gamblers and

gunmen of his era. A mean-tempered, unfriendly, nervous
fellow with a quick trigger finger, Holliday fought his way
out of numerous scrapes and into a reputation. The strange
friendship that developed between the gunman and the
marshal has been the subject of considerable speculation,
for the two men had little in common except courage and
a steady gunhand. But from the beginning Doc and Wyatt
were drawn together like two members of an exclusive
club who form an alliance through the mutual recognition
of some unspoken sign or mannerism. It may have been
that to Doc, living with his fatal illness so long, death had
lost much of its terror, and that now, like Wyatt, he had
nothing but bitter contempt for it. In any case, when Earp
returned to Dodge City in the spring of 1878, Doc Holliday followed him.

In Wyatt's absence all hell had broken loose. On April
9, Ed Masterson had been killed in a gunfight with two
outlaws, and, despite the fact that Bat Masterson had
promptly cut down both of the killers, the incident had
ignited the smouldering emotions of the gunmen. During
the summer several attempts were made to collect the
$1,000 bounty on the marshal's head, but he managed to
keep the situation under control. Then, in September,
Wyatt led a civilian posse to reinforce U. S. Cavalry units
fighting an Indian uprising around Cimarron. While he
was gone, Tobe Driskill and Ed Morrison, his arch ene-
mies, decided to "tree" Dodge City. Returning unexpectedly with some Indian prisoners on the night of the 24th,
Wyatt walked right into the middle of a full-scale raid.

The Texans moved into town by way of Front Street,
swept quickly through the South Side, crossed the tracks
and began to shoot up the "better" part of Dodge with
methodical savagery. Wyatt was at the jailhouse feeding
his prisoners. When he heard the gunfire, he headed across
town at a fast trot. He reached Front Street just as the

gang was passing Second Avenue, raking the street with
their crossfire. At this point he made a bad guess that
almost cost him his life. Stored away behind the counter
of the Long Branch was a shotgun he had put there for
just such an emergency. Wyatt estimated that he could
reach the doorway ahead of the rioting cowboys. It was
a dead heat. Before he could get to the shotgun or draw
his Colts, a dozen Texas men stepped out of the shadows
and covered him with their guns.

"I been waitin' all my life for this moment," Ed Morrison crowed.

"If you've got any praying to do, you better do it,"
Tobe Driskill said as the Texans converged on him, fingers
tight on the triggers of their .45's.

Wyatt later admitted that it was one of the few times
in his career that he was sure his number was up. His
only hope was to take a few cowboys with him.

"Draw, you son-of-a-bitch!" Driskill screamed, and
Wyatt's muscles coiled as he saw the tendons in the cattleman's gun hand tighten. As twenty-five cowboys and the
marshal went for their guns simultaneously, an alien voice
broke sharply on their ears. "Hold it!" They froze like
figures in a tableau.

"Reach, you miserable bastards!" the voice commanded. Wyatt Earp grinned as he listened to the long
string of profanity. There was only one man he knew who
could curse like that. He squinted into the shadows of the
doorway and verified his hunch. The thin, haunting coun-
tenance of Doc Holliday stared back at him. As the cowmen hesitated, Wyatt whipped out his own guns, realizing
that his reprieve would be shortlived unless the Texans
could be decisively buffaloed before their bewilderment
gave way to reason; he and Doc were outnumbered better
than twelve to one. But Holliday was already a step ahead
of him. In a matter-of-fact voice that implied there was
no doubt about who was in charge, he growled, "Well,

do we lock 'em up, Wyatt?" Taking the cue, Earp slashed his gun down on Ed Morrison's skull, then turned savagely on Driskill. "Drop those guns, Tobe, or you're next!"

The cattle boss hastened to comply. The other cowboys were set to follow suit when one of the rioters who had faded back into the shadows made a last-ditch bid. Drawing a bead on the marshal's badge, he squeezed the trigger of his .45. But another shot rang out a fraction of a second ahead of his, and, as he pulled the trigger, the cowboy twisted in pain and clutched at his shoulder. His bullet pinged harmlessly into the wall above Wyatt's head.

"Don't anybody else try that," Doc Holliday said calmly, blowing the smoke from the barrel of one of his six-guns. The rest of the Driskill-Morrison gang couldn't get rid of their guns fast enough.

Wyatt knew better than to thank Doc for saving his life. It would only have embarrassed him. When the cowboys were safely locked up, he made only a slight reference to the incident. "Nice shooting, Doc," he said casually. "I couldn't have done better myself."

Doc's stony face cracked in a rare smile.

The great Driskill-Morrison fiasco marked the end of the warfare in Dodge City. With outlawry and gunplay on the decline, Wyatt's duties were limited primarily to paper work. It wasn't long before he was overcome with restlessness. He was ripe for a change.

On December 1, 1879, Wyatt Earp tackled the last and toughest assignment of his career—bringing law and order to Tombstone, Arizona. Tombstone was the Sodom of the plains, a composite of all that was bad in the West. A drab mining camp perched on a mile-high ledge of rock in the middle of the desert, Tombstone came to life spectacularly when Ed Schieffelin struck a vein of silver ore that was assayed at $20,000 a ton. Within a year and a half, the population jumped from 500 to 15,000.

In its heyday, Tombstone was a boom town in the real

sense of the word. It was common to see old men who looked like vagrants flashing $100,000 rolls in saloons and gambling houses. In the middle of the main street, there was a forty-five foot hole, carefully fenced off like a monument, from which a cool million dollars in metal had been taken. In the midst of rudely constructed frame and adobe buildings, luxurious palaces of pleasure sprang up that would have done credit to Monte Carlo. In the Oriental, the Crystal Palace, and the Alhambra, hobnailed boots ground the mud and dust of unpaved streets into the finest Brussels carpet, ten-gallon hats graced elaborately carved mahogany bars, and one establishment boasted the bizarre phenomenon of a string quartet, decked out in white ties and tails, grinding out cowboy tunes.

Silver was God in Arizona, and Tombstone was the shrine where the greedy came to worship. For every man who came to Tombstone to seek his fortune honestly, there were a half dozen who came to take it away from him. And the officials of the Arizona Territory showed remarkably little interest in controlling the thieves. Operating virtually with official sanction, smugglers, murderers, rustlers, and criminals of all types had a field day.

Typical of the organized outlawry that operated out of Tombstone was the Clanton Gang, a band of 300 outlaws under the guise of ranchers who worked a lucrative "protection racket" on the businessmen of Tombstone and the legitimate ranchers in the surrounding districts. The officers of the Clanton Gang included such notorious gunmen as Ike, Phin, and Billy Clanton, Curly Bill Brocious, John Ringo, Frank and Tom McLowery, Frank Stillwell, and Pete Spence.

Wyatt was first appointed sheriff of Tombstone, but in 1880 he received a federal appointment as U. S. marshal of the district. For two years, his efforts at reform were hamstrung by the politicians, chiefly by Johnny Behan, the sheriff of Cochise County and puppet of the Clanton crowd. As senior local peace officer in the community, Behan sabotaged the clean-up campaign by artfully bungling arrests, allowing prisoners to escape, and tipping off the outlaws concerning all the marshal's movements and plans.

In 1881, the scandalous administration of the Arizona Territory became a matter of national attention. On the recommendation of a Congressional investigating committee, President Arthur appointed John J. Gosper, an avowed supporter of Wyatt Earp, as governor of the territory. As soon as he took office, Gosper gave the marshal the green light to clean up Tombstone and promised him that all the resources of the state government would be placed at his disposal.

The Clantons were frightened. They realized that from this point on, Wyatt's position would become progressively stronger. It was apparent to them that if they were ever to stop him, it had to be done quickly.

On October 23, Earp received an ultimatum: "You have forty-eight hours to get out of town." The alternative was obvious. Two days later, a somber party that included Ike Clanton, Billy Clanton, Tom McLowery, Frank McLowery, Bill Claiborne, and Wes Fuller rode into Tombstone and staked out in the O. K. Corral. They left their horses in the stables on Allen Street, then walked back into the corral at the rear that fronted Fremont Street. Ike Clanton stopped a passerby and gave him a message to Wyatt Earp. "Tell him we're waiting for him at the O. K. Corral."

Wyatt was in Hafford's Store on Fourth Avenue with his brothers, Virgil and Morgan, when he got the challenge. The three brothers looked at each other and without a word headed for the door. Halfway down the block they passed Doc Holliday.

"What's up, Wyatt?" he demanded.

"Got a date at the O. K. Corral."

Doc brightened. "Good. I'll come with you."

"This is a personal matter, Doc."

Holliday was insulted. "That ain't no way to talk to a friend."

A tight smile played on Wyatt's face. "It's going to be rough."

"It's right up my alley, then," Doc said, and without waiting for an invitation, he fell into step beside his friend.

At the corner of Fourth and Fremont, Sheriff Behan hurried up to them breathlessly. "Everything's under control, Wyatt. I got their guns."

"Did you run 'em in?" Wyatt asked suspiciously.

"No," the sheriff hedged, "I'll arrest them later."

"Let's go then," Wyatt shot back.

Behan went pale. "Look here, I'm the sheriff of this here county, and I'm ordering you not to go down there. I'll arrest them myself."

Doc Holliday favored the sheriff with a few of his choice profanities, and the party pushed on down Fremont with Behan tagging along, pleading now. "You'll be cut down like dogs. Stay away from those hombres, I'm warnin' you."

On the west, the O. K. Corral was flanked by the Assay Office; on the east, by C. S. Fly's photo gallery. When the Earps came abreast of Fly's, Behan ducked into the front door and took up a position near a side window that commanded a view of the corral.

Maintaining a wide interval between them, the three brothers turned into the corral while Doc Holliday stationed himself at the entrance to forestall an ambush. The five rustlers were standing with their backs against the Assay Office. They had placed two horses on their left flank to block any fire from the corner of the building. As the distance closed between the two factions, Virgil Earp called out, "Put up your hands. You're under arrest!"

Frank McLowery's hand dropped to the handle of his
.45. It was a cue to the others.

Thousands of words and a dozen motion pictures have
immortalized the action of the next thirty seconds.

Frank McLowery and Billy Clanton opened fire on
Wyatt Earp. Both shots were wide; one perforated the
skirt of his long coat, the other nicked his sleeve. Frank
McLowery took a slug from Wyatt's Buntline square in
the belly. At the opening salvo, Tom McLowery leaped
behind one of the horses and fired at Morgan Earp.
Morgan twisted half-around, hit in the shoulder. Ignoring
Billy Clanton, Wyatt pumped a bullet into the pony that
was shielding Tom McLowery. Both horses stampeded
for the street.

Like so many others before them, Billy Claiborne and
Ike Clanton panicked at the sight of the ominous Earps.
Fanning his gun wildly at Virgil, Claiborne bolted for
the side door of Fly's gallery. Ike didn't even go for his
gun. With his hands up, he headed straight for Wyatt,
pleading, "Don't shoot me, Wyatt, please don't shoot me."
Brushing Ike aside contemptuously while he tried to sight
on Tom McLowery, Wyatt snapped, "If you're not going
to fight, get out of the way." Sprinting as if his life de-
pended on it, Ike followed Claiborne through the gallery
door—which was held open by Johnny Behan.

Meanwhile, Doc Holliday cut loose with a shotgun
that Virgil Earp had handed him when he first joined the
party. Riddled with buckshot, Tom McLowery ran for
the street. As he turned the corner, Wyatt dropped him
with a slug in the ribs. Billy Clanton tossed his Colt from
his right hand to his left as Virgil winged his gun arm.
A second later, Morgan Earp, firing from a prone position,
drilled Clanton in the chest. Badly wounded, Frank Mc-
Lowery and Billy Clanton kept coming on, their guns
blazing. Suddenly, two shots rang out behind them. "Look

out, boys," Doc Holliday shouted. He winged a volley through the gallery window, and the threat from that quarter was silenced.

Three bullets spun Frank McLowery clear around as Doc, Morgan, and Wyatt fired together. He was dead before he hit the ground. Virgil took one of Billy Clanton's slugs high in the leg. Then Wyatt dropped Billy with one in the spine. Abruptly the O. K. Corral was quiet. Minutes later, when a posse of vigilantes arrived on the scene, the Earps were all on their feet. The wounds suffered by Morgan and Virgil weren't serious, and Doc Holliday had only an ugly scratch across his back from a ricochet. Wyatt's luck held good; there wasn't a single mark on him anywhere.

The outlaw band hadn't fared so well. Three were dead, and two were still running.

Writhing under Wyatt's heel like a dying rattlesnake, the Clanton empire struck out blindly. With the knowledge that his own days of power were numbered, Sheriff Behan threatened to arrest the Earps and Doc Holliday for murder. Wyatt dared him to try it. A coroner's jury quashed the ridiculous charge in short order. But on the night of December 28, as Virgil Earp stepped from the Oriental saloon, the blast of five shotguns sprayed across Allen Street. Virgil collapsed with a gaping hole in his side, his left arm shattered. For months, it was uncertain whether he would live or die. Eleven weeks later, Morgan Earp was playing billiards in Bob Hatch's pool hall. Wyatt, comfortably relaxed in a chair against the wall, was watching the game. At the rear of the building, a door led into the alley running between Fourth Street and Fifth. At about 10:30, Morgan was standing with his back to this door, chalking his cue, when suddenly the glass panes in the upper half of the panel shattered in a roar of gunfire. Two shots spat into the plaster above Wyatt's head, but

Morgan wasn't so lucky. One of the bullets severed his
spine. He died minutes later in Wyatt's arms.

The next morning, after he had testified at a coroner's
hearing, Wyatt made plans to put Virgil on a train for
California. "I've got a job to do," he said grimly. "I can't
do it if I have to worry about you. Doc and I will ride as
far as Tucson with you. There's a half-hour stopover there
and I don't want to take any chances. They got one Earp.
Maybe they'll figure to push their luck."

It was a good hunch. When the California train was
ready to pull out of the Tucson station, Wyatt and Doc
Holliday said goodbye to Virgil and separated to patrol
the darkened railroad yard through which the train would
shortly pass. Cat-footing along the tracks, Wyatt spotted
a group of figures huddled on a flat car among a string of
empties on a siding. He moved into the shadows alongside
the car and brought up the sawed-off shotgun he was
carrying. In his haste the barrel twisted in his hands and
clanked against metal. Two orange flashes mushroomed
in the blackness, and the would-be assassins scattered in
all directions from the flatcar before Wyatt could return
the fire. He sprinted after one of the retreating figures
through the maze of the deserted yard. The chase ended
abruptly when his quarry doubled back to the tracks and
found the way blocked by the California train. Frantically
the man whirled, and in the light from the sluggishly
moving coaches, Wyatt recognized Frank Stillwell. Telling
about it later, Wyatt said he would never forget the look
of terror on the rustler's face. As he closed in on him,
Stillwell lunged for the shotgun. Wyatt wrenched it loose,
jammed it underneath his heart, and fired both barrels.
A second later, he looked up to see Virgil's white face
flattened against a window as the train slid past. With
his eyes glued on the ghostlike mask staring out into the
night, Wyatt ran alongside the coach, holding one finger
in the air. "We got one, Virg! We got one for Morg!"

Three days later, Wyatt cornered Indian Charlie at Pete Spence's ranch. The halfbreed admitted freely that Curly Bill, Frank Stillwell, and Hank Swilling had paid him $25 to help dry-gulch Morgan Earp. Wyatt's face was terrible in its fury. "Go ahead and draw, Charlie," he said. "Here's your chance to earn another $25."

Indian Charlie fell to his knees and begged for mercy, but Wyatt regarded him without pity. "I tell you what. I'll count slow from one to three. At one, you can go for your guns. I won't touch mine until I reach three." There was a murmur of protest from the rest of the posse. Indian Charlie was no gunfighter, but who could lose with odds like those? A gleam of hope brightened the half-breed's eyes.

"You mean it?" he asked guardedly.

"I'm going to start counting," Wyatt warned. "One . . ." Indian Charlie lunged for his six-gun. Overanxious, he tried to bring up the barrel before it was clear of the holster . . . "Two . . ." Panicky, the half-breed struggled with the gun as the front sight caught in the leather. "Three . . ." Wyatt's Buntline leaped from its holster. Indian Charlie had his gun free now, but before he could fire it, Wyatt had squeezed off three shots. Indian Charlie sagged to the ground, hit in the belly, chest, and head.

On Thursday afternoon, Wyatt's posse surprised a band of outlaws led by Curly Bill near a waterhole at Iron Springs. Wyatt, riding at the head of the column on a narrow mountain trail, rounded a shoulder and came face to face with Curly Bill. Both men were armed with shotguns. Bill fired first, and a double load of buckshot shredded Wyatt's coat. The short-snouted gun in Wyatt's hands roared twice. Curly Bill pitched forward on his face, his body almost cut in half. In the confusion, the rest of the outlaws escaped through a grove of cottonwood trees, but the score was mounting. In less than a week three of the men who had murdered Morgan Earp were dead.

In the weeks that followed, Wyatt put the heat on the rustlers relentlessly. Word spread across the prairie that he was out to kill them all. Morgan's murder had become a two-edged sword. A tranquil Wyatt Earp was bad enough, but a vengeful one was a prospect too frightening to face. Saddlebags were packed hurriedly and the boys of the Clanton Gang streamed out of their holes like rats and scattered to Mexico and the Indian Territory. A few hid out in the mountains where they launched occasional forays on hapless travelers, but organized crime in Tombstone was finished forever.

Late in 1882, after Wyatt Earp had left Arizona, Ike and Phin Clanton, John Ringo, Billy Claiborne, and Pony Deal drifted back to Tombstone. Within a year all were killed in gunfights, with the exception of Phin, who was sentenced to a long term in Yuma prison.

With the conclusion of the Tombstone affair, Wyatt Earp hung up his guns. He had been fighting almost continuously for ten years, and that was enough for any man. All he wanted now was peace. Too young to retire, he tried his luck as a gambler, as a real estate agent, and as a saloon keeper. In later years, he became a minor tycoon with considerable properties in gold, copper, and oil.

In 1929, he died in his sleep at the age of eighty-one, not a very auspicious ending if, like the old-timers, you believe that all good gunfighters should die with their boots on. But, as Doc Holliday once put it, "That's all right for *just good* gunfighters—but Wyatt Earp was the *best*."

The Saga of Sam Bass

By Clair Huffaker

~~~~~~

Sam and his outlaw "army" almost put the Texas railroads out of business and had the best lawmen in the nation tearing out their hair—until a traitor did him in

Sam Bass was born in Indiana—that was his native home.
And at the age of seventeen, young Sam began to roam.
He first came out to Texas, a cowboy for to be
A kinder-hearted feller, you scarcely ever see.

Daniel and Elizabeth Bass raised a big family on their farm outside Mitchell, Indiana. Their fourth son, Samuel, was born on the 21st day of July in 1851. As a boy, Sam was a hard worker, quiet and industrious. His proud parents often boasted that he was the solid, dependable sort of lad who would grow up, marry one of the gingham-clad girls around Mitchell, and settle down on his own farm to be a respected citizen, raise up a family, and live a long, peaceful life.

They had no way of knowing that their youngster would never have time to marry or settle down, that he was to lead a short, violent life that would be hammered to a close by the pounding bullets of Texas Ranger Colts. As for Sam's being a respected citizen, this surmise was not quite true either. Sam was to become Texas' most beloved bandit, adored and venerated by half the people in his adopted state—but the other half would angrily insist hanging was too good for him. He was to become an almost mythical figure in the Southwest, a sort of legendary six-gun Robin Hood surrounded by lean-hipped Merry Men who thundered down out of the hills to rob the rich and give to the poor and who blithely drove a legion of confused law officers almost to insanity—until a traitor entered his camp.

When he was ten, Sam's mother died. Then, while the boy was just getting over this great blow, his older brothers went off to fight the Civil War and news quickly came back that two of them had been killed. Sam's father never recovered from these shocks, and a little later, his health gone, the old man departed from this world too.

Now an orphan, a tall, skinny youth who talked in a shy whisper and whose face reflected the thought that life was a pretty grim prospect, Sam was sent to a nearby farm to live with his mother's well-to-do brother, Dave Sheeks. They say that Uncle David welcomed the distraught boy with open arms—in one outstretched arm was a shovel and in the other a pitchfork. Sheeks worked the boy day and night, seven days a week. In return, he generously saw to it that Sam had something to eat every now and then and enough clothes to just barely cover his lanky frame.

During the years that Sam was literally in bondage to his uncle, his schooling was completely ignored. He never did master the complexities of reading and writing. Later in life, when he made his heavy, laborious signature, he often rested after printing the "B" so that the name sometimes had an unhappy way of looking like Sam B. Ass, a point over which even his closest friends never failed to chuckle.

The only cheerful moments that brightened the otherwise gloomy years Sam spent with his uncle were the times when he would hear exciting (and highly exaggerated) stories of the Reno Gang, a tough bunch of badmen marauding through the territory. They staged one holdup only a few miles from Sheeks' farm, and by the time the news reached Sam, their loot was being estimated at $100,000.

That, Sam felt, must be the life. No worries, no cares. Just wander around having fun—and when you run short of cash, simply pull out your gun and take some.

When he was seventeen, young Sam told his tyrannical uncle he wanted some sort of an allowance or wages in return for his hard labor. Sheeks had never in his life parted willingly with a penny, and he wasn't about to change his ways, so the two reached an impasse. Around his eighteenth birthday, Sam saw clearly that he had to choose between being a serf for Uncle Dave indefinitely or striking out on his own. He didn't have the problem of what to pack; he simply walked off the farm and worked his way to St. Louis, from there moving on to Rosedale.

In Rosedale, Sam got a job in a lumbermill and decided life might turn out to be fun after all. He spent about a year there, and people just naturally liked the quiet, easygoing young man. It was at this time that Sam bought his first brace of revolvers and taught himself how to use them with notable expertness, although he thought too much of people to shoot them up in the then accepted manner and made up his mind never to do so if it could be avoided.

One of his many friends, a man named Mays, told Sam he was taking his family to Texas, and young Bass decided to go along with them. They made their way in a prairie schooner to the town of Denton in the Lone Star State, and Sam went to work at a variety of jobs. He rode as a cowpuncher, then became a stablehand at the Lacey House, a hotel in Denton. Colonel William Eagan, a prominent Denton citizen who owned considerable real estate in the town and was also the sheriff, took a liking to Sam.

He hired him as general handyman and later took to swearing him in as special deputy whenever Sam's particular talents were needed. These talents consisted of the rare ability to make friends right away with anyone. They say young Sam Bass could slap a coiled rattlesnake on the shoulder and invite it for a drink, and the rattler would insist on buying. Sam had the knack of making a happy-go-lucky pal out of anyone, and he caused many potential gun battles in the streets of Denton to wind up as good-natured discussions in the nearest bar.

Sam was doing fine. But then, just after his twenty-fourth birthday, he did something that made him some easy money and eventually plunged him into a life of lawlessness. Sam bought a horse, and that was the beginning of the end.

> He made a deal in race stock, one called the Denton
>   Mare,
> He matched her in scrub races and took her to the fair.
> Sam always coined the money, and spent it just as
>   free,
> He always drank good whisky, wherever he might be.

The horse's name was Jenny, and while she had no thoroughbred pretentions, the Denton Mare did have a wide streak of jackrabbit in her. Sam had always thought a salary of $25 a month was real riches, but when his friends talked him into running Jenny in a local scrub race and he wound up holding $100 in his slightly trembling hand, he suddenly had an entirely new idea of money. "Holy smoke!" he muttered. "This is a season's wages!"

When Sam drank, everyone drank, and that night everyone got roaring drunk, with Sam leading off at the bar.

Sheriff Eagan tried to talk him out of the horse-racing business, but Sam wouldn't listen to him. He had worked hard all his life, and he had been poor all his life. He could plainly see that hard work and poverty are too often stablemates. Sam quit Eagan and made a small vow never to do another day's work as long as he lived. And whatever his critics may say, it must be admitted that Sam fulfilled that vow with the utmost tenacity.

He made a science of horse racing. He hired a tiny Negro jockey named Dick Eidson, who weighed only a little more than the bridle Jenny wore. To cut down weight even farther, Dick used no saddle. On days when the diminutive rider had a hangover, they would spread a little sorghum on Jenny's back to keep the jock glued on when the mare whizzed down the track. Sam found that Jenny could do even better if she started from a two-foot bank built up behind her hind heels. At the races, in plain sight of the crowd, he and Dick would patiently dig up the track and pack a starting bank for the Denton Mare. If there were any complaints, Sam would begrudgingly offer his opponents a two-length handicap, knowing perfectly well that Jenny would shoot out from the bank like a low-flying rocket. Even with a three- and four-length handicap, Jenny rarely lost a quarter-mile race.

The money was rolling in at a rate almost equal to Jenny's uncanny pace. Sam paid Dick as much as $300 a race and treated his sorrel mare like a four-legged princess. At the same time he started going around with some high-living characters of the kind you always encounter around race tracks. He met Henry Underwood, a connoisseur of United States and Mexican jails, and he met a part-time badman, Joel Collins. His association with such men caused folks to begin to pay some attention to the evil rumors a few hard losers were spreading. They said Sam doped horses. They said he paid stablemen to twist thin strands of baling wire around other horses' legs, wire that would tighten into the flesh as they ran and cripple them.

Such talk wasn't true. Sam loved horses too much to mistreat them. But he did work a little confidence game with Joel Collins.

Joel would come into a town acting like a stranger to Sam and sneer openly at Jenny. He would say he had seen the Denton Mare run and that she was nothing but an overrated plow horse who couldn't outdistance a flat-footed turtle with a sprained ankle. "As a matter of plain fact, stranger," Joel would say, "they got a horse in this town that can run circles around your nag. I got $200 that says Speedwell, the local champ, can win in a walk!"

"Why, my Jenny can beat that broken-down mule running backwards!" Sam would snort contemptuously.

The outraged citizenry, spurred on by patriotism and by Joel's confidence, would then zealously lay it on the line in support of the local horse, and the team would move on to the next town, considerably richer. They took in most of Texas with this simple dodge, then moved up into Oklahoma. A few miles from Fort Sill, Sam found some Cherokee Indians who had justifiable pride in their swift mounts. He put Jenny up against the fastest pony the tribe could produce, betting cold cash against several of the Redskins' horses. Jenny won, but the race was close, and the Cherokees refused to pay up. Since there were about thirty of them, outnumbering Sam and his friends ten-to-one, Bass just shrugged his shoulders and left the camp. But that night he came back and took the Cherokee horses he had won—plus a few extra for interest—and started back for Texas.

The Cherokees had long boasted that no white man could ever get into their camp undetected. When they discovered their loss, they were furious. They sent a rider to report the incident to the nearest sheriff, who immediately collected a posse and headed Sam off near the border.

The sheriff drew up a hundred yards from where Sam

faced him on Jenny and called out, "Stop in the name of the law! I'm taking them ponies back to their rightful owners!"

"They're with their rightful owners!" Sam yelled back. He put a hand on each of his revolvers and added, "Before you take them, we'll wade knee deep in blood!"

Such was Sam's manner when angered that the sheriff thought his words over quietly and then rode back to tell the Cherokees their horses couldn't be found.

Jenny went lame after they got back to Texas, and Sam regretfully put her out to pasture on a friend's farm. He was drinking down his sorrow over the loss of the Denton Mare when Joel Collins had an idea how Sam might invest the money he hadn't yet thrown away. He suggested that they buy some longhorns and drive them up north where prices were high. Sam forthwith bought a herd.

Sam left the Collins ranch in the merry month of May,
With a herd of Texas cattle that grew some on the way.
Sold out in Custer City and then got on a spree,
A jollier set of cowboys, you seldom ever see.

Sam made Joel his ramrod, and they left Joel's ranch for Dodge City with a few forgetful cowboys they had picked up in various saloons around town. These *vaqueros* were so forgetful that they couldn't quite remember what Sam's trail brand was, and they were forever accidentally picking up stray cattle along the way. By the time they got to Dodge City, the herd had doubled in size, and the authorities in that town raised an embarrassing technical point of ownership. Naturally Sam couldn't remember where all the extra steers had come from, and he couldn't rightly recall where he had put the nonexistent bills of sale, so they drove the herd on into Nebraska where the authorities at that time were much less inclined to ask questions. The poor memories of everyone involved re-

sulted in Sam's netting $8,000 after the boys had been
paid off and all expenses met.

He and Joel next wandered down into Ogallala where
the town was frantic with talk of the gold strike in Deadwood. It didn't take them long to catch the fever. They
traveled to the Black Hills and joined the wild colony
hastily assembling there.

Winter hit within a few weeks. The thermometer plum-
meted to thirty below zero and stayed there.

Sam promptly dropped most of his $8,000 in a worth-
less mining claim. He and Joel tried everything from
professional gambling to running a bordello in the sprawling red-light district, but they went steadily down in
funds. Even Sam's good nature was strained when spring
came and they found themselves stone broke. Things were
so black, it looked as though Sam might have to break
his vow and go to work again.

When knee-deep mud had replaced the snow along
Deadwood's main drag, Sam told Joel, "Hell, I guess the
only thing to do is rob a stagecoach." They found three
other men low on their luck—Jim Berry, Frank Towle, and
Bill Reddy, who liked Sam's simple, straightforward idea.
The five rookie robbers were so poor they had to steal the
horses they needed for the job, but on March 25th, 1877,
they galloped their stolen steeds to a gulch three miles
outside of Deadwood, tied red bandannas around their
faces, and waited patiently for the coach. When the stage
lumbered into the draw beneath them, Sam called out,
"Haul on those reins! This is a holdup!"

Johnny Slaughter, the driver, did exactly that. He
stopped and held up his hands. Johnny was a fine, cooper-
ative driver to stick up. But Bill Reddy aimed his scattergun at the tranquil man in the driver's seat and blasted
poor Johnny nearly in two. The horses panicked at the
thundering echoes of the shotgun volley and took off in a

dead run for town, a strong box holding $15,000 bouncing safely in the boot.

Sam threatened to kill Reddy for the senseless murder. Reddy was so impressed with the way Sam expressed himself on this topic that he galloped away and was never heard of again.

Disgusted beyond words, the others rode into Deadwood to join in the general outcry over Johnny's untimely demise and to curse the blackhearted villains who had tried to rob the stage. Sam was so well liked that the law in Deadwood never did tie him up with the evil doing. Half a dozen stages were held up for minor sums during the following weeks. After each one, Sam was richer. But the local peace officers put his wealth down to luck at blackjack.

The trouble with robbing stages was, there wasn't any real money in it. You could count on a brass watch or two from the passengers and maybe $100 or so from the strongbox, but that was all. With so many coaches being held up, the shippers became wary; big shipments of gold were sent through when they were least expected, and, even then, the dust was cleverly hidden. One stage that Sam held up for its gold contained exactly nothing. The driver had only $30 on him, and since he told Sam he was getting married, Sam didn't take his money.

"Joel," Sam confessed later on, "I'm getting tired of risking my neck for flapjack money and a few brass watches."

Joel agreed that their plight was a sad one, and they were lamenting the deplorable state of the stage-coach-robbing business when a California renegade by the name of Jack Davis approached them. "Sam," Jack said, "if you're looking for gold, the place to find it is on the Union Pacific trains."

This was a pleasing thought. No one particularly liked

trains anyway. They were thought of generally as the ten-
tacles of a corporate octopus back East which was greedily
grabbing up all the West. Also, rumor had it that a young
fellow named Jesse James was doing well by sticking up
trains. Sam liked the idea and made plans accordingly.

On their way back to Texas they robbed the U.P.
*   train,*
And then split up in couples and started out again.
Joel Collins and his partner were overtaken soon.
With all their stolen money, they had to meet their
*   doom.*

On the night of September 19, Sam rode at the head
of five men toward the tiny station at Big Springs, Nebraska, where the eastbound Union Pacific was scheduled
to make a water stop. Along with Joel and Jack Davis, he
had recruited Jim Berry, Bill Heffridge, and Tom Nixon.
At a little before 10 o'clock, they halted their horses outside the ring of light cast from the stationhouse and put
bandannas around their faces. Their horses snorted nervously as the ten o'clock train rumbled out of the darkness
and screeched to a stop. Sam rode up to the express car,
while his companions appeared out of the night to cover
the conductor, engineer, brakeman, and station attendant.
Holding a .45 on the petrified express-car messenger, Sam
hoisted himself out of the saddle and into the car.

"Friend," he said softly, "how would you like to open
that safe?"

The attendant stuttered that he didn't know how, and
Sam believed him. Exploring the interior of the car, Sam
found a heavy pouch near the safe. Opening it, he saw
that it was filled with $20 gold pieces. "This is my meat,"
he told the messenger. "We won't have to bother with the
safe." He called for Joel to come and pick up the pouch,
then vaulted into the saddle and joined the others as they
headed for the hills.

When they were some distance out of Big Springs, Sam ordered a halt. They spent nearly two hours counting the gold pieces. There were 3,000 of them. "Sixty thousand dollars!" Joel whistled. "That's what I call a good night's work!"

"Thing to do now," Sam told them, "is divide the money and split up. Posses all over Nebraska will be looking for six men. I'm going back down to Denton, and one of you can come along. Two of you go east, and two west. Chances are better that way."

Joel and Bill Heffridge decided to head west, while Nixon and Berry went east. Jack Davis elected to go south with Sam.

By sunup Sam and Jack were twenty miles along the trail. When the sun's beams flashed across the prairie at them, Sam took one of the $20 gold pieces out of his saddle bags and looked at it. It shone brightly in the sun. It was a newly minted coin with the year 1877 printed on it. The coins were brand-new.

"Almost too pretty to spend," Sam laughed.

In Kansas City the two riders heard that lawmen were fanning out all over the state searching for the desperate gang of train robbers. It wasn't rightly known who they were, but it was expected that they would be spending 1877 gold pieces right and left. Sam and Jack didn't spend any money. They traded their two good horses for an old plow horse and a beaten-down rig to escape suspicion. On their way south from Kansas City they were joined and escorted by a troop of soldiers who had been detailed to help in the manhunt. They were on the road together for several days, and Sam often remarked of that time, "I felt right safe with them soldiers to look out for me."

At Fort Worth, Jack Davis took a train for New Orleans. "I'm going down to South America and get me a ranch," he told Sam. "Why don't you come along? The States'll be too hot for you."

"Oh, I reckon not," Sam said. "I kind of like Denton. It's sort of like a hometown to me. You be careful on that train," he cautioned. "No telling where them desperadoes will pop up next."

After Jack's train had pulled out, Sam visited a nearby saloon for a bit of refreshment. In the bar he listened with interest while others discussed the robbery. After half an hour a man rushed in with the latest report. An hombre named Joel Collins and his sidekick, Bill Heffridge, had been halted as a routine matter by a sheriff who had two deputies and a squad of ten soldiers with him. The two suspects had made a break and gone for their guns. They had been cut to pieces by murderous, point-blank fire from the soldiers' rifles.

Feeling slightly sick, Sam left the bar. He bought a fast horse and outfitted it the next day. Before he left Fort Worth, he got his second shock. Jim Berry had been cornered in Missouri by a posse and was now lying near death. Within three weeks, half of the gang had been shot up.

> Sam made it back to Texas, all right side up with care,
> Rode into the town of Denton, with all his friends to share.
> Sam's life was short in Texas, four robberies did he do,
> He robbed all the passengers, mail and express cars too.

Following little-known trails, Sam rode on toward Denton. He stopped at Cove Hollow, a lonely spot thickly overrun with trees and underbrush thirty miles outside of Denton, and set up a camp. Living there in the Hollow, he gradually began to regain his confidence. Sometimes he even rode into Denton at night to see some of his old buddies and cut up a few touches in the saloons. He ran

into Hank Underwood again, and, along with a likable
gunslinger named Frank Jackson, they spent considerable
time drinking and rousting about. Sam decided that no
one outside of his close friends knew he was a holdup
man after all, and, with Bass picking up the bills, the trio
outfitted themselves with new clothes, new horses, and
new guns and whooped out for San Antonio to go on a
spree. In San Antonio they went on a wild round of
wine, women, and song—but Sam was throwing around
too many of those shiny gold pieces. He often paid $20
for a meal, a cigar or a shoeshine, telling the astonished
recipient to keep the change.

But then one night a venturesome blonde whom Sam
had availed himself of from time to time came to where
he was living. "There's some cops in town looking for
you," she told Sam. "One of them's a Pinkerton man, and
he's got two deputies from Denton with him."

"They interested in anything in particular?" Sam
asked.

"I hear they're curious about a trail of 1877 gold pieces
you've left all the way from Denton."

Sam thanked the girl, hunted up Underwood and
Jackson, and headed out of San Antonio. He could have
made it across the border into Mexico, but he told Jackson, "God damn it, Texas is where all my friends are. No
one's going to drive me out of the state."

They rode back to their camp in Cove Hollow and,
against Sam's advice, Underwood went on into Denton.
"They'll claim you had a part in the Big Springs holdup,
Hank," Sam told him.

Underwood had been in Denton exactly fifteen minutes when Sheriff Eagan and three deputies jailed him.
They suspected that he was the "Tom Nixon," who had
been in on the U.P. robbery. Hank was so enraged at this
"terrible miscarriage of justice" that he was speechless. A
special deputy had him halfway to Nebraska for trial

before the shock wore off, and he started cussing at the top of his voice.

Sam and Frank hurried into Denton as soon as they heard of Hank's arrest. But the news had traveled too slowly, and poor Hank was already over the state line. They ran smack into Deputy Sheriff Tom Gerrin, who yelled for help and started blazing away at them with his revolver. Sam emptied his gun into the air. Gerrin, sure that he was about to have his head blown off, was so nervous he couldn't have hit the ground beneath him twice in a row.

Riding back to Cove Hollow, Sam realized that once a man is on the Hoot Owl trail, there is no turning back. He had been pretty idle lately, half thinking that no one would associate him with the U.P. holdup, hoping that it would blow over in time. But obviously he was now in the outlaw game for keeps. Sam and Frank moved to Hickory Creek, a little closer to Denton, where no one would be likely to think to look for them, then held up the stage at Weatherford just to keep in practice. Frank was jubilant over the $500 they got from the stage, but Sam told him it was nothing. "We'll round up a couple of boys and take on a train the next time," he promised.

Frank then uttered a classic understatement of the West. He shook his head thoughtfully and said, "It looks to me as if train robbin' might be gettin' kind of dangerous."

"I reckon," Sam admitted, "that there is some truth in what you say."

They put the deal up to an old friend of Sam's, Jim Murphy, who had a farm not far out of Denton. Jim liked the idea of robbing trains but didn't have the guts to go along. He used his father as an excuse, saying that the old man couldn't be left alone. Then they talked to Seab Barnes and Tom Spottswood about train robbing, and both Seab and Tom thought it offered a fine future.

Within the next two months, Sam completely revolutionized the railroad industry in Texas. He held up four trains in forty-eight days, a record that stands unbroken in all the gaudy history of the West. Lawmen from all over the nation swarmed into Texas until it was said that two out of every three people on the streets of Denton and Dallas were private detectives or official police—and the third man was one of Sam's gang. Newspapers all over the country outdid each other in front page spreads devoted to accounts of Sam and his "outlaw army." Estimates as to the number of the gang ran from fifty to 150.

On the night of February 22, 1878, Sam led his three men to Allen Station on the outskirts of Dallas. When the Houston and Texas Central train chugged into the station, Sam entered the express car while the others held guns on the surprised railroad employees. They cleared out with $1,300 amid the usual hail of angry shots and made it back to Hickory Creek. Tom Spottswood wandered off and soon got himself arrested in town. Seab took sick. Sam's "army" of 150 men was now cut to one man. He and Frank helped Seab over his illness and, then, on March 18, rode over to Hutchins to rob the Houston and Texas Central all over again. This time they only got $500, and the railroad men decided to put up a real fight as the boys galloped away. The air was filled with bullets, and the express messenger chased them down the road on foot, yelling and shaking his fist. He might even have caught them except that the brakeman on his own train brought him down with a rifle ball in the leg.

The boys made it back to Hickory Creek and found Hank Underwood waiting for them there with another jailbird named Arkansas Johnson. Hank had broken out of jail and brought Arkansas along with him. They went through a few bottles of whisky by way of celebrating the reunion, then got down to planning future operations.

On April 4, they tackled the Texas and Pacific Railroad

at Eagle Ford, practically in the downtown area of Dallas. Only six nights later they popped up in Mesquite in time to catch the eleven o'clock train at the station. Frank Jackson lined up the station agent, engineer, and brakeman on the platform while the other boys placed themselves at strategic points. Sam started for the mail car. Suddenly the conductor appeared on the platform with a small caliber pocket pistol and started shooting. The gun sounded like a little, yapping dog, and the conductor wasn't hitting within ten feet of where he was aiming, so the boys just laughed at him. Angered, the conductor ducked back into the train and came out a moment later with a heavy pair of .45 Colts. When he started blowing the station down in an irresponsible way with these small cannons, Sam regretfully shot him through the shoulder—just to keep him from killing anyone. Several passengers added to the confusion by shooting from the train windows, and two armed guards on the train proved to be trigger-happy too.

In the deafening roar of gunfire, Sam found that the messenger had locked the mail-car door from the inside. He had to threaten to burn the car down before the stubborn little man would open it. Sam found only a miserable $150 in the car, and, on top of that, the messenger timidly inquired if he could have a receipt for the money so his boss would know that he hadn't stolen it himself. Any bandit but Sam Bass, listening to the good-sized war going on outside and finding a negligible $150 in loot, would have shot the messenger. But good-natured Sam patiently scrawled his signature at the bottom of a receipt and handed it over.

By the time Sam and his boys ran for their horses and rode into the night, the station was so pockmarked with bullet holes it looked as though the whole Civil War had been fought right there. Fortunately, no one had been killed. A few minutes after the shooting was over, a man named Gross came into the light of the station, pushing a reluctant figure before him. "Lookit here!" he bellowed. "I caught Sam Bass hisself, singlehanded!"

Gross had succeeded in capturing the train's fireman.

Sam had four companions, each a bold and daring lad,
Underwood and Jackson, Tom Spottswood and Seab,
Four of the boldest cowboys the ranges ever knew,
They whupped the Texas Rangers and ran the boys in blue.

The four holdups very nearly ruined railroading in Texas. People knew that Sam wasn't robbing passengers, but they didn't know when he might start, and they were cashing in tickets and refusing to ride trains all over the state. Express company officers were frantic as the harried officials tore their hair and tried to think of hiding places for valuables being shipped.

Figuring that Sam wouldn't let the banks off forever, citizens all over the state began drawing out their deposits.

Newspaper writers began to flock to Denton County, only to find all available hotel space taken up by police. U.S. Marshal Stilwell H. Russel was at the Windsor Hotel with nineteen men. William Pinkerton, Allen Pinkerton's son, had taken over the LeGrand Hotel with a battalion of assistant investigators. Hordes of detectives hired by the railroads and express companies flocked through the territory. Federal investigators and local lawmen added to the chaos, while privatte sleuths, eager to catch Sam and collect the rewards that were growing every day, helped to make Sam's pursuit a comedy of errors. A be-whiskered gentleman in the streets of Denton dropped his beard. Blushing furiously, he tried to replace the false whiskers as he hurried around a corner. Two special deputies proudly brought in "Sam Bass," only to discover that their victim was another special deputy.

Topping the crest of the flood of lawmen, Major John
Jones and Captain June Peak of the Texas Rangers arrived
with thirty handpicked men to try their luck at catching
Bass. Major Jones knew Sam couldn't be far away. He also
knew Sam was even coming into Denton upon occasion,
but was so well thought of among the townspeople that
no one would inform on him. Indeed, because he was so
generous with the proceeds of his train robberies, they
thought of him as a kind of Robin Hood.

Jones devised a simple plan. He began arresting everyone who had ever been known to be on particularly good
terms with Sam and trying to pump them for information.
This meant arresting a goodly portion of Denton County,
but Jones was a determined man. He quizzed Spottswood
unsuccessfully, arrested Albert Pipes, Henry Herndon, and
Jim Murphy, all of whom were intimates of Sam and all
of whom were suspected of belonging to his gang. Within
a few days he had made dozens of arrests and had even
picked up Jim Murphy's old dad, for it was known that
he had spoken to Sam on numerous occasions.

In the meantime, Captain Peak was scouring the area
with his contingent of Rangers. They ran into other posses
more than anything else, but they did have occasional
brushes with Sam. Once the two groups spotted each
other from clear across Cove Hollow, a distance of nearly
2,500 feet. One of the Rangers took a shot at the bandits,
and the slug tore a hole in Sam's rifle stock. The shot was
pure luck, of course, but it made Sam so mad the others
had to talk him out of going back to battle the Rangers
at odds of about eight to one.

They even had the army searching for Sam, and it got
so the boys couldn't get a good night's sleep at the Hickory
Creek camp. No one ever actually looked there, since it
was so close to Denton, but troops of horses going by at
all hours made too much noise for relaxation.

Sam moved out to Salt Creek to avoid the crowds.

On the way there, they met two posses. In each case Sam passed his gang off as a team of express company agents and solemnly agreed with the other posses that Sam Bass was a very elusive cuss.

At Salt Creek they found things a little quieter. They stayed there calmly while peace officers roamed in droves about the county, shooting at each other. Then, by sheer accident, the Rangers stumbled on the Salt Creek hideout.

> Sam had another companion called Arkansas for
> short,
> He was shot by a Texas Ranger by the name of
> Thomas Floyd.
> Tom is a big six-shooter, and he acts mighty shy,
> But I can tell you his racket, he's a deadbeat on
> the sly.

Sam only had a few seconds' notice. The Rangers were coming noisily through the underbrush on horseback, unaware that they were wandering right into Sam's camp. He warned his boys in a whisper and they hurried away, leading the nearest horses. When the Rangers found the camp, there was no one in sight, but they did succeed in getting Sam's provisions and half of his horses.

The next day the Rangers dropped off their captured horses in Denton and took out for the hills to continue their search. As they disappeared out of town in one direction, three riders came into town from the other direction. Sam had brought along Frank Jackson and Seab Barnes to reclaim their "stolen" horses. By high noon they had the stablehand tied up and they led their mounts at a leisurely trot down the main street of Denton under the noses of countless lawmen who were telling each other where and how to catch Sam Bass.

An hour later, Sheriff Eagan, Sam's ex-employer, found that Sam had reclaimed his horses. Eagan led a posse of fifty men out of Denton after the gang. A few miles from

town the sheriff found a six-man party of Rangers who had
run into Sam. Sam had wounded one of them and put all
six afoot so they couldn't follow him. Eagan put a professional tracker to work, and they kept on the trail until
late at night. They finally heard the Bass gang moving up
ahead of them and opened fire. There was a violent gun
battle that lasted most of the night. In the morning it was
discovered that two men had been wounded in the fray.
It was also discovered that the "Bass gang" was a posse
who thought Eagan's bunch was the Bass gang.

Where Sam had disappeared to, no one knew. Reports
coming in from all over Texas indicated that every twenty-
four hours Sam was in at least 200 places over an area of
several thousand square miles. The most plausible tale
was that of a Denton man who claimed he saw Sam
sitting on his horse near Hickory Creek. In the distance
a posse was kicking up dust as they hell-for-leathered it
toward Palo Pinto where, according to the latest reports,
Sam was in hiding. The Denton man added further that
Sam was grinning a very quiet grin, like a fox watching a
pack of yelping hounds who had gone off the trail.

Captain June Peak was in for a second break though.
On May 12, he and several men bumped into Sam's camp
again. This time they drew blood. Hank Underwood was
shot in the arm, an outlaw named Carter who had just
teamed up with the gang was shot through the leg, and
Arkansas Johnson was shot in the neck, a wound that
turned out to be fatal. Even with his boys shot up some-
what, Sam managed to hold the Rangers off until night-
fall when he got the survivors away. Underwood and
Carter decided while nursing their wounds that this wild
life was beginning to be a strain on them, and they left
the gang to head for Mexico. Although newspapers across
the country were still filled with stories about Sam's
whopping big army of desperadoes, the number of badmen under his command was now exactly two. He had

faithful Frank Jackson and Seab Barnes still with him.
He didn't know it, but he was about to get a new recruit.

*Jim Murphy was arrested and then released on
    bail.*
*He jumped his bond at Tyler and took the train
    for Terrell.*
*But Major Jones had posted Jim, and that was all
    a stall,*
*'Twas only a plan to capture Sam before the
    coming fall.*

Major Jones had been busy all this time. He had talked
to every person who knew Sam Bass and arrested everyone who could even vaguely be charged with aiding and
abetting the fugitive. Jones was a shrewd psychologist,
and he figured the weakest friend Sam had was Jim
Murphy. He told Jim that he sure hated to hold him and
his dad in jail, but there wasn't much else he could do.
It was especially a pity since at the rate things were going
Sam never would be caught, and the Murphys would
likely rot away in prison before the law would have time
to bring them to trial. When the idea of betraying Sam
first came to Jim, he thought the plan was his own, but
Jones had planted the thought very carefully.

"Maybe I could help you catch Sam," Jim told the
major. "He trusts me. He told me I could join his gang
any time I wanted."

With Jones filling in, Jim evolved this plan of action:
If he and his dad would be released from jail by the major,
he would undertake to join Bass. Posing as the pal he
had always been taken for, he would ride with them, find
out when and where they were going to be at any given
spot, and sneak that information to Jones so that the
Rangers could be there waiting for them.

The major believed the plan worth trying—especially
since it was his own. He let Jim go, and Murphy went

back to his farm outside Denton. He spent nearly three
weeks trying to contact Sam. Then one morning, Sam,
Frank, and Seab all rode up to the front of the Murphy
cabin.

"Does what you said about my joining up with you
still go?" Jim asked Sam.

"Sure does. Always room for one more friend," Sam
told him.

Jim said he had to do a few things around the farm,
and they all agreed to meet at Hickory Creek that evening. As soon as they were out of sight, Jim rode toward
Denton where he met Sheriff Everheart of Grayson
County. He told Everheart where the boys would be that
night, and the sheriff promised to be there with as many
deputies as he could gather. Jim rode away feeling that
the business of playing traitor wasn't as hard as it was
cracked up to be.

There was just one thing wrong. Everheart never did
show up. Either he thought Jim was drunk, or he simply
didn't want to be the one to arrest Sam Bass. In any case
Jim was now one of the band, and he didn't like it. It
seemed to him they spotted a new and bigger posse every
ten minutes. As he remarked later on, "It was plumb risky
for a fella to go ridin' around with them fellers." In Jim's
defense it must be said that he was not the callous Judas
he has often been painted. Perhaps he honestly felt the
only way to get his father out of jail was by double-
crossing Sam. Perhaps he was too much of a coward to
defy the dreaded Texas Rangers. But, like everyone else
who knew the outlaw, he loved Sam, and his conscience
would, within a few months after his betrayal, drive him
to committing suicide by taking poison.

> Sam met his fate at Round Rock, July the
> twenty-first,

> They pierced poor Sam with rifle balls and
> emptied out his purse.
> Poor Sam he is a corpse and six foot under clay,
> And Jackson's in the bushes, tryin' to get away.

Sam decided the thing to do now was rob a bank.
Since most of the trains were carrying more guards than
passengers, and the banks had been left alone up to now,
they offered the most likely target. The band left Denton
and started south. At Rockwall, Sam spent a chunk of his
rapidly diminishing money buying Jim Murphy some new
guns and equipment. He had always had a soft spot for
the kid and had often helped him and his father out with
money in the past.

They then wandered down through Terrell, Kaufman,
Ennis, Waco, and Belton. On the way, they posed as
lawmen looking for the Bass gang, and the worse they
were treated, the happier Sam was. One old rancher
refused to sell or give them anything to eat. "I've heard
a heap about that Sam Bass," he said. "And I think a heap
of him. I hope you never do catch him."

"Well," Sam told him, passing the old man a $20 gold
piece with 1877 stamped on it, "I think the chances are
pretty good he never *will* be caught."

The oldster looked the coin over carefully, grinned at
Sam, and said, "You Rangers are welcome here as long
as you want to stay. And I don't want no money, so keep
this."

At one point they purchased a dozen eggs from a
woman. A posse appeared just as they rode out of sight.
The woman was still holding the $20 coin in her hand
when the sheriff asked her if she had seen any men who
might possibly be from the Bass gang. She said no one had
passed her house in days.

Jim Murphy went into Belton on a pretext and managed to get a letter off to Major Jones. He told Jones that the gang was headed into Round Rock where they planned to stick up the bank. Jones got the letter and every Ranger in that section of the country headed for the little town.

On the way down to Round Rock, the outlaws stopped off at a bar in a tiny village along the way. Toward the end of the evening, Sam threw a $20 gold piece on the bar. "Let her gush," he philosophized. "It all goes in a lifetime." It was his last 1877 coin.

On the morning of July 19, they arrived at the outskirts of Round Rock. Frank Jackson went into town to look the place over. He came back and said, "I don't care for the looks of that town. There's a feller I saw down there who looks like a Ranger to me."

That afternoon Sam and Seab moseyed down into the town to check on Frank's findings. Round Rock looked peaceful and calm to them, and they found nothing suspicious about the loiterers they saw along the main street.

The next morning the boys rode slowly into the quiet town. There was only a few people on the sidewalks. They didn't pull up in front of the bank, but reined in their horses a few feet down the street in front of Kopperel's tobacco store. They walked casually into the store and bought some tobacco. They wanted to size things up before moving on to the bank.

Jim Murphy whispered to Sam that he was going outside to keep an eye on things. Once out on the street, he hurried away from his friends and the bank, certain that his letter had got to Jones all right and that the quiet town was going to explode at any minute.

In the tobacco store, Sam was just turning from the counter when Sheriff Grimes of Round Rock and a deputy came in. Grimes looked Seab Barnes over critically and made a slighting remark about Seab's having "too many guns." This was not the sort of thing to tell Seab Barnes when he was about to rob a bank. Seab was touchy under the best circumstances, but at this particular moment, he was downright argumentative. He took one of his "too many guns" from its holster and nearly blew the sheriff's head off with it. Frank Jackson shot the deputy through the lungs as a wild slug from the deputy's pistol hit Sam in the hand. The three of them ran out onto the street to find that almost deserted thoroughfare suddenly filled to overflowing with Texas Rangers.

Seab was killed instantly by a slug through his head. Sam turned to help him and saw that he was dead. Sam's hesitation gave a Ranger the chance to shoot him square in the chest. Sam went down on both knees, then struggled to his feet. Frank Jackson, moving calmly and deliberately, got off his horse in the middle of the murderous fusillade, went over to Sam, and helped him up onto his horse. With bullets pounding and whining all around them, they galloped back out of town, Frank helping to support Sam in the saddle.

Sitting on some wooden steps, his head buried in his arms, Jim Murphy cried as the two men galloped past him.

> Jim sold out Sam and Barnes and left their
> friends to mourn,
> Oh what a scorching Jim will get when Gabriel
> blows his horn.
> Perhaps Jim's got to heaven, there's none of us
> to say,
> But if I'm right in my surmise, he's gone the
> other way.

The following morning, the Rangers found Sam lying under a tree. Frank had done everything possible for him and had left a horse nearby in case Sam came around enough to ride. Then, at Sam's insistence, he had cleared out before the law came. Sam was still alive, and they took him back into Round Rock.

Major Jones tried all day to get him to tell who had ridden with him, but Sam would say nothing about them. He talked freely about the boys who were dead, but as for telling Jones anything that might help him catch those still living, he said simply, "It's against my profession."

When Jones brought up Jim Murphy's name, Sam said nothing, but his lips set themselves into a faint, sad grin. The long afternoon was settling into evening when Sam finally said, "The world is bobbin' around," and died. It was July 21, 1878, Sam's twenty-seventh birthday.

An outlaw he was, but folks realized he had made it a point never to kill anyone, and he had given generously of himself and his money to all those around him. Texans proudly claimed the Indiana boy as their own, and any gun Sam had ever shot, any horse he had ever ridden, any glass he had ever taken a drink from became a priceless treasure to its owner. In the years to come thousands of "authentic" Sam Bass revolvers, gun belts, rifles, hats, boots, and spurs turned up all over the state. As the legend grew, it became clear that there wasn't one house Sam hadn't visited, there wasn't one fireplace he hadn't warmed his feet before, and there wasn't one old-timer in the state who hadn't sheltered Sam Bass while the Rangers were chasing him.

The people of Texas put a stone over Sam Bass' grave. On it they engraved a question about their beloved outlaw that no man could answer. "*A brave man reposes in death here. Why was he not true?*"

Sheriff Slaughter of Tombstone

By Edwin Johnson

~~~~~~

A pint-sized dude, he stood only a little over five feet, but his skill with a six-gun and his scorn for death made him the biggest man in the toughest town of the Old West

Word passed up and down the street. The citizens of Tombstone, Arizona, edged close to doors and windows. Only a few minutes before, a deputy had pounded into town on a lathered pony with news of another horse stealing. He had disappeared into the office of the recently appointed sheriff, John Slaughter. This was Slaughter's first test, and the people were anxious to see how he handled himself. They had watched other more famous sheriffs beat down the criminal element in blazing gun duels. Now they waited expectantly for Slaughter's door to bang open, the exciting call for possemen, the horses milling around in billowing clouds of dust, and the rifles unsheathed and waved menacingly.

There was none of this clamor. A small man in a wide-brimmed hat came out of the sheriff's office, unhitched a tall gray horse at the rail, and eased gracefully into the saddle. The news-bearing deputy, Burt Alvord, followed him out, looking about uncertainly.

"Just one horse," John Slaughter said from the saddle,

"means just one thief. You keep an eye on town, Burt.
I'll handle him."

The sheriff turned the big gray and rode slowly down
the street out of town. He sat ramrod-straight in the
saddle, making the most of his five-foot-six frame, and
he exuded a bristling air of importance. Expensively
carved leather boots, a fine, well-cut suit, and a fancy-Dan
pearl-handled .44 at his hip stamped him as a man of
money. He might have been a prosperous cattle buyer
going to a business meeting. Only the grim way his teeth
clenched a black Mexican cigar hinted that he might be
setting out on more deadly business.

Tombstone voiced its opinions as the sheriff faded into
a shifting blob of dust on the trail. This was the town they
had said was too tough to die, but now it had one foot
in a watery grave. The mines, which had paid out eighty
million dollars worth of high-grade silver ore in the ten-
year boom period, had become little more than sump
holes. Subterranean springs had flooded the shafts and
washed away ore deposits at workable depths. Washed
out of Tombstone along with the ore deposits were 12,000
miners, engineers, gamblers, businessmen, camp followers
—and professional lawmen. In the year 1887, the population had dwindled to a meager 3,000. Money was so
scarce that a man walking the board sidewalks with a
night's poker winnings in his pocket wasn't safe. Cowpunchers couldn't leave their ponies unwatched for fear
of horse thieves. Ranchers maintained tight guard over
their herds, wary of rustling gangs and the half-starved
residents of Cochise County. Big crime—stagecoach stick-
ups and the plundering of ore shipments—was in Tombstone's bawling, lusty past. But this new kind of crime,
small-time though it was, endangered the life and well-
being of the individual. Scores of families had already
been frightened off to safer territory. Tombstone couldn't
afford to lose any more.

Famous gun-slinging champions of law such as the Earps and Bat Masterson had departed with the rest of the boom element. Now the people had pinned the sheriff's star on their last hope, John Horton Slaughter, a Texan who had come to Arizona ten years before to build himself a cattle empire. There were many in town who said Slaughter was too rich, too soft, too much of a dude to be a lawman. They shook their heads skeptically as he rode out of town alone; he should have sworn in a posse, instead of going off on a one-man play for glory, they said.

Deputy Burt Alvord listened to the talk and shook his head. "That Slaughter," he said, "he's not like anybody else. He's got the damfool idea nobody can kill him."

Deputy Cesario Lucero slicked back his black hair under his floppy sombrero. "*Si*, he is a fighting fool. He has no fear. Who knows, maybe he can't be killed."

The discussions continued as the men straggled back to work. For twenty-four hours, at least one Tombstone eye was always watching the trail Slaughter had taken out of town. Finally, the sun glinted on a big white hat; a gray horse came into view, followed by a roan with an empty saddle.

Slaughter rode up to his office, dismounted, stamped his boots, and tossed the roan's reins to Alvord. "Take it back to the owner," he said, and went inside.

Alvord turned to face the crowd that was gathering in the street. He saw the questions in their eyes, and he wondered some himself. What had happened on the trail? Where was the horse thief who had taken the roan? Alvord shrugged. "That Slaughter's a damn silent cuss. Right surly."

Deputy Lucero grinned. "He didn't win that horse in a quiet poker game, my friend. Maybe now we will have less horse stealing."

Such was John Slaughter's inauguration as sheriff of the West's toughest town. His silence and the empty saddle on the roan spoke louder than a .45. Tombstone was going to have law—six-statute, pearl-handled law. In its short but bloody history, the town built on violence and silver was never to know a man like Slaughter again. He was the last of Tombstone's fabulous gunmen-sheriffs, its least publicized—and perhaps its greatest.

Born in Louisiana on October 2, 1841, Slaughter fought his way to manhood on the Texas steppes, rugged buffalo country where even the children had to outfight Kiowas and Comanches in order to survive. He enlisted briefly in the Confederate army, but was discharged when he became sick. Upon his recovery, Slaughter joined the Texas Rangers and served under famous Captain Tom in his campaigns against the Indians and outlaws. During this rough-riding period, young Slaughter learned the art of the fast draw, long-gun marksmanship, and hand-to-hand Indian fighting. These skills came in handy when he was discharged from the Rangers and went to the Texas Panhandle to start a ranch in Atascosa County.

Cattle ranching in those days was a constant war against the elements, hostile tribes, and rustlers, but the little man with the quick gun won out. Then the railroad came in from the East, opening up a new market for beef. Cattle prices shot from a dollar a head to $20, and overnight Slaughter became a rich man.

The birth of the Slaughter gun-fighter legend took place on a cattle-buying trip the young rancher made to the Devils River area of southwest Texas. Slaughter was returning to the Panhandle ranch with his trail-herd crew, when a gang of strange riders angled down a slope and poked through his bawling cattle. Slaughter soon found himself face to face with the leader of the group, Curly Bill Gallagher, a notorious two-gun murderer with thirteen notches proudly cut in the handles of his Colts.

"About a hundred of them cows look like lost stock

of mine," Curly Bill said pointedly. "I'm aiming to cut them out."

Slaughter's right hand dipped and flipped. His eyes snapped fire above the black hole of his six-gun. Rolling his cigar to the side of his mouth, he told Bill to "git."

The killer smiled. "Didn't say you stole them cows, exactly. Must have sorta strayed in with your herd. I usually take what's mine, friend. Maybe you heard of me —Curly Bill Gallagher?"

"I heard, and now I'm talking. Get going or take a bullet."

Gallagher saw deadly purpose glittering in the rancher's eyes. He scowled and wheeled his horse around. "By damn, mister, you'll hear from old Bill again."

Slaughter kept a bead on the tricky gunman until he and his gang were out of sight, then waved the trail herders on toward home. But he was destined to see Curly Bill Gallagher again—this time through the V-notch of a Winchester sight. Weeks later, Slaughter and his outfit were driving to Las Vegas to sell a load of prime beef on the hoof. They pitched camp near Fort Sumner, at the old Bosque Grande Ranch of New Mexico cattle baron John Chisum. As the last light of the setting sun fanned out across the plain, John Slaughter surveyed his bedded-down cows from a hillside. Suddenly he saw a lone horseman galloping across the plain toward him. As the rider spurred his mount up the slope, Slaughter recognized Bill Gallagher, a shotgun slung at the ready under one arm.

Curly Bill was closing rapidly, and once he was within shotgun range, Slaughter knew he wouldn't have a chance. He brought up his Winchester carbine and triggered it crisply.

Gallagher's horse folded under him, shot through the

head. The gunman was fuming as he disentangled himself from the animal. His shotgun was out-ranged, so he heaved it aside and pulled his six-guns. He fired a shot from each Colt, missed, and plunged forward.

Slaughter calmly lined up Gallagher in the sights of his carbine and pumped two slugs at him. One bullet crashed into his left arm, spinning him half around, but Gallagher staggered forward, triggering the Colt at his right hip. The Winchester cracked twice. Two .30-30's slammed into Curly Bill's chest and bowled him over.

The rancher advanced slowly and toed the notched-butt six-gun out of Gallagher's numbed fingers. The tough guy glared up at the man who had mortally wounded him, his bloody lips twisting in an awful grin. "You're real hell, Slaughter," he said. "Named right too."

In less than an hour Gallagher was dead, and the reputation of the man who had killed him began to grow. But no notches ever appeared on Slaughter's six-guns. Glory in his book was for the ignorant. A man killed another man for the same reason he might kill a plump rabbit—to survive. It was that cut and dried.

The aftermath of the Gallagher shooting taught Slaughter something; a good bluff was often more effective than a bullet. On the last leg of the Las Vegas trip, he learned the power of a killer reputation. A hand resting on a gun butt and a cold-eyed stare could put many a tough in his place.

During one cattle drive, Slaughter's trail herd was scattered by a wind storm. As he set about rounding up his stock, he found that many of his strays had mixed in with other steers grazing on the range. When he cut out sixty head from the great Chisum herd, John Chisum was enraged, claiming that the steers belonged to him. Slaughter laid his hand on his gun and commented, "Don't spoil a good deal with a bad one, John." The big cowman wasn't bargaining for bullets; he waved and rode off.

Slaughter pulled another 100 head of his stray stock from the herd of a rancher named Underwood. Two tough-looking henchmen accompanied Underwood to Slaughter's camp to protest. Slaughter went for his six-gun, and the three remembered Curly Bill Gallagher. They went home.

The gunslinger rap was snowballing. Four rustlers tried to muscle in on Slaughter's rebuilt herd, and their six-gun action frightened off one of Slaughter's men. Out came the Slaughter Winchester. The four thundered away, amid a hail of lead, to spread the Slaughter legend in saloons throughout the West.

Even the law decided discretion was the better part of valor—when valor meant mixing in with John Slaughter. A deputy sheriff was sent out with a warrant to prevent Slaughter from recovering some cattle from the herd of an influential rancher named John Richardson. Slaughter insisted they were his cows. The deputy put away the warrant and reluctantly groped for his sidearm. He stopped reaching and grinned helplessly when Slaughter's gun came out of leather with breathtaking quickness. Richardson, the man who had filed the complaint, withdrew it after a heart-to-gun-muzzle talk with Slaughter.

In 1877, John Slaughter eased the worries of fellow Texans by packing up his spread, cow by cow, and moving into the rich grazing around Arizona's Cochise County. About the same time Slaughter moved in his herd, Ed Schieflin made his big strike at Tombstone, and thousands of boomers flocked to the silver country. The Apaches, who had had the area to themselves, lashed out at the newcomers under the direction of the old terror himself, Geronimo.

When a band of redskin rustlers made a special target of Slaughter's big herd, a grim, unrelenting Slaughter tracked down and killed all of them.

His kills really shook the feathers on Geronimo's headpiece. Instead of giving out with a fiery war whoop, the chief looked at the bullet-riddled bodies of his best bucks and told his tribe to stay clear of the fast-shooting white devil. The fear-inspiring qualities of the quiet-talking gunman-rancher had reached even the great Indian warrior.

News of Slaughter's prowess as an Indian fighter interested Generals Crook and Miles, who were leading their troops against the clever Apache chief, and they enlisted Slaughter's help as a scout. Slaughter was with Miles at Skeleton Canyon in 1886 when Geronimo surrendered. The following year, Tombstone's boom fizzled, and John Slaughter was nominated for the job of restoring law and order to the chaos that was left.

More convincing than any electioneering speech Silent John Slaughter could have made was his run-in with notorious Ike Clanton, the man with courage enough to feud against fabulous Wyatt Earp—and sense enough to let little John Slaughter alone. Clanton was swinging a careless loop on the Slaughter range when he received his first visit from the cattle king. Ike heard himself called some choice words, but before he could make a move for his gun, he was looking at the business end of Slaughter's .44. Boiling with frustrated rage, he vowed he would kill Slaughter.

Several nights later, Slaughter was driving home from a shopping trip to Tombstone with his second wife, Viola. Instinct born of his life-or-death training against Indians gnawed at his sense of well-being. He turned to Viola and handed her the buggy reins.

"Drive the horse a while, dear," he said. "I want my gun in my hand."

He pulled the fancy six-gun and held it on his knee. There was the crackling roar of a horse being spurred from a standstill through heavy brush. Then a horseman drew abreast of the buggy—Ike Clanton. His gun gleamed in the moonlight. The same beams glinted on the cocked weapon in Slaughter's fist. Clanton rode past, dropping his gunhand slowly to his side, saying nothing and vanishing into the night.

"He meant to kill you, John!" Viola gasped. "How did you know?"

Slaughter shrugged. "Maybe I've got an angel watching over me."

His nose for danger was to come to John Slaughter's aid many times while he served as Tombstone's sheriff. Yet it was more than mere instinct that made Slaughter such a formidable foe. Day or night, his .44 was strapped on and ready. He invented the motto: "Shoot first and ask questions later." His deputies often joked that it was impossible to get behind the wary gunfighter. Slaughter once engaged in a conversation with Burt Alvord, turning in a complete circle as the deputy slyly tried to edge around behind him. His eyes, ever alert and of startling blue brilliance, perhaps made as much impact on Tombstone as did his trigger finger.

One of the many toughs who looked into Slaughter's eyes and got a frozen gun in hand was Ed Lyle. Lyle, Cap Stilwell, and four other outlaws tried to ambush Slaughter and his wife on a trip to Santa Cruz. But the Slaughter buggy outraced the bushwhackers to safety. Thereafter, Cochise County was hotter than hell for the six gunmen. Lyle was cornered by Slaughter in Charleston and backed out of a fight by claiming he had no gun. Slaughter quietly warned him to be out of the country in twenty-four hours —and Lyle got. Cap Stilwell had his comedown a week later, also in Charleston. Cap was wearing a gun and went for it—like a slow freight compared to the express action of Slaughter's right mitt. Cap got the twenty-four-hour limit. He had about twenty hours to spare when he galloped out of town. Cochise County never saw either man again, or missed them.

A few men called Slaughter's bluff, but they were never heard from again. Others only pretended to call it. Juan Soto, a Spaniard from California, beat a rustling charge when Burt Alvord failed to turn up sufficient evidence to convince the court of Soto's guilt. Alvord, however, pretending to be Soto's bar buddy, had pumped enough from the tequila-dizzy Spaniard to convince Slaughter that he was a rustler. A great non-believer in formal justice, Slaughter personally sentenced Soto after the man was legally acquitted. He gave Soto ten days to clear up his business in Tombstone and get out.

Soto wouldn't be bluffed, or so it seemed. Slaughter had got away without pulling a gun too many times, Soto proclaimed, but *he* would force the sheriff's hand. The Spaniard stayed around town, drinking and boasting about how he would fix Slaughter. Nine days he boasted; on the tenth day his bar chums couldn't locate him. A year later, word drifted back that Soto had settled down in nearby Pierce. Slaughter saddled up, visited Soto, and told him to vamoose real far.

Another shady character who never got court justice was Van Wyck Coster of Willcox. Slaughter had reason to believe that Coster, though a businessman of good reputation, was actually a chiseler trading in sharp land transactions. There wasn't enough evidence for a court conviction, so Slaughter gave Coster the move-along treatment. Tried and found guilty in the sheriff's mind, Coster had no choice but to leave the country. Rarely did Tombstone ever again see a character whom Slaughter told to get out of town.

When a Mexican stole his mother-in-law's favorite mount, the sheriff moved out of town in his usual quiet manner and returned the next day with the black and white pinto pony. Weeks later some prospectors came across the remains of the Mexican horse thief's body in a lonely canyon.

Like most law officers, Slaughter inherited some troubles. One of the more bothersome things was the constant needling from the U. S. marshal at Albuquerque, New Mexico. Wanted notices originally sent to Tombstone on two bandits, Tom Winters and John Gallick, had been written off by Wyatt Earp, Slaughter's predecessor. Earp had tracked the men to two graves near a cabin at Dead Horse Mesa in the Dragoon Mountains, and a witness had identified the graves as those of Gallick and Winters. But after Slaughter got into office, the New Mexico marshal kept sending wires, insisting that Winters and Gallick were still pulling stagecoach robberies in the Albuquerque area. Slaughter checked with Earp, then set out to the isolated cabin in the mountains.

He found the place unoccupied and padlocked. Breaking in, he came across Wells Fargo bags containing $4,000 in gold and currency—precisely the amount that had recently been stolen from a railroad station in Albuquerque. Slaughter left the cabin, but returned suddenly three days later. He took two occupants of the lonely shack by surprise. Holding his gun on them, he found papers in their wallets that identified them as Tom Winters and John Gallick. The latter, grinning sheepishly, admitted his identity and said there was only one body in the graves. He refused to identify the unknown corpse. Returned to New Mexico, Gallick was convicted of murder and died on the gallows. Winters received a twenty-year sentence for armed robbery. The identity of the body in the fake graves was never established, but Slaughter believed it was an old prospector who had vanished somewhere in the Dragoons.

While Slaughter kept the local element under control in his first year at Tombstone, there were those in the West who were not yet aware that the ex-boom town was also an ex-tough town. Four bandits fled from a $15,000 train stick-up twelve miles south of Nogales on May 11,

1888, and headed for "wide-open" Tombstone to hide
out. Two other members of the gang had already been
captured, and wanted bulletins were circulated across the
Sonora plains to Tombstone. Slaughter learned that the
four fugitives had a sweetie who shook her hips in the
floorshow of a Tombstone saloon. He posted deputies
Alvord and Lucero to watch the woman's home, but the
bandits got wise and fled.

Slaughter checked the wanted bulletins again. The
four bandits were Geronimo Mirando, Manuel Robles,
Neives Deron, and another man known only as Federico.
Manuel Robles, Slaughter learned, had a brother Guadalope Robles, who lived in Contention. Robles made his
living by selling firewood, which he cut at a wood ranch
in Frenchy's Canyon, near Miscal Springs in the wilder-
ness of the Whetstone Mountains. John Slaughter put a
man on Guadalope, who relayed back the information
that the firewood chopper was taking mighty big lunches
with him when he set out in his wagon to gather wood.

Slaughter was certain Guadalope was hiding the bandits in Frenchy's Canyon, but this time he didn't tackle
the manhunt alone. He was a pro in the sense that he
never let himself be out-manipulated or outnumbered.
Deputies Cesario Lucero and Alvord rode to the wood
ranch near Frenchy's Canyon with the sheriff. They
arrived on a dark night filled with disturbing croaks and
howls.

Slaughter could barely see the bulky outlines of his
mounted deputies. "Better go the rest of the way on foot,"
he told them. "Thick woods ahead. If Guadalope is hiding
'em, they'll hear us coming miles away. I don't want to be
picked off without a chance to get in my shot."

They dismounted and concealed the animals in heavy
brush. With Slaughter leading, they pushed into the
woods toward Frenchy's Canyon, moving as silently as

Indians. The two deputies had never worked with Slaughter on a manhunt, since he preferred to lonewolf it. Now, knowing his fearlessness, they were sure he was taking them directly into a six-gun showdown.

Burt Alvord began to walk slower and fell slightly behind. Slaughter stopped. "Better take off our boots and hang them around our necks," he said. "We should be getting near their camp. Keep it as quiet as possible—and stick together. I don't aim to tackle four men by myself, unless I have to." The dry click of a Colt hammer being thumbed back sounded in Alvord's ears. "You run away, Burt, and I'll kill you," Slaughter said casually.

The deputies realized it was a question of dying under Slaughter's impersonal gun or risking a battle with the bandits. They moved ahead to face the four guns, rather than the one.

Dawn was sending thin shafts of light down through the thick foliage as the men came to a clearing at the bottom of Frenchy's Canyon. Less than a hundred feet from them, they saw three sleeping figures, rolled into blankets against the cold. Slaughter motioned his men into position, stepped into the clearing, and drew his handgun.

"Get your paws up!" he shouted.

The sleeping trio leaped up as one. Guns kept close at hand whipped into action, spitting flame. Manuel Robles and Deron blasted away from crouching positions, edging slowly up the far slope. Guadalope Robles, less versed in gunplay, made the mistake of standing up and pegging lead from the hip.

Slaughter killed him with one shot. Deron, stumbling backward up the hill, completely disregarded the two greenhorn deputies and concentrated his fire on the sheriff. Three slugs hummed past Slaughter's hat; one nicked the lobe of his ear and drew blood. Slaughter snapped a fast shot at Deron, dropping him flat. At this point, Manuel Robles darted down the slope toward the canyon.

Burt Alvord, less green with each bullet, squeezed off several shots at Robles. Slaughter whirled toward the fleeing man and smiled at Alvord. "You're too high, Burt."

His own gun kicked in his hand, and Manuel Robles was slammed down by a high-powered .44. Robles promptly jumped up again, and Slaughter cut loose a second shot at him. The bandit went down again, bounced right back up, and ran like hell.

A third shot, at extreme long range, punched Robles' hat from his head, but he didn't stop for it. He rammed bull-like into the brush, and the stocking-footed lawmen were unable to keep up with him. A trail of bloodstains testified to the accuracy of Slaughter's bullets though. Later, they pulled on their boots and followed the bloody path. Further along, hoof prints in the dust indicated that Manuel had met someone on horseback and ridden away with him.

"Probably Federico, the fourth bandit," Slaughter said. "Had him posted out here somewhere as lookout. Not much chance catching those two now."

They loaded Guadalope Robles' corpse onto his wagon like a stick of his firewood. Deron, still alive, was fading fast. On the trip back to Contention, he confessed that it was he who had shot and killed two men during the attack on the Nogales train; he died of bullet wounds before the wagon reached town.

Slaughter had emphatically declared, through his blazing six-gun, that Tombstone was no longer a hideout for riff-raff. But he had done something more. He had aroused the fury of Federico and the remaining members of the train-robbery gang. Rumor floated across the border that the gang had vowed to kill the Tombstone sheriff. That vengeful vow brought about the death of easygoing

Deputy Lucero. Slaughter was scheduled to make a trip to San Bernardino several days after the Robles-Deron shooting, but, at the last moment, other business tied him up, and Lucero was dispatched from Tombstone to attend to the San Bernardino matter.

The unsuspecting deputy rode into an ambush and was killed by the savage crossfire of two hidden gunmen. White with rage, Slaughter set out on the trail of the murderers with death in his eyes. But Federico and his unknown bushwhacking accomplice scooted frantically across the border out of his reach. Several months later, the rurales pressed the two bandits northward toward the border. Rather than cross over into Slaughter territory, they surrendered meekly.

Manuel Robles, who had kept on running until he reached the comparative safety of Sonora, joined the last member of the gang, Geronimo Mirando, in a foolhardy shoot-out with the Mexican police. Both were killed. Though Slaughter was cheated out of pulling the trigger on the men who had slain his deputy, he had the satisfaction of knowing that it was his gunfighter reputation that had kept the killers bottled up in Mexico.

Slaughter's headaches were not all of the Mexican variety. Less than three weeks after the gunplay in Frenchy's Canyon, Irishman Mike Brady, stagecoach bandit and two-gun killer, sashayed boldly into Tombstone territory. When the Benson stage, never late even in the boom years, failed to pull into Tombstone on schedule one afternoon, Slaughter and Burt Alvord rode out into the hot, dusty desert to look for it. Two miles from town, they found the stage overturned, its team struggling against the harnesses that had dragged it to the ground. Pete Latham, the guard, was sprawled out several yards away, a bullet in his brains. Inside were two passengers, also shot through the head. Bill Gates, the tough old driver, groaned from a clump of sagebrush. Slaughter gently propped up the grizzled man, frowned at the bloodstained shirt front, and felt the weak, uncertain pulse.

Gates gasped out a story of robbery, murder, and kidnapping—the kidnap victim being a shapely dancing girl. "She's Buckskin Frank Leslie's wife, Elsie. She was running out on him because he was too rough on her . . ."

The driver revealed that in addition to the dancer, the three bandits had taken $20,000 in currency destined for the Tombstone bank and four mail sacks. "That poor gal," Alvord said.

Slaughter nodded grimly. "She's alone with three men who take what they want. Looks like we've got a real job for us, Burt."

They took Gates into Tombstone and notified Wells Fargo and the federal postal department of the theft. Then Slaughter and his deputies prowled through Cochise County, trying to get a lead on a man or men spending unusual amounts of cash. They hit pay dirt in Bisbee. A hell-raiser named Mike Brady had blown into town, leaving bartenders and saloon girls a little dazed at the wads of money he thrust into their fists. Like most tornadoes, he had just melted away, and nobody knew where he had gone. Slaughter visited other towns and heard other items about Mike Brady. He followed Brady's weaving trail to an isolated little canyon in the Whetstone Mountains—and fell into a trap. Brady sneaked up behind Slaughter with a sidekick, Ned McNeal, and got the drop on him before his fingers could flip the pearl-handled Colt.

"Undo that fancy shooting-iron," Brady snapped, "and drop her."

Slaughter, never a man to lose his composure and do something foolish, unbuckled his six-gun. Brady and McNeal tied him hand and foot and shoved him into a cabin. Lying there, Slaughter noticed several items of female clothing which obviously belonged to the kidnapped Elsie Leslie. He noticed, too, a brace of Winchester carbines stacked just inside the cabin door.

A man who had tied up many prisoners himself, Slaughter knew all the tricks. While they were tying him, he had tensed against the ropes, and, now that he was relaxed, there was some play in them. Before too long, he had his hands free. He was contemplating making a risky leap toward the carbines when McNeal heard a noise outside the cabin and went to investigate. There was a sudden, muffled gunshot, and Slaughter went for the carbines.

Brady wheeled about and drew. John Slaughter grabbed a gun, then levered and triggered from the hip in one motion. Six-gun and carbine roared together. Brady toppled over, mortally wounded.

Slaughter barged outside and saw McNeal sprawled on the ground. He snapped a quick bead on a tall stranger with a smoking gun in hand. The man held out the badge of a United States Postal Service detective. He had been on the trail of the stage bandits because of the stolen mail bags and had been about to crash into the cabin when McNeal came out and surprised him.

Cached in the cabin, they found all but a few thousand of the stolen bank money, plus the sacks of mail. From the dying McNeal, Slaughter learned the full story of the robbery.

"Ringo," McNeal said through clenched teeth "Kill-crazy, skirt-crazy fool! The whole thing was his idea." He died before they could question him about the kidnapped girl.

Elsie Leslie turned up safe, and as brassy as ever, in San Francisco a few weeks later. John Ringo turned up dead, his body propped up in sitting position under a cottonwood tree in Sulphur Springs Valley. One shot had been fired from Ringo's revolver, and there was a bullet hole dead-center in his forehead. No one knew who had gunned him down, or much cared. Some said it was Buckskin Frank Leslie, but Buckskin was slower than Ringo on the draw. Only a gunslinger like Earp or Hickok or Masterson could have got him—or maybe Slaughter, who had a habit of leaving them where they fell.

Slaughter's code of law and order at any price was bound to bring him trouble, and when it came, it was from the south.

The border gangs were not yet through with Sheriff Slaughter. Too many good Mexican thugs had crossed over to Tombstone and never returned. Finally, Chacon, the biggest bandit chieftain south of the border, put a death tag on the little sheriff from Tombstone. The hotheaded killer sent a message to Slaughter: "Am coming to Tombstone to kill you." Chacon, for all his bragging, was a rough individual, lethally fast and accurate with gun and knife. Alvord voiced the question in all Tombstone's minds—would Chacon come alone or with a stream of raiding terrorists?

"He'll come alone," Slaughter decided. "He won't give any warning, either. It'll come from an alley or a dark doorway. So I better start packing a scattergun."

Slaughter carried a shotgun with him faithfully during the next few days. Then Tombstone grew silent and tense, and the sheriff knew Chacon was in town. He did some quick thinking. Better to flush him into the open than to wait for a knife in the back. Slaughter knew the bandit chief was a lusty liver and thought he would most likely spend a day or two in the warm embrace of a friendly senorita. He checked upon some of Tombstone's prettiest girls and soon spotted the Chacon hideout, a long canvas-and-wood frame house in a gulch behind the courthouse.

Slaughter solicited Alvord's help for this job. "Burt," he told him, "all you gotta do is to knock on the front door of the house, then go home."

A more sporting man might have preferred a six-gun to a shotgun, but for Slaughter there was no sport to killing. Once he made up his mind that a man needed to be killed, he did the job in the quickest and surest way possible. When Slaughter took up his position at the rear of the hideout house, the scattergun was up to his shoulder, ready to blast.

Alvord, steeling himself for his part of the ordeal, walked up to the front door, pistol in hand, knocked loudly, then ducked around to the side of the house. Seconds later, there was the devastating roar of a shotgun. Alvord raced around to the rear, just as Slaughter threw the shotgun down and drew his .44.

"All right, Burt," Slaughter said. "Better get a lantern. I think I blew Chacon's head clear off!"

A lantern was fired up, and under its flickering glow, the lawmen searched for the corpse. They found nothing but a patch of scuffed-up earth, where one of the guy wires that supported the canvas house had snapped.

"Can you beat that?" Slaughter said. "He tripped over that guy wire just as I cut loose with the shotgun. Must have just missed him as he fell. Probably I'll never catch him now."

Slaughter never did. Chacon's flying feet carried him back to the old country, where he had to contend only with the *rurales*. The heavy shotgun charge sizzling through the air near his head had been the convincer. Tombstone was no place to play bold. Some years later, Chacon took the deep step into space from a gallows at Solomonville, after being captured by a posse led by Burt Alvord, Slaughter's pistol protegé.

Tombstone's wild days were over forever when John Horton Slaughter unpinned his silver star in 1891. Now fifty and turning gray, Slaughter packed up his guns and ammunition and returned to his big cattle spread and his prosperous ranching business. Perhaps the knowledge that the little man and his .44 were on call only a few miles away sobered the lawless element in Tombstone in the years that followed. It is a matter of public record that law and order prevailed in the former boom town thereafter.

Because of his modest silence about his lone-wolf escapades, Slaughter has received much less publicity than other gunmen sheriffs of his day. Estimates of the men he killed range from six to twenty-six. Some say his total tops that of any Western gunfighter. The people of the Old Southwest who knew John Slaughter personally always called him "the real article." One incident from his later life suggests the tremendous impact Slaughter made upon the community he served as sheriff.

At the age of eighty, John Slaughter was slightly stooped and his hair and beard were snow white. He had stopped smoking his long black cigars some years back, and the fancy Colt, once strapped to his hip twenty-four hours a day, had been relegated to an honored spot on the mantelpiece of his big ranchhouse. It was there on the night of May 4, 1921, when four bandits invaded Slaughter's spread.

In the darkness of the yard, one of the bandits drew a bead on Slaughter, who was sitting at a lighted window reading a book. But before he could squeeze the trigger, the old man suddenly stood up and stepped across the room to his .44, prompted by an inexplicable sense of danger. Three shots rang out in the darkness. Slaughter rushed to the door and hurled it open. A few yards away his foreman, Jess Fisher, lay dead upon the ground.

Investigation by the police disclosed that $80 had been taken from the foreman's wallet. Weeks later, four Mexican bandits were captured and quickly confessed to the robbery-murder. They admitted they had moved in on the Slaughter ranchhouse intending to kill the wealthy ex-sheriff, his entire family, and all hands on the premises before looting the place.

They had been concealed in the brush when Slaughter came to the door. Outlined by the light behind him, he had offered a perfect target, but not one of the bandits possessed the nerve to squeeze a trigger. All four had fled in terror.

"The sight of him standing there with a gun," one of the Mexicans recalled in an awed voice, "was too much. What he says is true. No man *can* kill him."

A year later one of the Southwest's greatest lawmen passed on. After exposing himself to savage Indians and cutthroat thugs for so many years, Slaughter died in bed of natural causes—and that was the way he wanted it. Whenever he heard a gunslinger talk about dying with his boots on, the hardheaded Slaughter would lift one eyebrow deprecatingly.

"Kid stuff," he would grunt. "Nothin' to be proud of, lettin' another man get the drop on you."

John Slaughter was proud.

The Saga of Buffalo Bill

By Jack Pearl

~~~~~~

He shot his first Indian when he was twelve, was a
master buffalo hunter at fifteen, and became the
most daring of the Pony Express riders before he
finished his seventeenth year

The five cavalry officers sat ramrod-stiff in the saddle as
their ponies jogged across the Kansas prairie toward a
knot of buffalo grazing about a half mile from the fort.
As they came abreast of a rolling hill, a lone horseman
rode over the crest and hailed them.

"Hey there! You boys from Fort Hayes?" He urged his
horse to catch up to them.

"That's right," the captain in charge of the party
answered. "We aim to get us some buffalo."

"Well now," the stranger said. "So am I. I'll join you."

The officers regarded their uninvited guest with
humorous curiosity. He was an ordinary enough looking
plainsman; big, muscular, broad-of-shoulder and narrow
through the waist and hips. His yellow beard and hair
were shaggy and unkempt. Undeniably, his face was more
sensitive than most, and his blue eyes were keen and alert.
He grinned, showing strong tobacco-stained teeth. "My
camp is runnin' low on fresh meat. Figgered me and Old
Lucretia Borgia here would tend to that." He patted the
enormous breech-loading Springfield rifle held lightly in
the crook of his elbow.

One of the young lieutenants in the party laughed. "It looks more like a cannon than a rifle."

The stranger winked. "She's a needle gun, fifty caliber. When she hits 'em they stay hit. That's why I call her Lucretia. She makes a poor enemy."

The captain eyed the stranger's horse rather critically. She was a big, bony, awkward-looking gray with a trace of swayback. Her owner rode bareback like an Indian, without even a blanket. In fact, the only rig she wore was a simple blind bridle made of rope. "You expect to catch buffalo with that outfit, my friend?" he inquired.

"I hope so."

"It takes an extremely fast horse to catch a buffalo," the captain said, as diplomatically as he could.

"I suppose so." The man dropped his eyes sheepishly— or so the captain thought.

The captain was suddenly filled with magnanimity toward the forlorn figure in buckskin. "I tell you what, friend. We're out for sport more than anything else. You're welcome to whatever we bring down after we take the tongues and a piece of the tenderloin."

The stranger's eyes gleamed. "Why that *is* nice of you, sir. I'll just keep out of your way." As they approached the buffalo, he dropped behind the five officers. There were eleven big bulls who apparently had wandered off from the main herd to forage for themselves. Their great shaggy heads rolled from side to side as they muzzled low in the grass, and their rockline humps jutted prominently in the air. When the officers were about 200 yards off, the biggest bull threw his nose high in the air and began to bleat nervously.

"They got our scent, boys!" the captain roared. "Let's get 'em!" He dug his spurs into his mount and catapulted into the lead.

The yellow-haired plainsman felt the big gray tremble under him. "Steady, Brigham," he whispered in its ear. "You ain't gonna be left out, don't worry. May as well let the soldier boys flush 'em for us." The cavalrymen were hooting and screaming like Indians as they swooped down on the buffalo at a rate that threatened to overtake the lumbering beasts in short order. The buffalo ran with mincing, almost dainty, steps for animals so ponderous. Like bulky locomotives, they accelerated slowly but steadily. By the time the horses were 100 yards from them, they had hit their stride. Then they began to make back the ground they had lost. As the officers fired wildly, the stranger grinned and shook his head condescendingly. As he had expected, the buffalo swerved to the left and described a great semicircle in the direction of the river about a half mile to the east. That was what he had been waiting for. He nudged the horse gently with his knees and slipped the blind bridle clear. "All right, Brigham, take over." The big gray shot forward like an arrow. Showing almost human intelligence, the horse headed off to the left in a forty-five degree diagonal that would eventually intersect the circular path of the stampeding buffalo. It soon became apparent to the cavalrymen who had fallen back almost 300 yards behind their quarry that the gray's appearance had been deceiving. The long legs that had made him seem gangling carried him along in extraordinary leaping strides. Even more extraordinary was the way the rider sat him without benefit of bridle or saddle, clinging with his legs like an Apache as he hefted the big Springfield to his shoulder. His buckskins stood straight out in the breeze, along with the bay's flowing tail. The gray caught the herd easily and stayed even with the rear buffalo until his master pumped a single shot into the animal's head. Then he spurted until he was abreast of the next buffalo in the line. Each time a buffalo stumbled and fell, he would pass on to another. When the last one crashed to earth, he slowed down to a lope.

"Whoa boy!" the rider said and turned him to wait for the army to bring up the rear. Four very red-faced lieutenants and one sheepish captain arrived.

"Good hunting, gentlemen," the stranger grinned. "Eleven buffalo with twelve shots."

"Twelve shots!" one of the lieutenants exclaimed.

"I feel awful about wastin' that one," the stranger said deadpanned. "But old Brigham stepped in a gopher hole and spoilt my aim onct."

The officers, appreciating that the joke was on them, began to laugh heartily. Then the captain performed introductions. "Lieutenants Redd, Thompson, Emmick, and Ezekial. I'm Captain Graham."

The plainsman whipped off his wide-brimmed slouch hat. "Bill Cody at your service, gentlemen."

"Bill Cody," Lieutenant Thompson repeated. "Buffalo Bill Cody?"

"You've got me dead to rights."

Captain Graham chuckled. "Buffalo Bill! Well now, that is something. And *we* were going to show *you* how to hunt buffalo." He studied Brigham closely. "And I guess we owe your gray an apology too."

Cody grinned. "He don't look like much, but he's the best buffalo horse in the country. Hell, he knows more about it than I do. I just give him his head, and he does the rest. All I do is put old Lucretia against their heads and pull the trigger."

Graham passed around cigars and they talked and smoked without dismounting. Then he had an inspiration. "I expect to lead a scouting expedition west within a few weeks. Would you consider being my guide, Mr. Cody?"

Cody combed his beard with his fingers. "I'm honored that you asked me, Captain, but I've got a contract with the Kansas Pacific Railroad to supply their construction camps with meat."

The Kansas Pacific employed over 1,200 men to lay their rails across the western prairie. Supplying these hardworking, ravenous hands with fresh meat was no small problem in this desolate land. Fortunately, the road ran through the heart of the buffalo country, so the company decided to hire expert hunters to keep the camp larders full. Goddard Brothers, who had the contract to feed the railroad crews, hired Bill Cody, a young army scout and guide with a reputation for being an expert marksman, for their chief hunter. The terms were that Cody would supply them with twelve buffaloes a day for $500 a month. It was a large salary for those days, but the risks were great, for the section was infested with hostile Indians. Cody's phenomenal success in this job won him the title of Buffalo Bill. In less than eighteen months, he killed over 4,280 buffaloes.

The title, "Buffalo Bill," and the romantic picture it evoked stuck with William Cody throughout his lifetime and has been perpetuated in all the books written about him ever since. Cody himself never did anything to discourage it. He enjoyed the image that people had of him as a simple, homespun hero, spouting homey philosophy, unaffected by fame and wealth. He kept the myth alive by retaining the buckskins, the shoulder-length hair and the slow, drawling vernacular of the plainsman. He never let an opportunity pass to assure folks that he slept sounder on a bedroll on the prairie than he did in a satin coverlet at the Waldorf; that to eat he preferred beans off a tin plate beside a campfire with a jug at his elbow to balancing a china plate full of *hors d'œuvres* on one knee and a cocktail on the other; that he would rather shoot buffalo on the range than play roulette at Monte Carlo—yet he was never deficient in practicing all the pastimes civilization had to offer. For throughout his varied career as a scout, hunter, soldier, actor, businessman, and Grover Whelan of the Wild West, Bill Cody was above all else a master showman.

When Bill Cody was eleven years old, his father, an abolitionist, was killed in the bitter pre-Civil War struggle between the Free-Soilers and the pro-Slavers in "Bloody Kansas." As the oldest boy in the family, the burden of supporting his mother and four younger sisters and brothers fell on him. Big for his age, he managed to get a job as a cattle herder for Russell, Majors, and Wadell, the firm who had the government contract to transport supplies to Colonel Albert Sidney Johnston's troops in the Utah territory, where the United States was trying to put down the Mormon insurrection. The supply trains were made up of twenty-five horse-drawn wagons, with the cattle tagging along at the rear. Inevitably, the wagons outdistanced the cattle, so that for most of the trip, the cavayard drivers, as the cowhands were called, were pretty much on their own.

On Bill's first trip, his outfit was ambushed by Indians as they were setting up a camp one night on the banks of the Platte River, about thirty-six miles west of Fort Kearney. The Platte flowed between high banks that formed a natural barricade, but still the Indians killed two of the herders and stampeded the cattle before they were driven off. As darkness settled over the prairie, Bill McCarthy, the boss of the drive, outlined a plan to his men: "The river's low this time of year. With luck we can wade her all the way down to Kearney." Before the moon came up, the herders were sloshing downstream, knee-deep in water. After they had gone about ten miles, they relaxed, for it seemed certain that they had eluded the Sioux.

Physically and emotionally exhausted from the excitement, and with water dragging at his feet every time he took a step, young Cody lagged behind the others. Soon their dim figures ahead of him faded into the night. As the moon rose from behind a bluff high above the river up ahead, it silhouetted the figure of a single Sioux warrior against the sky. Crouching at the edge of the bluff, the Indian raised a rifle to his shoulder and aimed at something below him. For an instant, panic immobilized Bill. Then almost reflexively, he threw up the old muzzle-loader he was armed with. It was an ancient Mississippi Yeager that fired a ball and two buckshot and had a trajectory like a boomerang. But Bill had practiced with it extensively on the march. The Yeager belched fire as he pulled the trigger, and a tremendous explosion rolled down the river gorge. The figure on the bluff lurched upright, then pitched forward into space. Bill heard a splash, followed by the excited voices of his herders up ahead. When he staggered up to them, they were crowded around the body of the dead Sioux, lying half submerged in the shallow water near the bank. McCarthy tested the barrel of the Yeager with his palm. "It's hot." He turned to the other men in amazement. "Billy's killed himself an Injun."

They reached the fort just before daybreak, and a detachment of cavalry was sent out to recover the bodies of the two dead herders and round up the cattle. That day Bill Cody was the object of much attention and admiration at Kearney. It was his first taste of notoriety, and it whetted his appetite for more of the same.

Not long after that, Bill was assigned to a wagon-train carrying tools and equipment to the Cheyenne Pass, where the army was constructing a new fort. There was a stopover at Fort Laramie, and Bill was left behind to guard a load of wagon beds. To a great extent, this experience helped to shape his future life in the West. Fort Laramie, one of the oldest frontier outposts, was literally the crossroads of the plains. Almost 5,000 Sioux, Arapahoes, and Cheyennes had built their villages around the once-famous trading post, and even after the military took it over, it was still a favorite meeting place for the Indians through force of habit. The government did not discourage them—welcomed them in fact—for many of the greatest chiefs and warriors made Laramie their headquarters, and some of the most important Indian councils were held there. For the price of a little hospitality, the Army was able to keep a finger on the pulse of the whole

Red Nation. Bill Cody met some of the most famous
Indian fighters, hunters, and trappers at the fort: Kit
Carson and Jim Bridger among them. He was fascinated
at the way these plainsmen would sit cross-legged in a
circle, smoking the pipe and pow-wowing with the Indians
and conversing easily in the redman's strange tongues and
sign language. In the summer that he spent at Laramie,
he won the friendship of these veteran frontiersmen and
made them his teachers. Determined to master the varied
dialects of the red tribes, he also cultivated the acquaint-
ance of Indian children. He played their games and
observed their customs and habits carefully. A born diplo-
mat, the twelve-year-old Cody built up a reputation of
trust and good-will among the redmen that was to save
his life many times in the future.

Throughout his personal and political life, Cody was
an active friend of the Indians. He once wrote: "They
were the inheritors of the land that we live in. They were
not capable of developing it, or of appreciating its possibilities, but they owned it when the White Man came and
the White Man took it away from them. It was only
natural that they should resist. . . . It was our business
as scouts to be continually on the warpath against them
when they committed depredations. But no scout ever
hated the Indians in general . . ."

It was on the Laramie expedition that Bill learned how
to fight the Indians too. One day he and two companions
were riding on mules, a good distance ahead of the wagon
train, when a war party of Sioux surrounded them. It
was flat country without cover. The man who was riding
next to Bill turned pale. "Damn! Not even an anthill to
get behind. We're goners."

The other man, a veteran Indian fighter named
Simpson, ordered them to dismount. He grabbed the
bridles and swung the three mules into a small triangle,
then drew his six-gun and shot each one cleanly through

the brain. They dropped in their tracks, forming a three-
sided barricade. "Now we got some cover, boys," Simpson
said. "Flatten out behind 'em." As the men dropped to the
ground, the Indians let go with a barrage of arrows and
bullets. In seconds, the carcasses of the mules looked like
pin-cushions.

"Poor old mules," Bill muttered. He was still shocked
at Simpson's casual brutality.

Simpson turned to him grimly. "Better them than us,
boy. If you expect to stay alive out here, you gotta think
fast and feel later . . . Oh, oh! Here they come!" The Sioux
were charging, hooting their piercing war cry, and twang-
ing arrows from their bows at a great rate. Luckily, only
a few of them were armed with rifles. When they were
about fifty yards away, the white men fired a volley into
the center of their ranks. Three Indians tumbled into the
dust. At twenty yards, another volley knocked down three
more. One of the riderless horses kept coming straight at
the barricade. "Duck!" Simpson screamed and tucked in
his head like a turtle. The pony vaulted the dead mules,
his hooves whistling no more than six inches over Bill's
head. With six of their number down, the Sioux broke
and regrouped out of range of the sharp-shooting plainsmen. While Bill reloaded their guns, Simpson examined
a flesh wound that Woods had received from a flying
arrow. "Looks clean to me. I don't think that arrow was
poisoned."

Woods laughed at his concern. "What the hell's the
difference? You don't figure we're goin' to get out of this,
do you? Them bastards outnumber us twenty to one.
Sooner or later they'll get us." He waved at the formidable force of Indians that was circling just out of range.

"You seem right anxious to give up your scalp,
partner," Simpson said acidly.

Bill bit his lip. "I was looking at one of them magazines the soldiers at Kearney brought from the East. All

about Indians attackin' settlers. In them stories the Cavalry always shows up at the last moment to save the white people."

"Oh Jesus!" Wood groaned. "Listen to him, will you."

They managed to pick off a few more of the attackers as the circle tightened about them. "Looks like they're about ready," Simpson decided. "Get set, boys." But before the Indians could start another charge, there was a sound off in the distance like the crack of a rifle, but sharper and clearer. Instantly, the Sioux began to mill about, shouting excitedly.

"What's the mattter with them?" Bill asked anxiously.

The strange sound was heard again, closer this time. Simpson grinned. "Don't you fellers know what that is? That's a bullwhip snappin'. The wagon train must be closeby. Them devils know it too. See?" He pointed to the Indians, who were turning away and riding off across the prairie. Soon after, the lead wagon came rumbling over a small rise to the west, its driver flicking his lone blacksnake whip over the mules' heads. "Yippee-eee!" Simpson ripped his slouch hat off and beat Woods playfully across the shoulders. "Just like the boy said, wasn't it. It ain't the cavalry, but it's the next best thing. Woodsie, old man, that'll teach you to have respect for them writer fellows."

Competing for man's wages in a man's world was quite a problem for a twelve-year-old. Bill soon found that to merit consideration from an employer, he not only had to prove that he could do the job as well as a man, but also that he could do it better. To offset the handicap of youth, he practiced the recognized skills of the frontier with fanatic zeal. By the time he was fifteen, Bill Cody was an expert horseman and a dead-shot with rifle or pistol. He could hunt and trap with the best of the mountain men, and whenever he drove cattle for pack trains, he sketched maps of the country they traveled through and committed them to memory. When the immortal "Pony Express" was organized by Russell, Majors, and Wadell in 1860, Bill, not quite fifteen, had the distinction of being the youngest rider picked to join this elite corps, which boasted the ruggedest specimens in the West. Riding the Pony required super-human stamina and strength. The route from St. Joseph, Missouri, to Sacramento, California, ran across 2,000 miles of alkali desert and snow-blocked mountain passes, swarming with hostile Indians and outlaws. The riders changed horses at each of the stations, which were located fifteen miles apart, and each rider rode forty-five miles at a stretch. The Pony Express made the first cross-country run in ten days and soon cut the time to eight. The salary was $125 a month, but after Indian ambushes and resignations took a heavy toll of personnel, the riders were paid overtime, plus bonuses for riding extra shifts. Bill set one of the notable records of the Pony when he rode 320 miles in twenty-one hours and forty minutes. Pulling into Three Crossings in the Rockies at the end of a seventy-six mile run from Red Buttes to Sweetwater, he discovered his relief had been killed the night before. There was nothing to do but jump on a fresh horse and take the deceased's run from Sweetwater to Rocky Ridge, a distance of eighty-five miles. That was a bad day for Pony riders. When Bill got to Rocky Ridge, he was informed that the rider who had been scheduled to take the first lap of the return trip was also missing. Bill shrugged, jumped on the ready horse, and started back.

At the outbreak of the Civil War, Bill joined the Red Legged Scouts, a Missouri Militia company cooperating with the Union Army to protect Missouri border settlements against Quantrell's Raiders and other Confederate guerillas. In 1864, he enlisted as a private in the Seventh Kansas Volunteers. Soon after the regiment was sent to Memphis Tennessee to join the command of General

A. J. Smith. Smith had the momentous assignment of checkmating General Forrest in southern Tennessee. The brilliant Confederate commander, whose hit-and-run tactics were part of the curriculum in Hitler's War Colleges before World War II, was as elusive as he was deadly, and he had to be found before he could be fought. Informed of Cody's reputation as a scout and guide, Smith asked Cody to perform a vital espionage assignment for him. Disguised as a farm boy, Bill slipped behind Confederate lines and located General Forrest's command. Armed with this information, General Smith caught the Confederate "Panzers" at Turpedo and defeated them badly.

At the end of the war, Bill was assigned as personal guide and interpreter to General Sherman, who had been commissioned to make peace with the hostile Indians on the border. At the completion of this mission, he married a girl who was determined to domesticate him. With the money Bill had saved, they opened a hotel in the Salt Creek Valley. But the life was too tame for an old plainsman like Bill, who, at the age of twenty, had lived through more excitement and adventure than most men twice his age. In 1866, Bill went back to scouting for the army.

Many of Cody's contemporaries, who were envious of the esteem in which he was held by high government officials and army brass, accused him of apple-polishing. The truth is that if it had not been for his uncommon talents, Bill Cody would have spent a good part of his army career in the guardhouse. He was always polite and respectful to his superiors, when they were polite and respectful to him, but he took malicious delight in deflating overblown egos. It was at Fort Hayes that he first met General George Custer, an opinionated, peppery man who had a reputation for being merciless to his subordinates. Custer was on his way to Fort Larned with an escort of ten cavalrymen, and when he heard that the

famed Bill Cody was at Hayes, a gleam came into his eye.
"I want him assigned to guide me," he snapped. "We'll
see if he's as good as they say."

Determined to humiliate Cody, he had his men out in
the courtyard a quarter-of-an-hour before they were due
to move out. When Bill reported at the scheduled time,
Custer blasted him: "Goddammit man! We've been waiting over an hour for you!"

Bill blinked. "I thought we were moving out at six
o'clock. That's what you told me last night."

"If you plainsmen washed your ears once in a while,
you'd hear better. I distinctly told you five o'clock and
answer 'Sir' when you're addressing an officer."

Bill swallowed hard. "Yes," he said between gritted
teeth, "sir!"

Suddenly Custer's eyes bulged. "What in hell is that
creature you're riding?"

"A mule—sir," Bill replied.

"A mule!" the General said in an apoplectic whisper.
"Mister Cody, are you aware that I am in a hurry to get
to Fort Larned?" He waved his hand in the direction of
the spirited Kentucky thoroughbreds his men were riding.
"With a mule setting the pace, our horses are likely to
roll over and go to sleep."

"He's a fast mule, General," Bill said.

"Bah!" Custer spit on the ground between the mule's
front feet. "I'm not sure who's the biggest jackass, you
or him . . . Well, I'm stuck with you now. May as well
make the best of it. Let's go."

Bill reddened, but said nothing. Swinging his mount
around, he led the way out of the fort. What General
Custer didn't know was that over fifty miles of sandhills
lay between him and his destination; loose fine sand that
gave a horse about as much footing as on a treadmill.
The stocky, big-footed mule was particularly endowed for
this sort of plodding. When they left the fort, Bill set a

pace that kept the cavalrymen moving at a half-trot. At
the end of twenty-five miles, he noticed that the horses
were sweating and breathing hard. "Any time you fellers
want to rest, say the word," he told Custer blandly.

The general snorted. "No time to waste. Push ahead,
Cody." They plunged on ahead into the sandhills. At the
end of an hour, the cavalrymen were lagging far behind
Custer and himself. Bill noted that Custer's horse was
badly winded, his sides trembling. The general coughed
and sputtered defensively. "I think maybe we're setting
too fast a pace."

"As you say—sir!" Bill turned to hide a grin. He slowed
down his mule during the next hour, but in spite of that,
they had to stop with increasing frequency to allow the
escort to catch up to them. When they reached Pawnee
Fork, it was obvious that the horses had reached the limit
of their endurance. Bill applied the *coup de grace*.
"General, sir," he said. "If you boys want to camp here,
I'll ride ahead to the fort. You won't have any trouble
findin' it now. Just follow the valley straight down."

"Blast you, Cody!" Custer roared. "That mouse-colored
mule can't outlast my stallion. I'll ride shoulder to shoulder
with you into Hell itself."

"Begging your pardon, Sir," a red-faced lieutenant
who had ridden up put in desperately. "I don't think the
rest of us can go another mile."

"One hell of an escort you men are," Custer muttered.
"Camp here then. For all I care you can stay here. But
I'm going with Cody."

Bill set a pace for the rest of the way that brought
Custer's thoroughbred down on his knees several times in
the tenacious sand. But the General never fell more than
a half-length behind him all the way. When they entered
the gates of the fort, however, it was evident that he was
one happy man.

The next morning Bill saddled his mule, who was as

fresh and frisky as a colt, and reported to Custer's head-quarters for further orders. The general looked glum as he returned Bill's snappy salute. "I don't feel so good, Cody," he said sheepishly. "My horse died in the night."

Bill nodded solemnly. "Sorry to hear it, sir. Too bad he got out of his class yesterday." As he turned to ride off, a broad grin broke through the shadows on Custer's face. "Say, Bill, maybe you can tell me where I can get a good mule?"

On another occasion, Bill cut another commander down to size. At the time, he was chief of scouts for the Fifth Cavalry, led by Colonel Royal, in an expedition against the Dog Soldier Indians, a band of unruly Cheyennes who refused to stay on a reservation. One night, when they were camped on the banks of the Saline River, Colonel Royal asked Bill to go out and shoot a few buffalo for fresh meat. "Glad to, Colonel," Bill said. "Just send a wagon along with me to bring in the meat."

The colonel, who liked to give orders but didn't like to get them, bridled. "I'll send the wagon *after* you've killed the buffalo, Cody. I don't intend to send a wagon on a wild goose chase."

Bill shrugged. "Have it your own way." Without another word, he mounted Brigham and scouted up a herd of buffalo about a quarter mile away from the camp. Cutting out a half-dozen from the herd, he stampeded them straight toward the company area. The buffalos stormed into the camp like Juggernauts, scattering the soldiers to all sides. One dashed right through the flap of the colonel's tent and burst through the other side. Bill, who was following right on their heels, picked them off neatly, one by one, within the space of 200 yards. The camp looked as if a twister had swept through it; pots, pans, messkits, rifles, and clothing were scattered to all sides. Colonel Royal, his panic overcoming his modesty, bolted out of his tent clad in only a pair of socks and garters, screaming, "To your arms, men. They're attacking. Get the—" Then he fell over a dead buffalo. Sprawled across the dead animal in his birthday suit, he made an extremely undignified picture. As he struggled to his feet, his reason returned in a series of logical steps. "Where are they? I don't see any Indians. Where did this buffalo come from? Where did all these buffalo come from? CODY! What's the meaning of this?"

Bill stepped forward and saluted smartly, and Royal returned it self-consciously. "Colonel," Bill said "Long as you were so stingy 'bout sendin' out a wagon, I figured to let the buffalo supply their own transportation." From chalk-white the colonel's face turned to brick-red. He opened his mouth, but nothing came out. Then with a whimper of frustration, he turned and marched back into his tent. Bill winked at a Captain nearby, who was having all he could do to control his laughter. "Damn! Did you ever see anything sillier than a man trying to act like an officer in his birthday suit?"

In 1868, while Bill was hunting buffalo for the Kansas and Pacific, a full-scale Indian war erupted on the frontier. Scouts and guides were scarce, so Bill quit his job and signed up again. He was assigned to Fort Larned, under the command of General Hazen. Because the fort was lightly garrisoned, General Hazen was doing his best to persuade the Comanche and Kiowa tribes in the region to remain neutral. Eventually, the negotiations fell through, and the army's Indian spies reported that Santana, one of the most powerful Comanche chieftains, was preparing to launch an assault on Larned. General Hazen asked for a man to carry a dispatch to General Sheridan at Fort Hayes asking for reinforcements, and since Bill knew the country better than any of the other scouts, he volunteered. It was sixty-five miles to Fort Hayes over treacherous terrain. Potholes, boulders, and quicksand made it an obstacle course for the most surefooted horses, even in daylight. And Bill had to ride under cover of darkness to avoid capture by the Indians. He had ridden only three miles when his horse stepped into a gopher hole, and Bill went sailing over his head. Before he could catch its bridle, the frightened animal scrambled to its feet and plunged on. Fortunately, Bill had taken precautions against just such an accident. When he started out, he had tied one end of his lariat to the bridle and the other end around his waist. Bracing his feet, he brought the horse to a standstill and climbed aboard once more. Shortly after reveille, he rode into Fort Hayes and delivered the dispatches to General Sheridan personally.

After breakfast Sheridan called him into his tent. "Cody," he said, "I've got some urgent dispatches that must reach Fort Dodge. None of my scouts will volunteer and . . ." He hesitated in embarrassment.

"I'll take 'em," Bill said quickly.

"I hate to ask you, after what you've been through, but it is an emergency."

Bill grinned. "Don't worry about me. Just give me a fresh horse, and it's as good as done." An hour later he was on his way. He rode all that afternoon and all night without a break, and by dawn the next morning he had covered seventy-five miles. At Saw Log River, he met a detachment of cavalry, which gave him a fresh horse, and after an hour's sleep, he was on his way again. He covered the twenty-five miles to Dodge by ten o'clock that morning.

The commander at the fort was amazed when Bill reported that he had not seen a single Indian in the area. "Hell, man," he said. "We're surrounded. They've run off our cattle and horses and killed a bunch of our sentries. They're thick as fleas between here and Fort Larned. I got some important dispatches here that should have been in General Hazen's hands two days ago, but I can't get anyone to take them."

"That's funny," Bill said without thinking, "I got through from Larned to Hayes all right, day before yesterday."

"Is that so?" the commander said, eyeing Bill with deference. "Say, you don't think . . ."

"Oh no!" Bill groaned. "I ain't had but an hour's sleep in two days."

The officer sighed. "Of course. It would be too much to ask, Cody. Forget it."

Bill gave the pot-bellied stove in the middle of the room a wicked kick. "Damn! Somebody's got to take them orders through." The officer shrugged. Bill wavered. "Well," he hedged, "I got there. I suppose I can get back. I'll take 'em for you."

The commander began to pound him across the shoulder blades. "I don't know what to say, Cody. You're a rare man. Thank you."

"I'll need a fresh horse though."

The commander laughed self-consciously. "A horse heh? Well, there isn't a decent horse in the fort. Tell you what though, I can give you an excellent mule?"

"A mule!" Bill said incredulously. "What's going to happen if I get some Injuns on my tail?"

"Cody," the commander said with perverse logic, "You told me yourself you didn't see an Indian all the way to Dodge. No doubt you'll be just as lucky on the return trip."

"No doubt," Bill mumbled sarcastically.

The first thirty miles of the trip were uneventful. Bill dismounted at Coon Creek and let the mule drink. Then it happened. Without warning, the animal pulled away from him and started down the wagon road for Larned at a half-trot. Cursing and shaking his fist, Bill sprinted after him. But the mule seemed possessed of a diabolical intelligence. At intervals he would slow down, twist his head around to stare at his pursuer, and blink gravely as

Bill narrowed the distance between them. Then, just when
Bill was set to pounce on him, he would wiggle his long
ears, let out a loud hee-haw, and put on a burst of speed.
So it went for the next thirty miles. The following morning, just after sunrise, a patrol scouting about a half-mile
outside Fort Larned was treated to an unusual sight.
Walking leisurely down the road toward them was a big
Army mule, and about ten paces in back of him was a
wild-eyed bedraggled man scuffling his feet in the dust.
The mule would stop occasionally to nibble at the grass
at the side of the road, prancing away nimbly whenever
the man came too close to him. The patrol rode forward
and took the mule in tow. When the man reached them,
he sat down in the middle of the road. "Whew!" he
groaned. "That was quite a trip."

"Who are you?" the lieutenant in charge inquired.

"Bill Cody. I'm running dispatches from Fort Dodge
to Fort Larned."

"Hell, man," the officer said. "You ought to be riding
that animal instead of walking him like that."

Bill squinted up at the lieutenant through bloodshot
eyes. "This here is a highly temperamental beast. The only
way he'd come at all was on his own terms. I ride him a
ways. Then I get off and we walk a ways. But you ain't
seen nothin' yet, boys. Now it's my turn to carry him."

As soon as Bill had delivered his dispatches, he turned
into his bedroll and slept through until dark—just in time
to get up and take another dispatch back to General
Sheridan's headquarters. He left that night and pulled
into Fort Hayes at daybreak. The general was flabber-
gasted when Bill handed him the dispatches from Larned.
"Why I thought you were up at Dodge, Cody," he asked.

"Hell, General," Bill grinned. "That was yesterday. I
get around." Over coffee and whiskey, Bill gave Sheridan
a detailed account of his odyssey—in fifty-eight hours he
had ridden and walked 365 miles through terrain that

was thick with Indians and presented more hazards than an obstacle course.

Although for some years Buffalo Bill served as chief U.S. detective for the army, as well as scout and guide, he never achieved a reputation for being a gun-slinger. By tradition, lawmen were supposed to be strong, silent, commanding figures, who held themselves aloof from the citizens they had been hired to keep in line. Experience had shown that a sheriff or marshal who became too friendly with the boys at the local tavern ran the risk of blunting his authority. Buffalo Bill was one of the rare law officers who could stand at the bar with his arm across the shoulder of a fast-drawing gambler and come away with his reputation intact. It was said that when he made an arrest, the prisoner usually ended up feeling like a heel because of the inconvenience he had caused Bill. Still he never ran away from a gun fight.

On one occasion, General Emory, the commander at Fort MacPherson appointed him Justice of the Peace to deal with an epidemic of civilian crimes over which the army had no jurisdiction. His first day on the job, a poor immigrant knocked on his door, hat in hand and trembling with emotion. He explained that one of his two horses, the only possessions he had in the world, had wandered off into a herd being driven to market. When he had timidly approached the herd boss and tried to claim his property, the man had laughed at him and refused to return the horse without a *writ of replevin*. For all intents the horse was as good as gone, for such legal technicalities were about as alien on the frontier as caviar and champagne.

Bill scratched his head. "Frankly," he told the immigrant, "I never heard of such a thing." Observing that the poor man was on the verge of nervous collapse, Bill had his wife prepare a hearty breakfast. "Let's talk about it over some bacon and eggs and whiskey. I figure we'll come up with something."

After they had eaten, Bill strapped on his six-shooter and saddled up his horse. "Now let's go find this feller," he said to the immigrant. "You lead the way."

About ten miles outside of the fort, they overtook the herd. The boss, a beefy, ugly-looking man with twin six-guns slung at his hips and a rifle in his saddle boot, was riding front of the herd. The two men rode up to him, and Bill calmly explained the nature of his business.

"How do I know that's his horse?" the boss scowled, spitting tobacco juice on the ground.

"You could round up your herd and count 'em," Bill suggested. "You must know how many horses you got."

The herder laughed. "I should go to that trouble. Lookie here, you a constable?"

"I'm a constable, all right," Bill said. "And the judge and jury too.

The herder slouched disarmingly in his saddle and regarded Bill from under eyelids, half-closed like a lizard. But Bill was alert to the tensed cords in the backs of his hands as they moved casually up his legs toward his holsters. "Where's your *writ of replevin?*" the herder asked.

"Right in my hand," Bill said easily. In a blur of motion, his Colt appeared in his hand, its muzzle pointing straight at the herder's belly.

The herder's hands fell limply to his sides. "Well, now," he drawled. "I don't see no sense in making a fuss over one horse. I'm in a hurry. You pick him out, and we'll let it go at that."

"You think so?" Bill said crisply. "Where I come from horse stealin' is a hanging offense. I think I'll just run your whole outfit back to the fort and give you the limit —six months in the pokey and a $500 fine."

The big man's jaw almost bounced off his saddle horn. "Listen, friend," he said nervously. "I swear I didn't know that damned horse had wandered into my herd. I'm right sorry 'bout all the trouble I caused this gentleman, and I'll be glad to make up for it."

Bill let him sweat it out for a few minutes, pretending to give the matter grave thought. "Hmmmm . . . I tell you," he finally said, "I figure this man is entitled to damages. You pay him $150 and we'll forget about the whole thing."

"Gladly, friend," the herder said with relief.

The immigrant picked out his horse, and the transaction was closed. Just as Bill was preparing to ride off, the herder asked him a question. "Say, you look familiar, friend. Who are you?"

"Buffalo Bill Cody."

The man's eyes snapped wide. "Buffalo Bill! Why didn't you say so in the first place?" He started to laugh. "Hell, it was worth $150 to meet up with you. What a story this will make to tell the boys in the bunkhouse."

In the last quarter of the nineteenth century, the American Wild West enjoyed an aura of romance and glamor seldom rivalled outside of the Arabian Nights. Part of it was deserved, but most of it was the invention of a cult of eastern writers, namely Ned Buntline, whose lurid stories of the West rocketed the circulations of the paperback magazines of the era. Small boys, Philadelphia debutantes, and the crowned heads of Europe devoured these tales with equal avidity. Their image of the frontier was a sweeping stage of cactus and desert where blood-thirsty Indians whirled around besieged wagon trains and cowboys shot each other over the turn of a card to the music of war whoops, thundering buffalo hooves, and death rattles, while Olympian sheriffs maintained what little sanity existed with smoking six-guns. Millionaires, artists, actors and writers, and nobility came from all over the world to witness this epic unfold first-hand. Buffalo Bill had some of his most bizarre adventures arranging and guiding these safaris of notables into the Wild West.

In 1874, Bill led the famous "Millionaires' Hunting Party" on an expedition to hunt buffalo. The group included such personalities as General Sheridan; James Gordon Bennett of the New York *Herald;* Samuel Johnson; General Anson Stager of the Western Union; and Charles Wilson, editor of the Chicago *Journal.* Frequently, the Wild West did not live up to the expectations of "wildness" that many of the visiting celebrities had entertained. On one occasion he was escorting a party of titled Englishmen and a wealthy financier, named McCarthy, from New York, who were eager to see some Indians on the warpath. At the time things were relatively peaceful, and neither Bill nor the army had any intentions of stirring up trouble to satisfy the whims of a couple of greenhorns. Nevertheless, Bill felt it was his duty to provide a little excitement for the visitors, who seemed a little disappointed at the lack of bloodshed around the post. "I can find more action than this in the Tenderloin," McCarthy would brag flippantly at the bar. And add with a touch of bravado, "I'd give anything to get a shot at some of these red beggars." Determined to oblige him, Bill arranged for a company of Pawnee Army scouts to deck themselves out in warpaint and battle regalia and to stage a mock attack one morning when he and McCarthy were riding outside the fort. The two white men were crossing a small creek when the redskins descended on them, firing their rifles in the air and whooping it up something fearsome. "Well," Bill said calmly, turning to McCarthy. "This is it. Shall we run for it or make a stand?"

Without a word, the cocky little financier dropped gun, hat, and a diamond-studded cigar-holder and galloped off in a cloud of dust. As Bill related later: "That man could have made a fortune as a jockey. Ain't another man on earth could have gotten such speed out of an old nag like he was ridin'."

Another time he was guiding a wealthy English Army

officer named Lord Flynn on a buffalo hunt when their
stock of liquid refreshments ran low. The closest saloon
was thirty miles away, and the sun had set some hours
before. After riding through the dark prairie most of the
evening, they arrived just as the saloon was closing down.
A man who was accustomed to getting what he wanted,
Lord Flynn bought the place—house, bar, and stock—had
his drink, then made a present of the saloon to one of the
plainsmen in his party.

But the weirdest expedition Bill ever took part in
was the one in honor of the Russian Grand Duke Alexis
and his coterie of Cossack guards. Every time the duke
brought down a buffalo, he would dismount and take a
bow while the prairie rang with the cheers of his men.
Then he would pass out caviar and champagne to everyone, and the expedition would drink to his health. This
ritual was repeated every time the duke killed a buffalo,
and after a half-dozen such celebrations, the West really
became "wild." Cossack riders went galloping in all directions over the plains, stampeding buffalo and bellowing
Russian marching songs as they stood in the saddle, hung
under their horses' bellies and performed other variations
of the trick-riding for which they were famous. "It was
a rather frightening spectacle," Bill said later, in what
was probably the understatement of that year.

To show his appreciation to Buffalo Bill for making all
that fun possible, the Duke presented him with a set of
diamond- and ruby-studded cuff links and a stickpin in the
shape of a buffalo head. Later in the year, the Millionaires'
Club invited Bill to New York to buy some dress shirts to
wear his jewelry on. Bill was feted in both Chicago and
New York by his influential friends. He went to Broadway
shows, was introduced to high society, and was outfitted
in ties, tails, and a stove pipe hat. He even went on a fox
hunt and was frightened to death at the reckless manner
in which the red-coated riders dashed madly over fences,

stone walls and under low-hanging branches—risking their
lives to catch one bushy-tailed little critter that they
couldn't even eat." Bill was greatly relieved when he
received emergency orders from the army to join General
Reynold's expedition into the northern Loup country. Bill
caught up with Reynolds at Pawnee Springs. As a joke
he dressed up in his evening clothes and cape, piled up
his long hair under his stovepipe hat, and rode into camp
like a London dude. The soldiers were standing reveille
when he arrived, and a good many raspberries greeted
him. Mincing up to the general, Bill saluted and in a
falsetto voice said: "I have come to report for duty, sir."

Reynold's face turned white, red, and purple in that
order as the formation disintegrated in laughter. "Who
in the hell are you, sir?" he roared.

"Why I am your guide," Bill said in his piping voice.

"My guide!" The general's eyes bulged.

"Yes, sir. In accordance with the new policy of the
War Department, I was sent direct from Washington.
Congress feels that it is time we started to give some consideration to the background of men in such responsible
positions. The old, uncouth order must go. I, sir, am a
graduate of a university. I have a degree in map-reading,
and I am sure I will meet with your satisfaction."

The general was panicky now. "Map reading!" he said
in a whisper. "Good God, what are those bastards in
Washington tryin' to do to us?" He turned frantically to
his aides. "The Injuns will push us back into the Atlantic
for certain."

Deciding that he had carried the joke far enough,
Bill raised his top hat, and his long hair tumbled down
round his shoulders. "Don't you know me, General?" he
said in his normal voice.

The general looked blank for a minute, then recognition came to him slowly. "No, it can't be . . . Buffalo
Bill . . . What in hell are you doing in that monkey suit?"

When he had recovered, he invited Bill into his tent for a drink. "I ain't had such a shock since my wife gave birth," the general said seriously as he downed a tumblerful of brandy.

The following spring, Bill was nominated and elected to the Nebraska legislature while he was away on a scouting expedition, but he didn't accept the office. There was a more intriguing offer to consider. Ned Buntline, the famous western writer wanted him, Wild Bill Hickok, and a few other prominent Western figures to come to New York and star in a Wild West melodrama he was producing on the stage. The show was a great success and ran for two seasons. By now, Bill was sold on show business and had ideas of organizing his own show. But just about then, the Sioux War broke out on the frontier, and he went back to duty as chief scout and guide for General Wesley Merritt's army in the Black Hills. Shortly after the massacre of General Custer and his command, Bill rode with Merritt and a detachment of 500 troopers to intercept an army of 800 Cheyennes, who had left the Red Cloud reservation to join Sitting Bull on the Little Big Horn.

The cavalry and the Indians met at War Bonnet Creek, and there were several preliminary skirmishes. Merritt soon discovered that not only did the Cheyennes outnumber him, but also that they were well equipped with arms. It was at this point that a heroic action by Buffalo Bill saved the day. One of the Cheyennes, whose war paint and dress proclaimed that he was a great chief, recognized Bill by his long yellow hair. Riding out in front of his men, he shouted a challenge: "I would fight with you, *Pa-ho-has-ka.*"

"What'd he say?" Merritt asked.

"He says he wants to have a go at it with Long-yellow-Hair—that's me." Bill checked his rifle and his .45 Colt to see they were in good working order.

"Don't be a damned fool, Bill," the general protested. "You can't fight him. The army can't afford to lose you."

Bill nodded at the chieftain who was strutting up and down on horseback out in front of his braves. "I can't afford to lose face either. These buggers are funny. If they see I'm afraid, it'll build up their confidence and give 'em a bigger edge on us than they got now."

While the red and white armies watched from the sidelines, Bill and the chief galloped toward each other at a fast clip. At fifty yards, the Indian raised his rifle and fired. The shot clipped past Bill's ear. At thirty yards, Bill shot the chief's horse out from under him. At the same instant, his own mount stumbled in a hole and pitched Bill over its head. The two battlers leaped to their feet simultaneously about ten feet apart and fired their rifles from the hip. Again the Indian missed, but took Bill's bullet in the chest. As he went down, Bill leaped on top of him and drove his hunting knife into the chief's heart. Enraged by the outcome of the duel, 200 of the Indians charged down the slope toward Cody. At the same time, a company of cavalrymen dashed out to head them off. Coolly, Bill scalped his victim and swung the bloody top-knot over his head: "The first scalp for Custer!" he roared. A great cheer went up from the troopers; and, yelling battle cries that were equally as frightening as the Indians', they waded into the Cheyennes. Disrupted by the loss of one of their chiefs and the ferocity of the cavalry attack, the renegades finally broke in confusion and headed back for the reservation. It was probably Buffalo Bill's single greatest act for his country. At the end of the campaign, he was commissioned a colonel in the reserves, in recognition of his services.

A free agent once more, he devoted himself earnestly to developing his ideas for a Wild West Show. Bill's active imagination spilled over the limitations of the stage. He wanted to show his audience what the West was really like. He staged his first show in an outdoor arena in Omaha. The grand opening featured Sioux, Arapahoes, Cheyennes, and Brueles decked out in war paint and feathers, charging around the ring, firing their guns into the air, and screaming war whoops. The Indians were followed by cowboys and cavalrymen, accurately costumed, with horse-drawn stagecoaches bringing up the rear. In authentic setting, the cowboys and soldiers engaged the redskins in mortal combat; stagecoaches careened around the arena pursued by gangs of masked bandits; wild horses and steers were roped and broken before the spectators' eyes; the customers were treated to the sight, hitherto denied the eyes of white men, of Indian ceremonial dances and sacrificial rituals. Overnight, Buffalo Bill's Wild West Show became a national and international sensation. Advance bookings extended two years into the future.

The show sailed to England and played a Command Performance at the huge London Amphitheater before King Edward VII. Bill outdid himself by staging a buffalo hunt and simulating a prairie cyclone that blew an entire Indian village away. The high point of the performance, however, was when the Kings of Denmark, Greece, Saxony, and the Crown Prince of Austria climbed on top of a coach and held on for dear life while Bill drove the horses at full speed around the arena, and a dozen mounted outlaws fired blank cartridges at the royal party. Buffalo Bill's Wild West Show toured all over Europe, piling up triumph after triumph. In Rome, a wealthy Italian nobleman tried to show up Bill's "rough riders." He had some wild horses in his stables that the best trainers in Europe had given up on, and he challenged anyone in the troupe to ride them. The contest was introduced as a climax to the regular show, and, in no time

at all, the western broncobusters had the beasts trotting
around the arena like show horses, while the audience
cheered madly.

As Buffalo Bill came down the gangplank in New York
after his European tour, he was handed a telegram from
General Miles informing him that the Indians were on the
warpath again and requesting his services. Nobody could
have blamed him if he had declined. For more than thirty
years he had placed duty to his country before his business, his family, and life itself. It was more than the
government expected from any soldier. Bill was middle-
aged now, and, for the first time in his life, he had a
good thing going for him financially. But within thirty-six
hours after he had set foot on land, Colonel Cody reported
for duty at General Miles' headquarters in Chicago.

In this campaign Bill devised a daring scheme to end
the Indian threat and volunteered to carry it out himself.
Disguised as an Indian, he hoped to infiltrate the head-
quarters of Sitting Bull, who was busy in the Dakotas
trying to recruit as many tribes as he could for the immi-
nent war against the whites. As an old and trusted friend
of the powerful Sioux chieftain, Bill hoped to persuade
him to settle his differences at the conference table. Even
if the plan failed, as many army men felt it would, the
delaying action would give the army time to move up and
evacuate the hundreds of helpless settlers in the district.
Bill was already on his way to Sitting Bull's camp when
a courier caught up to him with a telegram ordering him
back. It was signed by the President, Benjamin Harrison
himself. There was no choice but to obey the order. It
later developed that the President's advisors had per-
suaded him to overrule Bill's mission, because they were
afraid it would ignite, rather than prevent a war. Their
reasoning was that if Sitting Bull, the most influential
chieftain in the whole Indian nation, were killed, it would
destroy the hope of ever achieving a universal and lasting

peace with the redmen. Bill insisted it was a monumental
blunder, and subsequent events proved he was right.
Shortly afterward, Sitting Bull was killed in the Ghost
Dance War. Nevertheless, the Indian uprising was of short
duration, and Bill had the satisfaction of sitting in on the
peace conference, when all the tribes of North American
Indians surrendered unconditionally to General Miles—
after 300 years of warfare. Bill closed out his army career
as a Brigadier General and returned to civilian life for
good this time.

The remainder of his life was pleasant, prosperous,
and uneventful, and, to the relief of his wife, he became
a pretty fair family man. He continued to supervise his
Wild West Show, which was the forerunner of the modern
rodeo, and in 1901 he became president of the Cody Military College in Wyoming, in which capacity he served
until his death in 1917.

A dozen epitaphs come to mind that would be appro-
priate for a man like Buffalo Bill, all of them stressing
some aspect of his varied deeds and accomplishments. But
the most fitting of all is a simple phrase worked in dia-
monds at the bottom of a feathered crest presented to
Bill by the Prince of Wales: "I serve."

TWO'S COMPANY

BOOKS IN THE PUPPY PATROL SERIES ™

1. *TEACHER'S PET*
2. *BIG BEN*
3. *ABANDONED!*
4. *DOUBLE TROUBLE*
5. *STAR PAWS*
6. *TUG OF LOVE*
7. *SAVING SKYE*
8. *TUFF'S LUCK*
9. *RED ALERT*
10. *THE GREAT ESCAPE*
11. *PERFECT PUPPY*
12. *SAM AND DELILAH*
13. *THE SEA DOG*
14. *PUPPY SCHOOL*
15. *A WINTER'S TALE*
16. *PUPPY LOVE*
17. *BEST OF FRIENDS*
18. *KING OF THE CASTLE*
19. *POSH PUP*
20. *CHARLIE'S CHOICE*
21. *THE PUPPY PROJECT*
22. *SUPERDOG!*
23. *SHERLOCK'S HOME*
24. *FOREVER SAM*
25. *MILLY'S TRIUMPH*
26. *THE SNOW DOG*
27. *BOOMERANG BOB*
28. *WILLOW'S WOODS*
29. *DOGNAPPED!*
30. *PUPPY POWER!*
31. *TWO'S COMPANY*

COMING SOON

32. *DIGGER'S TREASURE*

TWO'S COMPANY

JENNY DALE

Illustrations by Mick Reid
Cover illustration by Michael Rowe

AN
APPLE
PAPERBACK

SCHOLASTIC INC.
New York   Toronto   London   Auckland   Sydney
Mexico City   New Delhi   Hong Kong   Buenos Aires

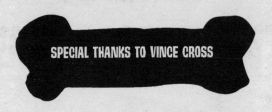

SPECIAL THANKS TO VINCE CROSS

ISBN 0-439-45352-6

All rights reserved. Published by Scholastic Inc., 557 Broadway, New York, NY 10012 by arrangement with Macmillan Children's Books, a division of Macmillan Publishers Ltd.

12 11 10 9 8 7 6 5 4 3 2 1   3 4 5 6 7 8/0

Printed in the U.S.A.   40
First Scholastic printing, August 2003

CHAPTER ONE

"**R**eady, Jake?" Neil Parker held the gaze of his young black-and-white Border collie for just a second or two more, then curled the Frisbee into the warm air of the May evening. Jake scrambled away eagerly across the exercise field that lay behind King Street Kennels. With all four feet clear off the ground, he tried to snatch the flying saucer out of the sky.

But the Frisbee hit him lightly on the nose and dropped into the grass. Jake shook himself and sneezed.

Eleven-year-old Neil laughed. Neil loved being with dogs. Playing with them, feeding them, looking after them when they were sick — he couldn't imagine a better way of spending his time. Luckily his parents, Bob and Carole Parker, ran King Street

1

Kennels — a boarding kennel and rescue center near the small country town of Compton. Neil would never want to live anywhere else.

Jake picked up the Frisbee and ran back to Neil for an affectionate scratch behind the ears.

"He's not much better than you at catching, is he, Neil?" shouted Emily, Neil's ten-year-old sister, as she watched Neil fuss over Jake.

Bob Parker was leaning on the gate next to her. "Personally, I blame the thrower," he chuckled.

"Let's see how well you do then, Dad," challenged Neil. He stooped down and delicately extracted the Frisbee from Jake's teeth, then quickly spun it out hard and flat toward Bob.

Jake dashed across the grass in hot pursuit.

Bob jumped to catch the Frisbee as it rose up to his right, but as he stretched out his hand for it, he stumbled and lost his footing. He was a big man and he fell heavily, his back twisting as he hit the ground.

Neil started to laugh, but then stopped abruptly when he realized his dad might really be hurt.

"Dad, are you all right?" asked Emily, running over to him. For a moment, there was no answer as Bob got his bearings. Jake licked his face.

Bob winced as he stood up. Then, as he tried to straighten up fully, he gave a grimace of pain.

"Dad, is your back OK?" asked Neil.

"I'll be fine . . . I think!" said his father ruefully,

rubbing his back. "There must be something wrong with that Frisbee. Either that or I'm getting too old for running and jumping."

"I'm sorry," said Neil. "I shouldn't have thrown it so hard."

"Don't worry," said Bob. "I'll be fine. Now, aren't you two supposed to be going over to the Grange to see Mr. Bradshaw? He'll think you're not coming if you don't get a move on."

"Yeah, I guess we should be leaving. Come on, Em."

Neil and Emily left their dad walking stiffly back to the house, and set off for the Grange with Jake.

The best route to the old people's home was by the path that led away from King Street Kennels and traced the foot of the hills surrounding Compton. It was a bright Friday evening, but there was no one around. Neil and Emily let Jake run ahead. Every now and then, the young Border collie would stop and turn to look at them, ears pricked and head to one side, checking to make sure they were keeping up.

It was always fun to visit Henry Bradshaw and Skye, his collie. It wasn't so long ago that there'd been a "No Pets" policy at the Grange. It had taken a lot of persuasion for Neil and his sister to convince the manager, Mrs. Dickens, that neither Henry nor Skye would ever be happy until they could be together full-time. But the collie's gentle nature had quickly won everyone's hearts, and over the months Mrs. Dickens had mellowed out. Now a couple of the other residents had their dogs with them, too. Even so, Neil knew that Jake would have to be on his best behavior or risk getting yelled at by Mrs. Dickens.

They walked through the imposing gates of the big, gray, stone house and up to its grand entrance hall. Tom Dewhurst, the young assistant manager, strolled down the steps from the front door.

"Good evening, you two!" he greeted them. "Hello, Jake! Henry's expecting you all. He told me he's been looking forward to seeing you all day." He picked up a stick and offered it to Jake for a game of tug-of-war.

"How's Mr. Bradshaw?" asked Neil.

"He's fine," replied Tom. "You know where to find him, don't you?"

Neil and Emily nodded and made their way inside.

The Grange was like a comfortable hotel. The staircase leading to the second floor and Mr. Bradshaw's room rose gracefully from the hall. Underneath Neil and Emily's feet was a new, bright blue carpet.

"There you are!" a voice called from above them.

Neil and Emily looked up to see Henry Bradshaw's deep blue eyes twinkling at them from over the banister.

"I thought you'd gotten lost," the old man said with a smile.

Neil, Emily, and Jake climbed the stairs to join Henry.

"Nice carpet, Mr. B," said Emily.

"Yes, they've had it decorated again," he said as he led them along the upper corridor, waving a hand at the flowery walls. "New wallpaper, too." He pulled at his white mustache. "Mind you, I thought it was alright beforehand. Now come in, come in! What have you two got to say for yourselves, eh? How's young Jake shaping up?" he added, bending down toward the dog. Jake rolled over shamelessly, demanding to be tickled and scratched.

Mr. Bradshaw welcomed them into his cozy room. From beside the fireplace, Skye barked a welcome, too, and shuffled her feet. She was in peak condition, her amber-and-white coat shining with health. She bent her sensitive, intelligent face down to meet Jake's as he skidded over the floor toward her.

"Careful, Jake!" warned Neil. "Best behavior, remember!"

"He'll be all right," said Henry. "If it's Mrs. Dickens you're worried about, she's a changed woman as far as dogs are concerned . . ."

And before Neil and Emily could get a word in edgewise, Henry was off telling a tale about how Skye had dug up some of the manager's beloved peonies in the Grange's garden.

". . . and you know, Neil, when I told her about it, all she said was, 'These things happen!' Now a year ago, she'd have gone through the roof. But having Skye around has changed things. And so did Willy Mannion's dog, Jasmine."

He suddenly dropped his head. Neil and Emily looked at each other. Even Jake and Skye, who had been busy reintroducing themselves, stopped sniffing and pawing each other and turned to watch Henry.

"Willy Mannion?" said Neil quietly.

"Yes," said Henry. "Loved animals, did Willy."

"Who is he?" asked Emily.

"He used to live here," said Henry, dabbing at his eyes with a red silk handkerchief from his jacket pocket. "I'm afraid he passed away last week."

Then the old man pulled himself upright in his armchair and, smiling bravely, said, "But you two don't want to hear about that."

"He was your friend?" asked Emily sympathetically.

"Yes," said Henry softly. "And a very good friend

he's been these last six months. We had a lot of laughs together in here, Willy and me. I'm going to miss him. And so will Skye." He dropped a hand to his side and ruffled Skye's fur.

For a moment, Neil and Emily thought Henry Bradshaw might break down and cry, but he pulled himself together.

Neil stood up. "Maybe it's time we went home, Mr. Bradshaw."

"I'm sorry to be such an old sad sack. You two must want to get back to the kennels." Mr. Bradshaw smiled. "I'll show you out," he offered.

As Henry and Skye led the way toward the staircase, Neil noticed that the door of the room next to Henry's was ajar. Jake suddenly tugged forward on the end of his leash and nosed the door wide open.

"Jake!" called Neil in embarrassment. "What do you think you're doing?"

Neil knocked politely on the door and leaned into the room, ready to apologize to whoever lived there. At first glance, the room looked empty and bare of any personal belongings. Even the bed was stripped down. But then Neil saw what had drawn Jake inside. By the bed lay a beautiful, elderly yellow Labrador, its head on its paws. The dog raised its head, and turned its sad, wet eyes toward Jake. The younger dog gave the Labrador's nose an exploratory nuzzle but was gently pushed away.

Henry stood by the door and shook his head. "That's Jasmine, Willy's dog. Goodness knows what will become of her."

"She looks so sad," said Emily.

"She's been like this for days," said Henry. "She still won't leave Willy's bed. I suppose she thinks he's coming back."

Neil bent down to where Jasmine lay and stroked the smooth, creamy fur of Willy's faithful companion. She licked his hand gently, and then put her head back on her paws. As Neil straightened up, he caught sight of a harness lying on the table. He'd seen similar ones on guide dogs before.

"So Willy was blind?" he asked.

"He was," Henry Bradshaw answered. "Jasmine here was his eyes these past eleven years. And a good team they were, too."

No wonder Jasmine was in mourning, thought Neil. *For those eleven years, she and Willy must have been inseparable.*

Neil and Emily said good-bye to Jasmine and walked slowly down to the entrance hall with Henry. They were reluctant to leave Jasmine behind — she looked so sad and lonely. As they got to the front door, Mrs. Dickens hurried through from the kitchen with a tray, her face flushed and her gray hair pinned up in a bun. She stopped when she saw them.

"Hello," she said. "What's with all the long faces?"

"They've just met Jasmine," said Henry.

"Oh," said Mrs. Dickens thoughtfully, nodding her head. "I see."

"What's going to happen to her?" asked Emily.

"Well, to be honest," said Mrs. Dickens, "we don't quite know yet, do we, Henry? I'm still waiting to hear from the Guide Dogs for the Blind Association."

Neil looked puzzled. "But I thought Jasmine belonged to Willy," he said.

"Well, not exactly," Mrs. Dickens explained. "Technically, she still belongs to the Association. But Jasmine's probably too old to retrain with someone else now."

"So who *is* going to take her?" Neil pressed anxiously.

"That's just it, son," said Henry sadly. "There's no one now. Besides us, there wasn't anyone at poor Willy's funeral. He was pretty much on his own."

"So it may well be that she'll end her days in a boarding kennel," Mrs. Dickens added. "Though I have to say, she looks so sad, perhaps it would be kinder if she were put down. Some dogs never really get over their owner's death. I don't know what you think, Henry?"

The old man shook his head wearily. "I do know we'll all miss her terribly when she goes."

"She can't be put down," said Neil quickly.

"I think that Jasmine deserves a vacation at the very least," said Emily eagerly. "Would you let us take her to King Street for a few days, Mrs. Dickens? We'll look after her, won't we, Neil? We promise!"

Neil nodded his enthusiastic agreement. "It's a great idea, Em. We'll give her some good food and lots of gentle exercise. And with the other dogs around her, she'll soon perk up. She looks like she needs company."

Mrs. Dickens frowned and looked doubtful. "I'm sure she's well fed here, Neil. Probably too well, knowing the residents. I don't know what to say. What do you think, Henry?"

Henry's blue eyes twinkled more brightly than ever. "I think it's a stroke of genius. No doubt about it. Give her a break. It's what Willy would have wanted."

"Great!" said Neil and Emily together.

CHAPTER TWO

Neil went to see Jasmine in her kennel at the rescue center first thing before breakfast the next day. She struggled out of her basket to greet him with a slow wag of the tail and a couple of woofs of recognition.

"You're looking better this morning, Jas," said Neil. "Give me half an hour for breakfast, and I'll be back to take you out."

Jasmine had seemed happy to go with Neil and Emily the previous night, but she had been tired and distracted. After explanations and introductions, the Labrador had taken to life at King Street Kennels surprisingly well. Neil had fed her and bedded her down, and she hadn't complained once about the change of scenery.

"Are you going to be all right, old girl?" asked Neil, smoothing down her beautiful creamy coat as he talked. She licked his nose reassuringly, and shuffled back on the bed, but when he left her to go inside the house, her sad eyes followed him hauntingly.

"Neil, will you call your dad down for breakfast?" asked Carole Parker as Neil walked into the kitchen.

"Where are Emily and Sarah?" asked Neil. Sarah was his five-year-old sister.

"How could you forget?" Carole teased as she put plates out on the kitchen table. "We're off to Colshaw Town Hall this morning for Sarah's ballet competition. Emily's helping her get ready upstairs. Would you call them for me?"

Neil went to the bottom of the stairs and called his sisters. His dad was already edging his way down, clutching at the banister.

"I feel like I'm seventy," he grumbled.

"If your back's that bad," said Carole, "you'd better see the doctor." Neil could see that his mom was concerned.

"I really don't want to worry Alex Harvey," Bob muttered. "The only advice doctors give about bad backs is to stay in bed until they're better. And how can I do that?"

"We'll cope. You know how efficient Kate and Bev are — and Neil and Emily can help out as well," reassured Carole.

Kate Paget and Bev Mitchell were King Street's kennel assistants. They were a great team — energetic and hardworking, too.

"Will you make it to the festival this afternoon, Dad?" asked Emily, taking her place at the breakfast table.

Bob looked puzzled.

"The town festival, Dad," Sarah reminded him as she breezed into the room with her pigtails swinging. "You hadn't forgotten, had you? Fudge is going to win the pets' competition. You've got to be there to see that!" Fudge was Sarah's hamster. She was convinced that he was the smartest animal in the world and she was always trying to teach him new tricks.

Bob clapped a hand to his forehead in mock despair. "I'd completely forgotten."

Carole shook her head. "Well, you don't have to *do* anything except show up. Kate and Bev have got it all under control."

"What's that? The festival?" said Kate as she appeared in the kitchen doorway. She brushed back her mane of blond hair with one hand. "Yeah, no problem. It's all sorted out."

"Do you need Neil and Emily to help you this morning, Kate?" asked Bob.

"I think I can manage without them," Kate smiled. "I'm sure you two are dying to take Jasmine out for a walk. She seems like a wonderful dog."

"She is," replied Neil. "Dad, do you think Mike Turner would have time to look at Jasmine when he comes in this morning?"

Mike Turner, the local vet, came in twice a week to check on King Street's residents and hold a walk-in dog clinic for the general public.

"I'm sure Mike would make time," said Bob. "But I think you should find out a little about guide dogs before you take Jasmine out. She'll be used to a particular way of doing things. I'm sure there's a book around here somewhere." Bob left the breakfast table and hobbled off to the office, returning a minute or two later with a heavy reference book in his hand.

"Look at this before you go out. If I remember correctly, there are standard commands all owners use with their guide dogs. If you don't use the right one, Jasmine might not know what's going on. And don't be surprised if she insists on walking to your left. It's what she's trained to do."

Neil leafed through the pages eagerly. Emily peered over his shoulder while Jake tugged at his jeans, anxious to be off.

"Don't be so impatient, Jake," Neil scolded gently. "We've got to get this right."

"Most of the commands are what you'd expect, Dad," Emily reported. "'Sit,' 'Down,' 'Wait,' 'Come,' and 'Leave' . . . That sort of thing."

"I thought I remembered it being more complicated than that," said Bob, frowning.

"There are commands like 'Forward' for moving ahead, and 'Over' and 'In' to bring the dog closer or farther away to you," said Neil. "Nothing very unusual, though."

"OK. Well just be careful, then," said Bob. He winced as he tried to sit down at the table again.

"Like you?" Neil laughed sheepishly.

The walk was no problem. Jake darted around Neil, Emily, and Jasmine as they went out through the fields behind the kennels and up the hill. Jasmine walked sedately at Neil's side, always to his left, cautiously examining this new, strange place with its expanse of lush, vivid green grass.

Neil and Emily let the Labrador briefly off the

leash, to see what she would do. She lumbered a few paces, halfheartedly following the scent of a rabbit in the brambles before returning to their side.

They came back an hour later to find Mrs. Atkinson in their kitchen, on a surprise visit from Railway Cottages, where she lived.

"Hello, Neil," said the old lady, pulling away slightly from Jake's muddy paws and brushing down her skirt. "How are you? I can see Jake's in a good mood."

"Down, Jake!" said Neil. "Keep your dirty paws to yourself."

"He's just like his grandma." The old lady sighed. "Same spirit. I could never get Betsy to restrain herself, either. She was always so good with people." Mrs. Atkinson reached down and tickled Jake's ears. Jake became quiet at once, nuzzling her hand affectionately.

Mrs. Atkinson's dog Betsy had died giving birth to Jake's father, Sam. Mrs. Atkinson hadn't been able to afford to look after Betsy's pups properly, and, in desperation, she had left them where she knew someone would find them. She had never had a dog since.

Fortunately, both Sam and his brother Skip had survived and ended up in good homes. Sam was very special to Neil. They had been inseparable while Neil was growing up, and Neil was devastated when Sam had died just a few months ago. The Border collie's damaged heart had failed after he'd saved his son Jake from drowning. It meant a lot to Neil that Jake was so much like his dad — strong, energetic, and loving.

"You know," Mrs. Atkinson said, looking up, "I could almost imagine having a dog again myself."

Carole looked at her questioningly.

"Well," she went on, "my brother Alf died a year ago. He left me quite a bit of money, you know. I could afford to keep a dog now and I'd love the company."

Jasmine padded around the kitchen and pushed at Mrs. Atkinson's leg, not wanting to be left out of the conversation.

"Mind you, he'd have to be nice and quiet. I don't have the energy to go rushing around after a puppy." Jasmine introduced herself again, this time more forcefully. "Hello!" said Mrs. Atkinson to the Labrador. "You're a beautiful dog, aren't you?"

Jasmine turned her doleful eyes on Mrs. Atkinson. The old lady met the dog's gaze and stroked her smooth nose.

Neil suddenly had an idea. "Meet Jasmine," he said. "A dog like her would be perfect for you, I bet. And she's looking for a new home."

Mrs. Atkinson looked doubtful. "I don't know about that," she said with regret in her voice. "I'm probably too old to look after a dog properly. It might be too much for me to handle now —"

"Not a dog of Jasmine's age," interrupted Neil. "She's very well-trained now." And he and Emily told her how Jasmine had come to stay with them.

"Hmm, very interesting," said Mrs. Atkinson, looking fondly at the dog. "I'm sure you'll find a good home for her," she added, though Neil was convinced she sounded uncertain.

"I hope so," he said, smiling.

Carole looked at her watch. "Now, I don't want to hurry you, Mrs. A," she said, "but I've got to dash into Colshaw with Sarah so that she can be a fairy at eleven-thirty. And Neil and Emily have got to take Jasmine to the vet, right?"

"Hello, you two!" said Mike Turner as Neil and Emily led Jasmine into the converted old rescue center where the vet held his clinic. "How're things? So this is the wonderful Jasmine. Bev's been telling me all about her!"

Neil watched as the vet ran an experienced eye over the elderly Labrador. "Looks healthy enough, for starters, Neil. Nice shine on that coat! She's obviously been well-cared for. Walk her around for me a moment, will you?"

Neil and Jasmine took a turn around the room.

"Hmm, she seems to move reasonably well, considering her age. What is she, about thirteen?"

"That's what Mrs. Dickens said," answered Neil.

"OK, let's put your dog knowledge to the test, Neil. What should I be looking for in an old Labrador like Jasmine?"

"Arthritis?" suggested Neil.

"That's right! It's common in Labs as they get older. So it's good that Jasmine's moving quite freely." Mike bent down and stroked her. "Let's get you up here, old girl," he said, coaxing her up onto the table.

Emily helped her up, and the vet gave her a thorough examination.

"What do you think?" asked Neil.

"She's in great shape," he announced. "Her breathing's good, too. She's a beautiful dog, but she's probably too old to go back to work now. Her reactions won't be what they were. She'd still make someone a great pet, though."

Just then, Bev slipped into the room and said something to Mike that Neil didn't catch. The vet raised his eyebrows.

"Perhaps you could take Jasmine to the kennel for a rest, Bev?" he suggested. "It sounds like I've got a patient Neil and Emily might find interesting."

"Why's that?" asked Neil curiously.

"Coincidentally, it's another guide dog. I don't think I've examined one in the last year, and now there's two in the same day. Strange!"

Bev led Jasmine away, and showed a family group into the clinic.

"Come in, Mrs. Elliott. Come in, all of you," said Mike with a welcoming smile.

The woman who entered the room was sharply dressed, and Neil thought she looked pretty chic. With her were two children and a lively, lean young Labrador, carrying much less weight than Jasmine. Neil recognized the boy as Tim Elliott, who'd recently joined his friend Chris Wilson's class at Meadowbank School in Compton. He was chunkily built, with cropped blond hair and a very pale complexion.

The girl was older. She was slightly built, with

very short dark hair, almost like a boy's. She was barely taller than her brother, but there was something challenging and confident about her despite her size, Neil thought. She was the one holding the Labrador, too, on the end of a familiar short, framed leash.

"What can I do for you folks?" Mike asked.

Mrs. Elliott cast a doubtful eye over Neil and Emily.

"This is Neil Parker and his sister Emily," said Mike reassuringly. "They live here at the kennel — and they love dogs. What's this one's name?"

The dog held herself alertly and seemed to be glowing with health. Its coat was darker than Jasmine's, a rich golden color.

The girl answered, "Chloe," in a cool, confident voice.

"OK, and what seems to be the problem with Chloe?" asked Mike.

"She's been sick, Mr. Turner," said Mrs. Elliott. "It's such a nuisance." She began a long and detailed description of a recent occasion when Chloe had been sick.

Mrs. Elliott doesn't seem to like her dog very much, Neil thought. There was something about the way she spoke about the Labrador that seemed all wrong for this beautiful, calmly behaved dog. Neil tried smiling at Tim, but he scowled at his feet and gave no sign of recognition. The girl was tapping her foot, waiting for her mother to finish.

"Well, let's take a look at her, then," said Mike. He examined Chloe thoroughly. She was every bit as good on the table as Jasmine had been.

"Chloe's got a great temperament, that's for sure," the vet said. The girl smiled, almost triumphantly. "Has she been eating well?" Mike Turner added.

"No problems at all," said the girl before her mother could get a word in. "It's stress, if you ask me."

"Oh?" said Mike, interested. "And what makes you say that?"

"You'd only have to live in our house for five minutes to know," the girl muttered under her breath.

"Charlie!" Her mother looked flustered. "If there's any stress, it's because of the way you behave. Don't listen to her, Mr. Turner. She doesn't know what she's talking about."

"Don't know what I'm talking about? Don't know?" Charlie was nearly shouting. "Whose dog is she? Who spends time with her? Who's the one who loves her? I knew this was a complete waste of time. Come on, Chloe!"

The Labrador rose and jumped down to Charlie before Mike could lay a restraining hand on her rump. Charlie turned and urged Chloe forward. She stomped her way through the door and out of the clinic.

Her mother blushed a deep shade of red and

seemed to be about to say something to Mike. Then, obviously on the verge of tears, she rushed after her daughter, mumbling an embarrassed apology. Tim shrugged his shoulders and, without raising his eyes, trailed off behind them, leaving Neil, Emily, and Mike looking at one another in astonishment.

CHAPTER THREE

For the first time in a few years, it wasn't raining on the day of the Compton town festival. Everyone was enjoying themselves on the large lawn in the park.

Having worked all morning to set up the King Street Kennels booth, Kate and Bev escaped to the refreshments tent, leaving Neil and Emily in charge, with Jake and Jasmine for company. Emily loved selling things to people. There were King Street Kennels sweatshirts, mugs, and bookmarks and, as she told anyone passing within earshot, it was all for a very good cause.

Neil's friend, Chris Wilson, appeared at the booth in the middle of the afternoon. Jake scurried around his feet and nibbled at the laces of his sneakers, while Jasmine lay in the shade of the booth, keeping cool.

"Hi, Chris! You look lost," said Neil.

"Saturday afternoons are for playing soccer!" Chris laughed.

"Buy a mug for your mom," suggested Emily.

Chris peered at the articles for sale, looking bored.

"Hey, is there a new kid in your class? Tim Elliott?" Neil asked.

"*Yeah*. He's all right. Even though he likes basketball better than soccer!" said Chris with a grimace.

"We ran into him this morning," continued Neil. "He didn't seem so all right then. Has he ever mentioned Chloe?"

"Who's Chloe? His sister?" said Chris, casually inspecting a sweatshirt.

"No, his sister's called Charlie," Neil replied. "Chloe's her guide dog."

"Oh, right," said Chris. "I'd better go. My mom's picking me up in twenty minutes, and I'm going to win a trophy if it's the last thing I do!"

"Are the Elliotts here now?" Neil shouted at Chris's retreating back.

"Yeah," Chris shouted back, waving a hand airily around the field. "They're somewhere around. With the dog."

"It's quite a coincidence, isn't it?" said Neil, stroking Jasmine as the old dog staggered to her feet for a gentle stroll around the booth.

"What is?" said Emily, counting change.

"The Guide Dogs for the Blind booth being almost next door to us. Hadn't you noticed?"

"Are they?" asked Emily. "I've been too busy selling things. Hello, Mr. Hamley. Buy a T-shirt! Please!"

The principal of their school walked on with a cheery wave, pleading poverty.

"When Kate and Bev get back, we should go over and introduce ourselves," said Emily. "Perhaps the Guide Dog people will tell us what they've got in mind for Jasmine. I'm desperate to know."

"Me, too, but it might be bad news," said Neil, suddenly worried. "They might want to send her away to a kennel. But I can't help thinking that we could find her a really good home. Jasmine and Mrs. Atkinson are perfect for each other."

"Are you sure she should have another dog? After all, she couldn't look after Betsy's pups properly — Sam and Skip had to be adopted," Emily reminded him.

"Yes, but she made sure someone would look after them — and you've seen how much she loves dogs," Neil said. "Mrs. Atkinson's definitely ready for another dog now. She's got enough money and she'd love the company."

Just then, Kate and Bev reappeared, with large chocolate ice creams. Jake jumped up at Kate and a melting spatter of chocolate landed on his nose.

"I just saw your dad," she said, laughing at the young Border collie. "He's not doing too well, is he?"

Neil frowned. "I still feel guilty about him getting injured," he said.

"He'll be OK," answered Kate.

Kate and Bev took over the booth, and Neil and Emily wandered over to the Guide Dogs for the Blind booth. Jake ran in front of them and sniffed curiously at the pictures of dogs that decorated it. Jasmine stayed close to Neil's side.

"Well, hi there! You're a little on the small side for a guide dog, I'm afraid!" a friendly voice said to Jake.

Standing behind the booth, was a woman in her

mid-twenties. She was grinning broadly. The dark fringe of her pageboy haircut framed a round face. The pictures surrounding her were of guide dogs and their blind human companions. There were golden and chocolate Labradors crossing roads and passing beside construction sites, and German shepherds threading their way through revolving doors and up staircases: dogs providing sight for humans.

"My name's Syd," said the woman. "I work at the Association's regional center in Bolton. It's where we train guide dogs and their new owners. How can I help —" She stopped suddenly as she caught sight of Jasmine. "Well now, I know *you,* don't I? What are you doing here?" she said in surprise.

Jasmine wagged her tail energetically and, with jaws wide open and tongue hanging out, she panted a greeting.

"This is Willy Mannion's dog, isn't it?" asked Syd. She came around from behind the booth and fondled Jasmine's neck affectionately. "Now, remind me," she said softly. "What's your name again? Janice . . . ? Jocelyn . . . ?"

"Jasmine," corrected Neil.

"Of course," said Syd. "I don't always remember the names, but I never forget the dogs and their owners. So where's Willy?"

Neil began to explain about Willy's death, and why Jasmine was with them. Syd looked sad for a moment, then cuddled the Labrador.

"Poor old Jasmine," she said. "How's she coping?"

As Neil and Emily looked at each other, Jasmine turned to lick Neil's hand. "Not very well, really, but she's perked up a lot since she's been with us," Neil said.

"Well, it's very sad about Willy, but it's very kind of you to look after her," said Syd. Then, suddenly, she seemed to put two and two together. "But of course! You're from King Street, aren't you? I've heard so much about you."

"Actually," said Neil, "we wanted to talk to you. You see, we're worried about Jasmine's future —"

Just then, a crowd of people began to drift by noisily. A few of them started to show interest in the booth, picking up leaflets and studying the pictures.

"Hey, kids," said Syd, "I'd like to talk some more, but it looks like we're getting busy. Do you want to come back in a while, when the rush has died down?"

"Sure," said Neil. "We'll be back."

They left Syd chatting to a stream of curious customers and wandered aimlessly between the booths.

"That was amazing," said Neil. "I can't believe Syd recognized Jasmine."

"Well, think about it," replied Emily. "We'd recognize a lot of the dogs that have passed through King Street, wouldn't we?"

Neil nodded in agreement. "Look who's heading our way!" he said.

About twenty yards across the grass and steering

straight for them were Charlie Elliott and Chloe, with a sulky-looking Tim trailing behind.

"Let's say hello," said Emily.

"You bet," replied Neil. "I want to know more about Chloe. Mike never even had a chance to find out if there was anything wrong with her."

At that moment, Jasmine took matters into her own paws. She went forward to meet Chloe, nuzzling and sniffing at her. Blocked by Jasmine, the Elliotts came to a halt.

"Hi there!" said Neil. "Do you remember us? I'm Neil and this is Emily. We were at King Street Kennels earlier when you brought Chloe in."

"Yes, I remember," Charlie answered in an offhand way.

"I'm in the same grade as Tim at Meadowbank," said Neil.

"Tough break," said Charlie. Tim just grunted and scowled. Neil noticed that he was staring at Jasmine.

"Chloe's a really cool dog," Neil went on, taking a deep breath and trying very hard not to be put off.

The girl softened slightly and said, "She's the best, aren't you, Chloe?" She reached down to caress the young Labrador's smooth neck.

"And is she really all right, like you said?" asked Neil. "Her stomach, I mean."

"Oh, that stuff with the vet this morning?" Charlie

sounded scornful. "It's just my mom being difficult. Chloe's not hers, and she doesn't understand her. Sure, Chloe was sick once, but it was no big deal. She's absolutely fine — if you know anything about dogs, you'll be able to see that for yourself!"

She reached over and gently felt Jasmine's head and neck. "So you've got a Labrador, too," she said, surprised. "What's her name?"

"She's called Jasmine," Emily replied. "Only she's not ours. We're just looking after her for a while." Tim gave Jasmine another hard stare and Charlie started with surprise.

"We know a Lab called Jasmine," she said. "But she belonged to a man named Willy Mannion. He lived in the same old people's home as my granddad."

Neil groaned inwardly. For the second time that day, he and Emily had to explain how Jasmine had come to be with them.

"Mom went to the funeral with Granddad," said Charlie quietly. "She said it was really sad that Willy had no relatives." She dropped to her knees and cupped Jasmine's face in her hands. "You're going to miss Willy terribly, aren't you, Jasmine? I've only been with Chloe a couple of months — since my sixteenth birthday — and we'd already be lost without each other." As if in reply, Chloe shouldered her way in to lick Charlie's nose, so that the girl was kneeling with an arm around each Labrador. The two dogs could have been mother and daughter.

As Charlie spoke, Tim turned away with a scowl.

"We're really worried about what's going to happen to Jasmine," said Emily.

"Have you met Syd from the Guide Dogs for the Blind Association?" asked Charlie, standing up again.

"Just now," replied Neil. "I was amazed that she recognized Jasmine."

"Oh, yeah, she knows most of the guide dogs for miles around. We were just on our way to see her. Do you want to tag along?"

"Sure," said Neil. "We'd already planned to go back and talk to her."

With a command of "Forward" and then "Straight on" to Chloe, they all moved across the grass toward the Guide Dogs for the Blind booth. Jake tore ahead of them, while Tim trailed along at the back, his head down.

"Wow, it's great to see you again, Charlie!" said Syd, grinning. "Chloe looks fantastic. How's it going?"

"So-so," said Charlie in reply. Syd looked disappointed and concerned. "It's just Mom." The younger girl sighed.

"Well, we knew it'd be difficult, didn't we?" said Syd. She turned to Neil and Emily. "It's often hard for relatives to adjust when someone gets a guide dog for the first time. We try to make sure the whole family can cope beforehand, but there's only so much we can do."

"I didn't think it'd be this hard!" Charlie moaned. "Chloe was sick once. It's nothing really, but Mom panics so quickly. I don't know what to do with her. We keep having fights."

"But she must be able to see what a great dog Chloe is," said Neil.

"You would think so — but things are difficult at the moment," said Charlie, scowling. Tim was standing a few feet away, watching the goldfish toss. "I think Mom's a bit lonely. We've only been in Compton three months, you see. I don't think she found the move very easy."

"Do you want me to come over and have a word with her later on? I've got time before I go back home," offered Syd.

"Oh, would you, Syd? That's be so nice of you!" Charlie said gratefully. "Now, come on, let's forget about me. Tell us what's going to happen to Jasmine? Will you let her stay with Neil and Emily?" she asked eagerly.

"I'm afraid I haven't heard anything about it at all, and the decision wouldn't be mine anyway," said Syd. "What would *you* like to happen, Neil?"

Without actually mentioning Mrs. Atkinson, Neil explained that he thought he might have found a possible home for Jasmine.

"The Association wouldn't have Jasmine put down, would they?" asked Charlie.

Syd shook her head. "Not unless she's ill — but she is quite old, and Labs are prone to arthritis."

"It won't come to that," said Neil, feeling less confident than he sounded. "Jasmine deserves a good home — just like Chloe. Considering you've been together just a couple of months," he said to Charlie, quickly changing the subject, "the bond between you and Chloe is incredible."

"Thank you," said Charlie quietly. "I think we're lucky to have each other."

"You do realize, of course," Syd said to Neil and Emily, "that you're in the presence of a genius!"

From out of the corner of his eye, Neil saw Tim shoot Syd another one of his grim looks.

"Oh, be quiet, Syd," said Charlie, embarrassed.

"This young woman's only going to Oxford University to study math in October — *two years early*," Syd continued.

"Are you really?" said Neil.

"Yeah," Charlie laughed.

"What's the secret?" asked Emily.

"I have no idea," said Charlie, looking genuinely mystified. "I've just always been very good at it."

Suddenly, Tim boiled over and, for the first time, Neil and Emily heard his voice. It quivered with anger. "Me, me, me! Charlie this and Charlie that! Why does everything in our family always have to revolve around you? I hate you and I hate living here, and I've had enough! I'm going!" He turned on his heel and half-stomped, half-ran across the field.

Neil was shocked. "What was that all about?" he asked.

CHAPTER FOUR

For a moment, Charlie and Syd were silent, unsure of what to do.

"Don't worry," said Syd gently. "He'll be OK. Things must be difficult for Tim right now. Look, the festival's winding down, and it doesn't seem as though I'm exactly going to be overwhelmed with business now. Let's go and have an ice-cream cone and see if Tim comes back."

They sat at a table outside the refreshments tent and watched as other booth-holders began to dismantle furniture and pack away unsold goods. Neil shot a look toward the King Street Kennels stand where Kate and Bev were packing up. It looked like they were nearly finished.

Chloe and Jasmine lay panting in the heat, nuzzling each other affectionately. "I've got a feeling those two are related, you know," mused Syd, wiping stray ice cream from her mouth.

"How's that?" said Neil.

"Well, most of our dogs come from the breeding center at Tollgate, near Warwick," Syd went on, "and I'm fairly sure that Chloe's mom was the granddaughter of Jasmine's mom."

"So that makes her Jasmine's great-grand-daughter, then?" asked Emily.

"No, a great-aunt," said Charlie, "I think!"

"That's amazing!" said Neil. "No wonder they get along so well."

"Tell you what," said Syd. "Charlie and I had agreed she'd come over to Bolton one Saturday when I was free, just for fun. We could do it next week, and you two could come along as well, if you like. Then you can see what we do. You never know, it might inspire you . . ."

"Inspire us to what?" asked Neil.

"Well," said Syd, her eyes twinkling, "you might get the urge to do some fund-raising. We can always use the cash."

"We could organize a collection!" said Emily enthusiastically. "Or a garage sale!"

"Good idea!" said Syd. "Although sponsored events sometimes rake in a bit more money."

"What about a sponsored walk?" Neil suggested. "For people *and* their dogs. I bet there are lots of people in Compton who'd be up for that."

"Now that sounds like a fantastic idea!" Syd leaned forward, her chin in her hands. "And I'll tell you something else. My boss, Martin Harrison, might well be the one with the say-so on Jasmine's future. Let's assume he hasn't decided anything yet. If you've got a suggestion as to where she might be placed *and* you're raising money for the Association, he's certainly going to listen to you, isn't he?"

Charlie smiled for the first time in a while. "Good thinking, Syd," she said.

That evening, as the Parkers relaxed in the living room at King Street, Neil and Emily told their mom and dad about their idea for a sponsored walk in support of the Guide Dogs for the Blind Association.

"It looks like everyone's so booked up, there's only one day it can be," said Neil. "Saturday, June fourteenth."

Bob Parker was lying flat on the floor, trying to get his back comfortable, while Jake, who thought this was great fun, licked his face and generally made a nuisance of himself. Bob pulled himself up into a sitting position. "Sounds like a great idea," he said. "But are you sure you've thought it through? Something as big as this has to be organized very carefully, and if it's got to be on June fourteenth, you've

only left yourselves three weeks to get everything together."

Carole looked thoughtful. "Well," she said, "since you're injured and can't be Mr. Action Man this week, maybe you'd be able to find more time than usual to help Neil and Emily set things up."

"I'm not exactly helpless, you know," said Bob.

"Could me and Fudge do the walk?" asked Sarah. The hamster peeped out between her hands to stare inquisitively at the rest of the family.

"Sure," said Neil encouragingly. "As long as you're with a dog, too. That's the important thing."

"Come on, Dad," pleaded Emily.

"Well," said Bob, ruffling Jake's glossy black-and-white fur, "I suppose, for starters, I could help you plan the route, and get the police involved." His eyes brightened. "It'd be good if we could use the grounds of Padsham Castle, wouldn't it? And we're going to have to work hard to persuade everyone to take part."

"Excellent! I can't wait!" said Neil. "Come on, Em, you're good at lists. We need to think of as many people as possible, and start writing letters now."

"And we can put posters up around Compton," said Emily eagerly. "This is going to be the best!"

As Mrs. Elliott drove them all to Bolton the following Saturday, Neil and Emily brought Charlie up-to-date on developments, while Chloe dozed behind them in the back of the Elliotts' battered old station wagon. There hadn't been enough room to bring Jasmine as well, and Tim had decided he'd rather stay at home.

Every spare minute of the last week had been spent on the phone and writing letters. Everyone at Meadowbank School had been told about the walk, and Emily had searched through the Kennels' database for even more people who would be willing and fit enough to spend a whole day walking with their dog.

"How's Chloe been this week?" Neil asked Charlie.

"No problems at all," she answered from the front seat. "She's definitely over it —"

"She still looks a bit run-down to me," interrupted Mrs. Elliott.

"I'd know if anything was really wrong, Mom," replied Charlie patiently. "She's got tons of energy and she's been right on the ball all week."

"She looks fine to me, Mrs. Elliott," said Neil, stroking the Labrador's golden fur through the grille behind him. Chloe pushed her nose against his hand and wagged her tail happily.

"Look, are you going to manage OK without me today, Charlie?" said Mrs. Elliott suddenly, as they left Compton. "You're still getting used to Chloe, you know, and I don't *have* to go clothes shopping."

"I think it's more of a question of you getting used to me being independent," Charlie snapped. "I trust Chloe. Can't you see how good we are together? And think of the money that's gone into training her. Twenty-five thousand pounds per dog! The Guide Dogs for the Blind Association wouldn't do that if it didn't work, would they?"

Mrs. Elliott didn't reply. There was an uncomfortable silence.

"We've mapped out a great route for the walk," said Neil eventually to Charlie. "It's more or less a circle. Mrs. Dickens is going to let us start and finish at the Grange. From there, we can go all the way to King Street on the bridle paths."

"And from home we'll go right up over the hill, before cutting back through the grounds of Padsham

Castle," picked up Emily. "Then we'll make our way to Colshaw, and finally back through the far side of Old Mill Farm to the Grange again. What do you think?"

"I'll have to take your word for it!" Charlie laughed. "I'm still getting used to where everything is around here. How far do you think the walk is?"

"Well, it looks like about twelve-and-a-half miles," said Neil.

"And we've worked out five stopping points where dogs — and walkers — can have a drink of water," said Emily. "If some people can't manage the whole walk, they can wait at one of the stopping points for a ride to the finish."

"Well, that doesn't leave me much to do," Charlie sighed.

Neil sensed her disappointment. "You're kidding! There's tons. We've really got to get our act together with publicity and sponsorship. Oh, and Em and I had a great idea. What do you think about going on local radio?"

"Whatever!" said Charlie jokingly. "Morning talk shows, too, if you like."

"She doesn't think we're serious," said Neil, smiling.

"We are, you know!" Emily laughed. "Wait and see! And if Tim wants to help, there's plenty for him to do, too."

Charlie was silent.

"How *is* Tim?" prompted Neil.

There was another pause before Charlie answered, and for a moment Neil was worried she might be annoyed with him for asking.

"He's not too happy at the moment," she said eventually. "I suppose a lot of it's about Cosmo."

"Who's Cosmo?" asked Neil.

"He was our dog, an Old English sheepdog. Well, *Tim's* dog, to be more accurate. When we came to Compton and I got Chloe, we were a bit short on money and space."

Neil saw Sylvia Elliott shoot an embarrassed glance at Charlie in the rearview mirror.

"Anyway, Cosmo had to go, and Tim was devastated," Charlie continued.

"You didn't have him put down, did you?" asked Neil, appalled at the thought.

"Of course not! But he's gone to live with my aunt in Preston, and Tim hasn't been the same since —"

"Oh, come on, Charlie," interrupted Mrs. Elliott. Her tone was one of annoyance, but she looked uneasy. "You're exaggerating. And anyway, we didn't have a choice."

"I know we didn't, but it's true, Mom. You know it is. He always seems so angry now," Charlie added.

"I bet it'd help if we tried to get him involved in the walk," Emily suggested.

"Maybe." Charlie didn't sound too hopeful.

"Well, here we are at last!" said Mrs. Elliott as the car swung into a wide driveway. Chloe stirred in the back and barked a loud greeting.

They drove through a small park and stopped in front of a jumble of buildings. An alert retriever loped past them on a path with a nervous-looking blind owner. Beside the pair walked a sighted person, offering encouragement.

Even before Mrs. Elliott had parked the car, Syd emerged from the main building and waved. "You found us all right, then?" she shouted. "Fantastic! Come in and have a cup of tea."

For the rest of the afternoon, while Sylvia Elliott went off shopping in Bolton, Neil and Emily met some of the smartest and most dedicated dogs they had ever seen.

"This is Brandy," said Syd as she showed them around the beautifully designed kennels. "She's fourteen months old, and just two months into her training with us. Before she came here, she was one of our best puppy-walkers at Leamington Spa."

The immaculately groomed Labrador's coat was a rich chocolate-brown. She kept perfectly still and poised as Neil stroked her.

"What's a puppy-walker?" Emily asked. "Or is that a silly question?"

"No," replied Charlie. "It's just someone from an ordinary family who takes one of the puppies from breeding and spends nine months or so doing the basic obedience training."

"Yes," Syd added. "We couldn't do without them. They make sure the puppies go out as much as possible so that they can cope with being near traffic or getting around obstacles. Later on, if Brandy does well, she'll be ready to be matched with an owner."

Chloe and Brandy stood shoulder to shoulder, completely relaxed in each other's company, as if they were old friends.

"How do you match the dogs with the owners?" asked Neil, curious about this whole new world of dogs.

"Some owners have preferences," Syd explained. "Older people might not want an animal that's too lively, and different people walk at different speeds. So we try to find everyone a dog that suits them. Labradors are the most popular breed, but we have a lot of retrievers and Labrador-retriever mixes, too. Perhaps ten percent are German shepherds, and very occasionally there are other breeds."

Back inside the main building, they found the corridor almost filled by a big man with a friendly grin.

"Martin, these are the friends of Charlie I told you about," said Syd. "Neil and Emily, this is my boss, Martin Harrison."

"Hi, folks! Good to see you again, Charlie," said Martin warmly. "So, come on, Neil and Emily! Tell me all about this rescue center of yours!"

They stopped and chatted for a few minutes about King Street Kennels and Charlie's progress with Chloe. After a while, Emily couldn't contain herself.

"Mr. Harrison?" she said.

"Call me Martin. Everyone else does."

"Martin, you know about Jasmine?" Emily continued.

"Willy Mannion's dog?" Martin asked with a grin. "Yes, Syd's told me you've taken her in."

"Will she be able to stay in Compton, if we find her a home?" Emily asked anxiously.

Martin Harrison looked directly at her. "Well, to be honest, I've just managed to find her a place in a kennel in Manchester."

Emily's face fell.

"But we haven't confirmed it yet," he continued. "Syd told me you two have got your heart set on Jasmine staying in Compton — and a possible home for her in mind. If you really can come up with a suitable alternative, we'll definitely consider it."

"Just give us a couple of weeks to work on it," pleaded Neil.

Martin's eyes crinkled into a smile. "That seems fair enough to me," he said.

CHAPTER FIVE

"**C**ome on, Jasmine! Keep up!" Neil bent down to encourage the Labrador. "She's getting fitter, you know," he said to Emily. "I'm sure she's lost some weight in the past week." Jake raced ahead of them and sprang over a low gate as they set off toward Old Mill Farm, which bordered King Street Kennels.

It was Sunday afternoon, and Neil and Emily had decided to check out the path that led through Richard and Jane Hammonds' farm to the Grange. It was an essential part of the sponsored walk, and, as Bob had pointed out, they'd never actually used it before.

The path widened into an old road with high, tangled hedges on both sides. Just when they thought they were nearing the farm, the path narrowed

again and nettles began to grow in from the sides,
forcing them to walk in single file. Then Neil came to
a dead stop. Jake barked in surprise at the sudden
halt.

"Hey, this is kind of a problem, isn't it?" said Neil,
wiping his brow.

"I didn't expect this!" said Emily. "Yuck, what
stinks?"

In front of them, the path was overgrown with nettles. Worse than that, it was completely blocked by a
pile of rubble and old machinery. Jake wandered up
to it and sniffed the air, while Jasmine stood obedi-
ently to Neil's left, waiting for his next move.

"What are we going to do?" said Emily. "If we can't get through this way, the whole walk will have to take a massive detour. The only other route back to the Grange is the main road through Compton."

"Mr. Hammond will just have to move this junk. We're on a public footpath. He's not allowed to block it!" Neil asserted. "Let's go and ask him to clean it up."

Emily thought for a moment. "No, let's go back home and talk to Dad first. We need to handle this properly."

"Yeah, you're probably right. Charlie and Tim will be coming over soon anyway."

They arrived back at King Street Kennels to find their dad attempting to help Kate with the evening rounds. Neil could see he was still in pain as he crouched down stiffly to pet an overexcited Jake. When Neil told him the news, Bob stroked his beard thoughtfully.

"That's strange. Richard Hammond should know better. I'm sure he wouldn't want to spoil the walk, but he's also a very busy man. I doubt he'll be able to clear the path in time."

"But the walk will be ruined!" Emily cried.

"And what he's doing is against the law," added Neil.

"Well, I suppose you could try talking to him, Neil. But I don't think you should get your hopes up," said Bob.

"Perhaps taking Charlie and Chloe along would make the point. They should be here any minute — we've got to talk about plans for the walk," said Neil.

"Good idea." Bob laughed. "If anyone can persuade him, Charlie can!"

Just then, Sylvia Elliott's car turned into the driveway. Charlie and Chloe piled out, followed by a reluctant Tim, and Mrs. Elliott waved and drove off. Tim took a soccer ball outside to practice against a wall, while the others settled themselves in the living room to talk. Chloe lay down loyally by Charlie's feet, and Jasmine lay next to her, obviously enjoying the younger dog's company.

Neil and Emily told Charlie about the problem with the path on Richard Hammond's land.

"Hmmm," she said. "We'll deal with him after we've gone through everything else on our list. What's first, Emily?"

They went through all the possible walkers, checking off people who'd agreed to take part and been given sponsor forms, and deciding who would target the remaining names on the hit list.

"We've lined up Mrs. Atkinson to walk with Jasmine," said Neil. "We told her that we didn't think Jas would be able to do more than one or two stages, and she actually offered to go with her. They're going to come to the starting line to see everyone off, and then Mom will give her a ride to King Street so that they can walk from there to Padsham Castle."

"You really are doing your best to pair those two up, aren't you?" Charlie laughed.

"Well, I'm positive that once Mrs. A gets to know Jas better, she won't be able to resist!" said Neil. "Oh, and by the way, Dad says he's arranged for someone special to come and open the event, but he won't say who it is! He's being very secretive."

Neil went to the kitchen to get a pitcher of lemonade from the fridge. Through the kitchen window, he could see Tim. Only he wasn't playing soccer. To Neil's surprise, he and Jake were fooling around with Jake's rubber bone. For the first time ever, Neil saw Tim laughing.

Neil opened the kitchen door and casually wandered outside. As soon as Tim saw him, he stopped playing with Jake and assumed his usual moody expression. He swung a foot at the soccer ball, slamming it against the wall.

"Jake looked as if he was enjoying himself," said Neil. "And so did you. You didn't have to stop for me."

Jake barked and ran off a few paces, daring Tim to give chase. Tim turned away.

Neil understood how awful Tim must feel, moving to a new house, a new school, and — worst of all — losing his dog. It wasn't long ago that he'd had to cope with the pain of losing Sam. And he could imagine how jealous Tim felt of Charlie. Not only was she always the center of attention, but now she had a new dog of her own.

"What was Cosmo like?" he asked gently. Tim just shook his head and stepped away a few more paces.

"OK," said Neil, "but if you ever want to talk, I'd be happy to listen. And you can visit the dogs here anytime."

Neil went back inside. "Now, about going on the radio," he said, handing out lemonade and cookies to Emily and Charlie, "what do you think?"

"Surely it's not as simple as all that?" Charlie replied uncertainly.

"It won't be a problem," said Emily. "All you need to do is phone Tony Bradley from the *Tell Tony* program. He's an old friend of ours. Why don't you try him now? We've got the number here."

"I don't know," murmured Charlie. "I'm not sure I want to."

"He's really easy to talk to," said Neil, trying to be helpful. "You never know, you might be able to get him to come along on the day of the walk."

"Wouldn't that be great?" Emily enthused.

"Look . . . can I think about it?" Charlie hesitated.

"I don't see what the problem is," Neil said irritably. Why was Charlie being so difficult when they were all working so hard?

Charlie got to her feet and pulled Chloe up with her. "There's a lot you don't understand, Neil. All right?" She spoke angrily. "You only want me to come with you to Richard Hammond's place to get his sympathy. And now you want me to do the same with the man at the radio station. Maybe I don't always want the most important thing about me to be that I'm blind. Now, can you ask your mom if she'll take us home? If not, we'll walk!"

Neil suddenly felt very small and couldn't think of anything to say.

The next evening, Neil and Emily came home from school to find a message on the answering machine.

"It's Charlie," the voice said. *"I'm really sorry about yesterday. Sometimes it just all gets to be too much, you know. It can feel like I'm always walking on eggshells with Mom and Tim. Anyway, I've done it. I'm going to be on Tony Bradley's show tomorrow afternoon, and we'll plug the walk and the cause of guide dogs for all we're worth, won't we, Chloe?"*

There was an answering woof in the background.

"So, if there's anything you want me to say, call me back. Otherwise, I'll come by tomorrow evening and we'll go to the Hammonds' farm. Bye!"

Neil breathed a sigh of relief.

Charlie was great on the radio. She sounded relaxed and confident as Tony interviewed her about the story of how she and Chloe met. He even asked Chloe jokingly if she had anything she wanted to say to the world, and Chloe responded with a barked message of her own. Then Tony asked people to phone in with offers of sponsorship for Charlie and

Chloe. He promised on the air that he'd try his very best to be at the Grange for the start of the walk.

"Great job, Charlie!" exclaimed Emily as they met outside Old Mill Farm later on that evening. "You were amazing." Jake bounced up at her to add his congratulations.

"And we can't forget Chloe," said Neil, bending over to ruffle the Lab's neck. "What a team!" Chloe wagged her tail in delight.

"Now let's see how good we are at getting Richard Hammond on our side," said Charlie. "Come on. You probably don't want to do this any more than I do."

Jane Hammond answered the door and showed them into the living room, where they all sank into the comfortable chairs and sofa. The Hammonds' dog Delilah was Jake's mother. She spotted Jake, and the two dogs greeted each other noisily, paws and noses locked in a friendly tussle, before settling down together by the fireplace. Chloe lay by Charlie's feet.

Richard Hammond was sitting reading the paper, but he put it down as they came in. In contrast to Jane, who was small and short, Richard's long, thin legs stuck out in front of him untidily.

"This is all very mysterious," he said. "A deputation! What's it all about?"

When they explained, Richard Hammond's ears turned red and Jane left the room hurriedly. For a moment, Neil feared the worst.

Richard cleared his throat. "I see," he said nervously. "Yes, well, I'm afraid you've caught me on that one. Jane's been telling me I should do something about it for months. I never meant to block the path, you know. It was those sloppy builders not cleaning up after themselves when we had some renovations done on the side of the house. Still, you don't want to know about that. You want to know what I'm going to do about it, right?"

They nodded their heads politely while Richard drank a cup of tea. He seemed determined to keep them in suspense.

"Well . . ." He looked at Neil, Emily, and Charlie. "I'll have all the junk removed by the weekend. And if there's anything more Jane and I can do to help the walk, we'd be delighted. I think it was very brave of you to come and see me."

As the day of the walk got closer, there were a lot of jobs to do and people to see. Carole arranged for members of the local Women's Institute to staff the stopping points. Bob made sure there'd be enough drinks available for walkers and their dogs. Neil, Emily, and Charlie checked that all the walkers had a copy of the route. Most important of all, everybody was working hard on finding as much sponsorship as possible, right up to the last minute.

The evening before the walk, Neil found Bob hanging by his hands from the frame of the barn door.

"What the heck are you up to, Dad? You'll hurt yourself."

"I've *already* hurt myself, Neil. I'm trying to *unhurt* myself now," said Bob. "This is supposed to be good for the back."

"It doesn't look like it's so good," replied Neil. Then he added, "Dad, I'm worried. Do you think it's going to be OK tomorrow? Will there be enough people there?"

Bob dropped down, wincing as his feet took the weight of his body. "Well, it's too late to worry now, Neil. But I've got a hunch it might be a day to remember. You'll see."

"And there's one other thing," added Neil. "I'm dying to know who this mystery guest is that you've got lined up."

Bob tapped his nose. "That's between me and this doorpost," he laughed. "But you'll find out soon enough, won't you?"

CHAPTER SIX

By nine o'clock on Saturday morning, June 14, it was already hot in the courtyard of King Street Kennels and it was getting hotter by the minute.

"We've provided enough water at the stopping points, haven't we? And they're all in the shade, aren't they?" Neil asked his dad, hopping from foot to foot. "I'm worried about the dogs in this heat."

"Neil, just relax," said Bob, smiling. "It's unlike you to be so wound up. From what I hear, the Women's Institute volunteers are going to make sure there's enough food and water for a small army, and the St. John's ambulance people have agreed to be on hand, too. It'll all be fine. Since we're not walking, your mom and I will keep an eye on things. And we'll keep in touch with each stopping point via cell phone."

"It's just so important that everything goes right," said Neil.

"Maybe next time we won't start the walk in the midday heat!" said Bob, laughing. "Then again, next time it'll probably snow."

The doorbell rang.

"Go ahead and answer it," prompted Bob.

Waiting on the doorstep were Max Hooper and Prince, Max's beautiful golden cocker spaniel. A taxi zoomed out of the driveway on its way back to the train station.

Max was the star of Neil and Emily's favorite TV show, *The Time Travelers*. When an episode of the series was filmed at Padsham Castle, Max and Neil became friends, drawn together by their love of dogs.

"Max, what are *you* doing here?" exclaimed Neil. "It's great to see you both, but you've picked kind of a funny day to drop by."

Max looked at him strangely. "I know," he said.

"What do you mean, 'you know'?"

"Neil, you're being thick-headed!" Max laughed. "Why do you think I'm here?"

A lightbulb went off. "*You're* the mystery guest who's going to start the walk! Now I get it!" yelled Neil. "Come in. Come and see Jake, Prince!" But before Prince could nose his way past Neil, Jake came tumbling through the house, falling over his feet in excitement at seeing his old friend.

"Where's Princess?" asked Neil. Princess was Max's new puppy and Prince's daughter.

"I had to get here by train," said Max, "and I didn't think I could manage them both by myself. Princess is quite a handful now!"

At eleven o'clock, everyone squeezed into the Range Rover for the short ride up to the Grange. Mrs. Dickens and her residents had done a fantastic job. Decorations were hung between the lampposts that lined the driveway and right across the front of the imposing building. A starting line had been constructed between two posts, and half a dozen tables with um-

brellas were scattered among the beech trees on the lawn. Already there were people and dogs waiting expectantly.

Syd was standing on the front steps talking to Charlie, Mr. Bradshaw, and another old gentleman wearing a bright blue shirt who looked as if he might be Charlie's granddad. Syd caught sight of Neil and Emily and called out, "Isn't this fantastic? And what a beautiful day for it!"

Tony Bradley was wandering around with a tape recorder and a microphone, talking to anyone who looked interesting — and desperately trying to avoid Mrs. Jepson, King Street Kennels' least favorite customer. She was dressed in a shiny blue tracksuit and had tied matching ribbons onto her two spoiled Westies, Sugar and Spice. She was following the radio DJ everywhere, obviously wanting to be interviewed, and her husband was shuffling after her, looking embarrassed. As soon as Tony Bradley saw Max and Prince arrive, he made a swift beeline for them.

"Hey, there's Mrs. Atkinson," said Emily. "Come on, Jasmine! Let's take you over to your partner for the day."

Jasmine picked herself up reluctantly and, already panting heavily, lumbered over to the old lady.

"Now, are you two going to be OK?" asked Neil anxiously. "You'll make sure to give Jasmine plenty to drink, won't you?"

"Oh, yes. I'll make sure she's just fine, won't I, Jas?" said Mrs. Atkinson, stooping down to stroke the Labrador fondly. "Don't you worry, Neil. Once your mother's taken us up to King Street, we'll have a couple of hours together to get used to each other before we do any walking. We'll wait for Mr. Brewster and Skip to arrive, and then we'll walk up to Padsham with them."

"That's good," said Neil to Emily as they left the pair to their own devices. "They'll be safe with Jim."

Skip, Jim Brewster's Border collie, was Sam's brother. He looked so much like Sam that every time Neil saw him, his heart missed a beat.

As the clock approached noon, Neil and Emily watched more and more walkers assemble. Eventually, Max and Prince climbed to the top step of The Grange's entrance. Max thanked everyone for agreeing to take part and introduced Syd. She said a few words about the Guide Dogs for the Blind Association and how important the money raised that day would be, then turned back to Max.

"Well, good luck everyone," he shouted. "Have a happy, safe walk. On your marks? Get set . . . *go!*"

At various speeds, the crowd made their way through the gate, around the corner, and off toward the footpath that would eventually lead them to King Street.

Neil and Emily had agreed that they and Jake would walk with Charlie and Chloe. Charlie's mom and Tim were walking, too, with Kip, an affectionate mongrel that had arrived at the rescue center two weeks ago.

"It'll be really good for her," said Charlie to Neil and Emily. "Mom's bound to make some friends today. That's what she needs."

"Be careful, Charlie," said Mrs. Elliott anxiously to her daughter as she and Tim set off. "I'm still not sure it's a good idea for you to do this walk."

"Don't nag me, Mom," muttered Charlie irritably. "It's a *very* good idea. Just try to enjoy it! Come on, let's go," she added to Neil and Emily.

"There's no need to rush," said Neil. "I'm sure we can walk faster than most of these people over the course of a whole afternoon. Anyway, despite what some people seem to think, it's not a race. Did you see the way Dr. Harvey took off with Finn and Sandy? It was like they had a train to catch."

"We actually *have* got a train to catch," said Max as he appeared behind them with Prince. "Sorry it was such a quick visit. It was great to see you. Put us down for ten pounds if you complete the course."

"*If?*" Neil snorted. "You might as well give us the ten pounds now!"

They left the Grange with the last group of stragglers and turned out onto the road. A signpost pointed the way across a large field, and Neil saw a gleaming Jaguar pull up at the curb a hundred yards or so farther on. Two Westies with bows between their ears and an unmistakable broad figure wearing a tight, bright blue tracksuit were piling into it hurriedly.

"Hey! Look over there!" whispered Neil.

"It's Mrs. Jepson!" said Emily. "What is she doing?"

"Well, it looks as though she's had enough already." Neil laughed.

"Poor Sugar and Spice!" said Emily. "I'm sure they could have used the exercise."

"Well, just as long as she doesn't claim they walked the whole way. It's not very fair to the people who've sponsored her," said Neil.

"Or to the rest of us!" Charlie laughed, too.

The walk was like one big party stretched out over a dozen miles. People chatted as they strolled along, and everyone was in high spirits. Most of the dogs were in a party mood, too, bounding ahead of their owners and chasing one another in circles in the empty, open fields.

Neil, Charlie, and Emily arrived at King Street just before one o'clock. It seemed like an open-house day, with dogs everywhere and walkers wandering the grounds with drinks and sandwiches in their hands.

"Bravo, Neil," said Mr. Hamley, trying not to spill his lemonade as Dotty, his boisterous Dalmatian, tugged at her leash impatiently, pulling him around in circles. "What a splendid event. I hope you're go-

ing to write something about this for the school paper."

As far as Neil could tell, the only person not in a
great mood was Tim. His mom was talking to Jake
Fielding from the *Compton News*, whose ponytail
bobbed up and down as he listened and took notes.
Tim stood apart from them, tapping his foot impatiently.

"At school last week, I asked Tim if he wanted to
come and visit the rescue center and help with the
dogs," said Neil to Charlie.

"It's no use, Neil." Charlie shook her head. "Maybe he'll get over Cosmo in time. But at the moment, no one can talk to him. I know it's hard, but you've just got to let him be."

They set off again, this time heading for the path that took them up over the hill. Here there was no escape from the full force of the sun, and it was a relief to eventually drop down into the woodland surrounding Padsham Castle. Neil found it fascinating to walk with Charlie and Chloe and see the marvelous trust that had developed between them, even in such a short time. Chloe seemed to really look after her human companion, giving Charlie the confidence to deal with the awkward obstacles she faced in the woods at Padsham. Neil learned as he tried to help that he should never *take* Charlie's arm to guide her over a fallen tree or a stream, but instead offer to help guide her.

At Padsham Castle, Neil spotted Syd in the crowd. She was busy chatting to as many of the walkers as she could, but she waved when she saw them and called over. "Isn't it going well? No real casualties yet, though I've heard a few complaints about blisters."

"Yes," said Emily. "I think I've got one myself. Ouch!"

Neil could see that a few of the walkers were beginning to feel the heat. He spotted Alex Harvey, flat out in the shade under a tree. The doctor's dogs seemed to be lasting better than him, and were licking his face, eager to set off again.

"Look at the difference between those two!" Neil said to Emily as they watched Jake and Chloe. "As soon as we arrive somewhere, Jake just can't wait to say hello to everybody, but Chloe always conserves her energy. You never see her rushing around."

"Do you think it's the breed or the training?" asked Emily.

"Probably both. Some Labs can be really slow!" replied Neil.

They pushed on toward Colshaw and the stopping point at Netherfield Farm, the farthest point of the walk. They were back in open country again now, and Neil's legs were beginning to ache. Where the paths crossed fields of corn or oilseed, or where there were sheep, Jake had to be reined in on his leash. Neil realized how hard the walk must be for Charlie.

"Are you OK?" he asked her.

Her head was down and she was concentrating hard. "Fine, thanks," she said in reply, flashing Neil a smile. "Getting a bit tired, though." Beside her, Chloe plowed gamely on, panting loudly but apparently eager to tackle the rest of the walk.

Charlie was visibly relieved when they reached Netherfield Farm. But as soon as they sat down in the cool courtyard in front of the farmhouse, Mr. Hamley rushed up to Neil.

"Your mom just phoned here," he said. "She wants

you to call her back right away. The phone's just inside, in the kitchen."

"Why, has something happened?" Neil asked, looking puzzled.

"Mrs. Atkinson and Jasmine are missing!"

CHAPTER SEVEN

"**S**o what's going on?" said Emily when Neil had spoken to Carole. "They can't have just disappeared!"

"Mom says Mrs. Atkinson and Jasmine never arrived at Padsham Castle. Apparently, it's a good two hours since they left King Street," replied Neil. "They should have been at the castle a long time ago."

"What about Jim Brewster and Skip?" asked Emily. "I thought they were supposed to be keeping them company."

"Hold on," said Neil, catching sight of a familiar black-and-white shape on the far side of the courtyard. "There's Skip. Jim Brewster can't be far behind."

"There he is!" cried Emily as Jim strolled around the side of the farm building, balancing a cup of tea.

"So perhaps Mrs. Atkinson's here after all. Maybe you mom just didn't see her and she decided to keep walking," Charlie added hopefully.

"Hey, Jim!" said Neil, calling him over. "Are Mrs. Atkinson and Jasmine with you?"

Skip's ears pricked up and his tail wagged when he saw Jake. The two dogs sniffed each other in a friendly greeting. Jim Brewster looked worried as he began to explain what had happened. Mrs. Atkinson had found the climb up the hill really tiring, and she'd started to worry that she and Jasmine were holding Jim and Skip back.

"I told her it wasn't a problem," explained Jim, "but she was insistent. She said she'd walk back to the previous stage and get a ride. In the end, I gave in, and we walked on ahead. We knew we shouldn't have, didn't we, Skip?" Skip put his head to one side and whined his agreement. "I wonder what she's gone and done?"

"Well, they can't have wandered far," Emily said calmly. "We know they're somewhere between King Street and Padsham. We'll just have to go and look for them."

"I'll come with you if you like," said Jim. "I feel really bad about this."

Neil thought for a moment, and then said, "No, Jim. You keep going. Don't worry, we'll find her."

He pulled a map of the area from his backpack. "They can't be out in the open," he said. "They'd have been spotted by now. I guess they must have gotten lost somehow — maybe in the woods behind the castle, though with all those people around I can't see how."

Emily peered over Neil's shoulder. "In which case, if we take that footpath there —" she pointed at a line on the map, "we can take a shortcut behind the castle and be searching the woods in half an hour. What do you think?"

"Good idea," agreed Neil. "I'll just go and call Mom to let her know, and then let's do it. Are you up for this, Charlie?"

Chloe was already on her feet, raring to go. "You bet!" Charlie answered right away.

The path they'd seen on the map did not seem like much of a shortcut as they walked back to the woods behind Padsham Castle. By the time they were close to the route the walk had taken, even Jake's head was drooping.

But Chloe was tireless. She never seemed to take a wrong step, and she never stopped watching out for Charlie.

"You're a champ, Chloe," said Neil. "What would we do without you?"

As soon as they were in the woods, they began to call Mrs. Atkinson's name, but there was no reply.

Eventually, the path began to run alongside a clearing. Suddenly, Chloe lurched forward on the end of her harness.

"What is it, Chloe?" asked Charlie urgently. "What have you spotted?"

The Labrador pulled Charlie forward toward a narrow path that led across the clearing and into the trees beyond.

"I think Chloe's on to something," said Charlie over her shoulder. "Maybe she's picked up Jasmine's scent."

"Careful, Charlie," said Neil, moving quickly through the undergrowth to her side and allowing her to slip her arm through his. "It's really rough around here."

They made their way carefully across the clearing. As they approached the other side, Chloe put down her nose and sniffed long and hard. Then, as she lifted her head, Jasmine casually wandered out from the trees to greet her, looking as if she didn't have a care in the world.

"Jasmine!" said Neil, falling on his knees and giving her a hug. "Where have you been? Where's Mrs. Atkinson?"

They shouted out Mrs. Atkinson's name once more. Jasmine wagged her tail, turned around, and ambled off again. With Jake now leading the way and Chloe pulling Charlie along, they followed her as quickly as they could.

The ground rose up ahead of them. It was littered with stones and it was difficult to walk, particularly for Charlie. Eventually, they heard a weak voice.

"Over here. Over here!" As they came up over the hill, there was Mrs. Atkinson, lying on the ground, her back against a boulder.

Jake reached her first. He pushed his wet nose straight into Mrs. Atkinson's face.

"Way to go, Chloe! And hooray for Jasmine!" Neil shouted. "Come back here, Jake, and give Mrs. Atkinson some space."

"Oh, I'm so glad to see you!" She sighed. "I'm really sorry to cause all this trouble."

"We're really glad to see you, too," said Emily. "Are you all right?"

"I've hurt my ankle." Mrs. Atkinson grimaced. "I was just beginning to think we were going to be here all night. Still, Jasmine would have been excellent company, wouldn't you, Jasmine? I'm sure we'd have lived to tell the tale!" Jasmine plodded up to her and swiped her face with her tongue.

"What made you come up here, Mrs. Atkinson?" asked Neil, trying very hard not to show his exasperation.

"Wild strawberries, Neil. It's a splendid place to go looking for them," said Mrs. Atkinson weakly. "I used to come up here years ago. I thought I'd say thank-you to Jim for walking with us by collecting some for him. We must have gone farther off the path than we intended, right Jasmine?"

Jasmine licked her face again.

"It's lucky you had Jasmine with you," said Neil. "How are we going to get you home? It looks as if we'll need a stretcher."

"I feel very embarrassed," said Mrs. Atkinson. "I should never have come all the way up here."

"Don't worry," said Charlie soothingly. "Chloe and I will stay here with you and Jasmine. Neil, why don't you and Emily go back to Padsham Castle for some help? It'll be quicker without us."

"OK," agreed Neil. "We'll be as fast as we can, Mrs. Atkinson."

Forgetting their tired legs and sore feet, Neil and Emily half-ran, half-walked across the rough ground back to the main path, and then sprinted down to the castle, where Bob and Carole were waiting anxiously. With them were Jim Brewster and Skip, who had come back to help.

"Well, we found her, Dad," said Neil, breathing heavily. "But I think we'll need to give the St. John's Ambulance people a call. She hurt her ankle. I think we can get pretty close to where she is if we take the Range Rover along one of the forest roads."

The St. John's Ambulance volunteers arrived quickly, and the Parkers, plus Jim and Skip, piled into the Range Rover and bounded up the stony track through the woods till they were near the clearing.

Neil led them quickly to where Mrs. Atkinson was waiting. Sitting patiently by her side were Jasmine, Chloe, and Charlie, the two dogs alert and watchful. The volunteers gently examined Mrs. Atkinson and eased her onto a stretcher. Jim rushed to help and said, "I don't know what came over me, Mrs. A. I knew it wasn't a good idea to leave you."

"No, no, it's my fault, Jim," she replied. "You mustn't blame yourself."

As they carefully picked their way back to the car, Jasmine walked faithfully beside the stretcher, always to Mrs. Atkinson's left, even when the ground was at its roughest.

"I think we're going to have to take you for an X-ray, Mrs. Atkinson," stated the St. John's team leader. "That ankle might be broken. Is there someone who can come with you? And who's going to look after your dog?"

"I'll go to the hospital with her," said Jim Brewster.

"And we'll look after Jasmine," said Emily. "Don't worry about that! She'll be a pleasure, won't you, girl?"

"Jasmine's just on loan, you see," Mrs. Atkinson explained. "She's not *my* dog at all, really."

"Not yet she isn't." Neil chuckled under his breath.

As they waved good-bye to Mrs. Atkinson, Jim, and Skip from Padsham Castle, Neil checked his watch. It was five o'clock. He groaned. "Look at the time!" he exclaimed. "Everyone else will be finishing the walk about now. Our day's been completely ruined. All that sponsorship up in smoke! What are we going to do now?"

CHAPTER EIGHT

There was no one left at Padsham Castle except Charlie and the Parkers. Maggie Jones, the caretaker, was making her rounds, picking up a few remaining pieces of litter. Jake went over to say hello to her, while Chloe and Jasmine settled down on the shady side of the Range Rover.

"Well," said Bob thoughtfully, "I suppose we *could* give the three of you a ride back to Netherfield, and you could try to complete the walk tonight . . ."

Charlie said, "I don't know about the others, but I think I'll pass on that. Sorry, but I've had enough for one day. And I think maybe Chloe has, too."

Emily nodded her head in agreement. Neil made a disappointed face, still reluctant to give in.

"Wouldn't it make more sense to complete the

walk tomorrow, Neil?" asked Bob. "I'm sure everyone would understand, considering what's happened."

Neil frowned, but inside he knew that what his dad was saying did make the most sense. "OK," he said. "I don't like it, but you're right."

Once they were back at the Grange, Neil, Emily, and Charlie quickly found themselves telling the tale of Mrs. Atkinson's rescue to a small crowd of people over a welcome glass of cold orange juice. Syd was there, with Charlie's mom and Tim, and assorted residents, including Henry Bradshaw and Skye. There hadn't been so much excitement at the Grange in a long while. Chloe was grateful to be out of her harness at last and was enjoying a romp with Jake under the trees. Jasmine took the opportunity for a well-earned nap by the greenhouse, in a cool spot that was clearly a favorite of hers.

"Chloe was the one who tracked down Mrs. Atkinson. We just followed," Neil explained. "You should have seen her and Charlie set off across the forest!"

From the corner of his eyes, Neil saw Tim's lip curl into a sneer. Tim broke off from the group, narrowing a look of pure jealousy in his sister's direction. His mom seemed to ignore him.

All the time, more walkers were arriving with their dogs. Mr. Hamley looked completely exhausted, though Dotty seemed to have the energy to go around a second time. The Jepsons were there and seemed

suspiciously sprightly. Mr. Jepson looked around nervously and fiddled with his scarf in an embarrassed way. Mrs. Jepson's bright blue tracksuit still looked immaculate, as did Sugar and Spice.

"Look, there's not a hair out of place!" whispered Emily. "No one's going to believe they've done the walk!"

Syd went to the top of the steps and cleared her throat. Someone banged a mug on a table for silence, and they all listened as Syd made a short speech thanking the walkers for their efforts. She told everyone how important fund-raising events were for the Association, and how impressed she was by Neil, Emily, and Charlie. Finally, she explained how Jasmine had been the real inspiration for the event, and asked everyone for a minute of silence in memory of Willy Mannion.

Afterward, they fell into groups of twos and threes, tidying up and chatting. Syd and Charlie sat down in the evening sun at the foot of the steps.

As he carried a tray of glasses past them into the house, Neil heard Charlie suddenly ask Syd in a panicky voice, "Where's Chloe?"

He turned around and cast an eye over the lawns of the Grange. Jake had joined Jasmine by the greenhouse, but Chloe was nowhere to be seen.

"That's strange," Neil said to Syd and Charlie. "Come to think of it, I haven't seen her for a while."

"Perhaps Chloe's with your mom?" Syd offered. "I heard her say she was going up with your granddad to his room."

"Doubt it," said Charlie. "Neil, I'm worried. I can't believe that Chloe would just wander off, but can you have a quick look around for her all the same? It was stupid of me to let her off the harness. I thought she'd be safe here, but if she wanders out into Compton, goodness knows what might happen."

Neil raced down toward the gates of the Grange.

On his way, he bumped into Emily and told her what had happened. She joined him, and Jake ran over to meet them at the gates, ears pricked. They looked both ways down the road outside and waited for a moment, hoping that a familiar doggy figure would bound out from behind a tree, or appear from around the bend in the road, but there was no sign of Chloe. The hot day had turned into a humid, sultry evening. Dark, threatening clouds were beginning to roll in from the west. Outside the Grange, there was no one around.

They turned back and began to search the edge of the grounds. But no Labrador came scrabbling from the shrubbery or running guiltily from the bottom of the vegetable garden.

"She's not here," said Emily.

"I know," answered Neil.

They went back to where Charlie and Syd were waiting by the steps.

"She's not with Mom, either," said Charlie. "Syd went and asked. I didn't think she would be."

At that moment, Mrs. Elliott appeared at the top of the steps. "Have you found that nuisance of a dog?" she asked. Charlie shook her head miserably.

"I knew this would happen," said Mrs. Elliott. She sounded so furious that Neil was quite shocked. "This is proof that the dog's just unreliable," she continued. "I never thought it would work out. Let's just suppose, Charlotte, that this is October and you're by yourself at Oxford. What would happen to you?"

"I imagine my friends would help me," said Charlie through gritted teeth. "Like Neil, Emily, and Syd are doing now."

"Your *family* would be quite willing to help you," said her mom with anger, "if only you'd let them!"

"I'm sixteen, Mom," snapped Charlie. "I'm sorry, but I don't always want to be with my family. I want to do other things with my life, too."

Her mother's voice softened, "You're *only* sixteen, darling. I worry constantly that something dreadful will happen to you. Can't you understand that?"

By now, Charlie wasn't really listening. "Let's face it, Mom," she said resentfully, "you don't want me to grow up. Has it occurred to you that you want me around for yourself, so that *you're* not lonely, and *you* don't have to try to make new friends?"

Neil and Emily studied the floor, embarrassed by this family fight. Jasmine, hearing the sudden noise, woke up and strolled over, curious to see what was going on.

"Why won't you just admit," said Mrs. Elliott, sounding close to tears herself, "that Chloe isn't ready to be left with someone like you? I'm sorry to have to say this, but clearly she must not have been trained properly. What with all that sickness —"

"Once!" interrupted Charlie. "And it was nothing —"

"What with all that sickness," her mom continued

stubbornly, "she hasn't been right from the very be-ginning. Even if we do find her again, I'm afraid she'll have to go back to Bolton."

Syd intervened gently. "I don't think that's very fair, Mrs. Elliott." She spoke softly. "Until we know what's really happened to Chloe, we shouldn't jump to any hasty conclusions. Obviously, I'm a bit anx-ious myself, because if there *have* been any problems with Chloe's training, I'd feel partially responsible myself. But standing here arguing isn't going to help us find Chloe, is it?"

The firm, calm way Syd spoke took the heat out of the situation.

"You're right, Syd," said Mrs. Elliott, looking em-barrassed. "I'm sorry. I really shouldn't have spoken like that about your work. It was uncalled for. Come on, let's have another look for Chloe. Tim can help, too."

"Where is Tim?" said Neil.

"Wasn't he with you? Don't you know where he is?" Mrs. Elliott asked Charlie.

"If he won't talk to me, how am I supposed to know where he is all the time?" Charlie's words had a bit-ter edge to them.

Neil thought quickly. He remembered the sneer-ing glances Tim had shot at his sister when they'd come back from finding Mrs. Atkinson. Tim was so jealous of Charlie and the attention he felt she was always getting, it wouldn't be at all surprising if he tried to get back at her somehow. And what more hurtful way could there be than through Chloe?

"I don't suppose Chloe could be with Tim?" Neil aimed his words at Mrs. Elliott. "Do you think he might have taken her somewhere? I mean, he doesn't always seem very happy, does he? I saw him playing with Jake the other day, and I think he misses having a dog terribly."

"I'm sure Tim would never harm Chloe," she said defensively.

"*I'm* not," muttered Charlie.

"No, Charlie," said Neil. "Your mom's right. He might be upset, but I'm sure he wouldn't do anything unkind."

"He's pretty unkind to me from time to time," was Charlie's sharp retort.

Bob and Carole Parker wandered over to the little group. Behind them trailed a weary-looking Sarah. With most of the walkers and their dogs on their way home, Carole had been helping Mrs. Dickens put away the tables and chairs and take down the decorations. Bob had Kip, the mongrel King Street had loaned to Tim and Sylvia Elliott for the walk, with him. He was leading Kip by the collar.

Neil and Charlie explained the situation. Bob looked serious.

"Well," he said, "maybe that explains why I found poor Kip roaming around without a leash."

"Do you think Tim borrowed it for Chloe?" said

Neil. "It certainly would make sense. I don't know how he'd persuade her to go with him otherwise."

"OK," said Bob, "it's eight o'clock now, and from the look of the sky, there's every chance of a storm. We might only have an hour or so of light left. How long have Tim and Chloe been gone?"

"Half an hour at the most," replied Neil.

"Normally, I'd say we should give them some time to see if they come back on their own," Bob thought out loud. "But I suppose I'm right in thinking that Tim doesn't know this area very well. Am I, Sylvia?"

Mrs. Elliott nodded.

"Well then, I think we should call Sergeant Moorhead right away so that the police can keep a lookout," Bob continued. "And perhaps we should also think about splitting up and searching for them ourselves."

Mrs. Elliott called Sergeant Moorhead from Bob's cell phone. After a quick conversation, she turned back to the group. "He'll be here shortly," she said.

"Good," said Neil. "But I think we should do as you said, Dad, and start searching now." Half an hour ago he'd felt really tired, but with the urgency of the situation, his energy had returned. "Why don't Charlie, Emily, and I take Jake with us to search the route we walked this morning, up toward the hill?" At the mention of his name, Jake stood to attention, tail wagging frantically. "And perhaps the rest of you could try the paths up behind the Grange? Will your back be OK, Dad?" Neil added.

"It stood up to today pretty well, actually. I'll be fine," Bob assured him, looking across at Mrs. Elliott. "I'm just concerned about you three going off on your own."

"We know those paths better than anyone, because we use them so often for walking the dogs," said Neil confidently. "Even on the hillside, the walking's easy enough. If Charlie holds on to one of us, she'll be fine." Charlie nodded her head vigorously.

Mrs. Elliott opened her mouth to protest, and then, seeing her daughter's stubborn look, thought twice about it and kept quiet.

"Why don't I give Neil my cell phone?" said Syd. "That way, we can all keep in touch. And I can't go off searching on my own, anyway. I haven't got a clue where I am!"

Mrs. Dickens had been standing behind them, listening to their plans.

"How about leaving Sarah with me?" she asked. "Come with me, sweetheart, and I'll read you a story."

"About hamsters?" asked a sleepy Sarah.

"Of course," answered Mrs. Dickens. "If that's what you'd like!"

At that moment, Jasmine picked herself up from her spot by the greenhouse, and perhaps as she always used to do, walked straight through the middle of them, into the Grange, and up the stairs, looking for Willy Mannion's room and her basket.

"Jasmine will be all right here, too," said the manager. "We'll make sure she's comfortable. You'd better go before it gets dark! Don't forget to take flashlights with you."

And with the skies darkening by the minute, they hurried off their separate ways to look for Tim and the missing guide dog.

CHAPTER NINE

The bars of the gates to the field were black against the indigo-blue of the evening sky as Neil, Emily, Charlie, and Jake turned off the road outside the Grange to begin the route of the sponsored walk for the second time that day.

"Ever get the feeling you've been somewhere before?" joked Charlie.

"Do you think we can get anyone to cough up money for the second time around?" said Neil. Suddenly serious again, he turned toward Charlie and asked, "Are you sure you're all right doing this?"

"You don't get it, do you, Neil?" replied Charlie angrily. "Chloe's my dog and Tim's my brother. I'm not exactly going to want to leave it to everyone else, am I?"

Jake gave a whine of distress at Charlie's sharp

voice, and nuzzled her hand. She stroked his head to comfort him.

"OK, OK!" said Neil defensively. "I get the point. I just didn't want you to do something you were unhappy about. Here we go, then."

They set out along the track. The light was getting dimmer by the minute and the detail of the bushes faded into dark, blurry shapes.

"It must be getting dark now. Hope you've all been eating your carrots!" said Charlie, trying to lighten the mood after her outburst. There was a moment's pause, and then she added sincerely, "I've been meaning to say to you guys how much I really appreciate everything you've tried to do for our family, and for the Association. No matter how this turns out, you've both been fantastic. I won't forget it, I promise you."

"No problem," said Neil, embarrassed by the sudden compliment. "It's all been fun — well, until now."

On their left, the fields fell away toward the river, which in the fading light was becoming a black gash across the landscape. On their right, the dark outline of a clump of woodland hung above them. As they reached its edge, there was a loud crash from the tree branches. All three of them jumped.

"What was that?" cried Charlie.

A bird with a huge wingspan slowly flapped its way out over the fields to begin its evening hunt.

"It's only a barn owl," Emily sighed in relief.

They walked on a couple of hundred yards with Jake in front of them, rooting through the grass at the side of the track. Suddenly, he came to a stop, ears pricked.

"What is it, Jake? What did you hear?" asked Neil, bending down and touching Jake's collar with his hand. Jake growled, shot a look at Neil over his shoulder, and bounded off into the undergrowth on the right.

"Stay here, you two. I'll follow him," shouted Neil, and he dived after Jake into the woodland. Even twenty feet from the track, Neil realized that he had no chance of keeping up with the young Border collie. The beam of the flashlight his dad had given him only covered a few feet in the dense thicket, and he was so unsure of his footing that it became impossible for him to go any farther.

"Jake!" he shouted. "Jake, come back!" Hoping that his dog had caught wind of Tim and Chloe, he tried calling for them, too, but there was no answer. All he heard was a crashing in the vegetation that could have been another person, or Jake, or a deer for that matter.

"What's going on?" called Charlie from behind him.

"Don't know," he yelled back. "Hold on!"

He waited and waited in the gloom. He was just beginning to think that he'd have to turn back, when Jake bounced into the beam of the flashlight and

shot past him back to where Charlie and Emily stood.

"Oh, Jake, we don't need this," Neil said in exasperation as he dragged himself out of the brambles. "This is no time for a game!"

"Whatever it was, I don't think it was Tim and Chloe," said Emily.

"Rabbits, probably," said Neil gloomily. "We're running out of time here. Emily, look at that sky."

Overhead, Neil and Emily could see a foreboding ceiling of clouds that threatened to block out the rising moon. From the distance came a rumble of thunder. Jake gave another low growl.

They plowed on up the track. They walked in silence now, and every crack of a twig, every scrape of their feet on the hard earth sounded deafening.

Suddenly, Charlie pulled on Neil's arm. "What's that?" she said breathlessly.

"Not you, too," said Neil. "I didn't hear anything."

"Maybe *you* didn't," Charlie replied sharply. "Just listen. *Really* listen, will you?"

They strained their ears, but no sound came back to Emily and Neil from the countryside around them.

Then Charlie gave another start. "There it is again," she cried. "It's a bark! From down there!" She gestured toward the river.

"I really can't hear anything," said Neil. "Are you sure?"

"Trust me," said Charlie. "I've got great hearing. Remember, I've always had to concentrate on sounds because I can't see. Is there a way down to the left?"

Neil and Emily peered down the track. They could just make out the hint of a path leading over the field.

"Could be," said Neil. "Let's give it a try."

They picked their way along the curving track as it snaked between hedges and through the corners of the fields, past the dark shapes of old farm machinery. Charlie stopped again. "Now can you hear?"

"You're right," said Emily. "It's definitely a bark."

"And it's definitely Chloe," said Charlie. "Quick, Neil, let's keep going. I just hope they're both OK."

Neil could hear the sound of the water now, and ahead of them he could see the shapes of stone buildings. Then, suddenly the barking became clearer and there was Chloe, bounding out of one of the buildings and up the track to greet them.

Chloe only cared about Charlie. Bottom wiggling with excitement and joy, Chloe clambered all over Charlie's crouched figure, licking her face, while Charlie, almost crying with relief, made a huge fuss over the now dirty Labrador.

"Where in the world have you been, you naughty girl?" she said. "And where's Tim?"

Chloe barked loudly and took a few steps toward the buildings, her tail wagging frantically. Jake went to join her.

"He must be down there," Neil said. "It looks like there are some ruins by the river. I'm sure I remember Mr. Bradshaw telling me there was an old water mill down here. Maybe that's where Chloe's taking us. She seems to know where she's going. Go, Chloe! Show us where Tim is! Good dog!"

The two dogs needed little encouragement and ran down to the buildings ahead of them.

Neil, Emily, and Charlie followed. As they came near the old water mill, they began to hear Tim's muffled voice calling out desperately from inside, matched by a chorus of barks from Chloe.

"Tim, are you OK?" shouted Charlie anxiously.

Even in the dim light, Neil could see the building

was in bad shape. The outer part had no roof, and where the front door should have been, there was only a pile of rubble.

He shined his flashlight into the darkness. It lit up a doorway leading into a second room. "Let me follow Chloe inside on my own," he said. "It's too difficult for all of us with only one flashlight. We don't want anyone else getting hurt today." Charlie and Emily reluctantly agreed.

Carefully, Neil clambered over the rubble and went through the second doorway. "Tim?" he called.

"I'm over here," answered a shaking, frightened voice, barely audible above the roar of the river water.

It took a while for Neil's eyes to adjust to the dark, even with the flashlight. There were gaping holes in the mill roof, through which the sky could be seen, and old rotting timbers lay piled up in one corner. Part of the river ran right through the mill, just inches from Chloe's paws, and the slot where the waterwheel and its paddles had once fitted was clearly visible. Sitting on top of a stone platform on the other side of the water was a miserable-looking Tim. He was drawn up into himself, hugging his knees. The remains of a makeshift wooden bridge trailed down into the stream in front of him. There was a drop of maybe ten feet into its churning flow.

"The wood broke," Tim said in a trembling voice. "It's too far to jump across. I thought no one would ever find us."

"Don't panic," said Neil, joining Chloe on the edge. "If you could make a run at the stream, you might be OK, but it's too tricky from a standing start. Give me a few seconds."

"What's going on?" shouted Charlie from behind him.

"Tim's OK," Neil reassured her, "but we've got a problem . . ."

"I'll call Dad and let them know we've found him," Emily said.

"Let's see what this wood is like," Neil shouted over to Tim, positioning the flashlight so that it pointed at the timber stacked in the corner. He pulled out a couple of pieces and tested them with his foot. They split and crumbled immediately.

"Then again, maybe not!" he muttered to himself. He pulled out more planks, testing them one by one until eventually he found two that seemed stable.

"As I push these over, grab them," he shouted to Tim. "They'll be able to support your weight."

Shakily, Tim got to his feet and looked down at the drop to the water below. In the flashlight's beam, Neil could see that Tim's face was white and scared. "It'll be OK. If this was a balance beam in gym class, you wouldn't think twice about it," encouraged Neil.

Tim put a foot onto the planks and then withdrew it. "I can't," he said.

"Of course you can," said Neil more firmly. "Just look at me. Come on!"

In the doorway, Emily crouched by Jake and held her breath.

"Tell me what's happening," Charlie cried desperately.

"It'll be all right. Really it will," Emily said, then quickly explained what was going on.

Suddenly, Chloe brushed past Neil and darted nimbly across the planks to Tim. She nudged him gently with her nose, then quickly turned around and walked back across the makeshift bridge to Neil.

"Look! Chloe's showing you the way," said Neil. "If she can do it, so can you! Way to go, girl," he added to Chloe, bending down to ruffle the Labrador's fur.

This was all the encouragement that Tim needed. Slowly, he inched his way onto the planks and, with arms stretched wide like a high-wire act, balanced his way across. In the middle, he teetered and doubled over. For a heart-stopping moment, Neil thought he would fall into the water, but he recovered and ran the last couple of feet. Behind him one of the planks loosened by the vibration, banged down into the stream.

"He made it!" cried Emily.

Charlie breathed again.

Tim clung to Chloe in sheer relief at having made it across.

"All right, Tim! Great work, Chloe!" said Neil. *What more does Chloe have to do to convince Mrs. Elliott she's made of the right stuff?* he thought.

CHAPTER TEN

Outside the water mill, Neil and Emily watched as Charlie slipped Chloe back into her harness, talking softly to her and stroking her back. Tim stood beside her, looking small and wretched. Charlie just frowned at him, for once lost for words.

They trudged back toward the Grange in a horrible silence. As Neil's flashlight picked out the bends of the track, Jake walked quietly beside him, apparently subdued.

Halfway to the road, a more powerful beam of light swung down the path toward them. It was Bob and Syd, with Sergeant Moorhead. There was relief in their voices when they saw that neither Chloe nor Tim were injured.

When they reached the Grange, Mrs. Elliott rushed

down the driveway to meet them, wrapping Tim in a hug. "Thank goodness, you're safe," she exclaimed. Then she took him by the shoulders and, looking him straight in the eyes, asked, "What were you thinking, Tim? We were *so* worried."

Tim explained haltingly that he hadn't meant to scare anyone or hurt Chloe. In fact, she'd gone with him willingly enough, once he'd clipped on Kip's leash.

A few months before, when he'd been visiting his granddad at the Grange, they'd got to chatting with old Willy Mannion. They'd been talking about local walks, and the old man had mentioned that when he wanted to think, he and Jasmine used to stroll down to the water mill and sit by the river.

"Willy played there when he was our age," said Tim. "When the water mill was still working." He stopped and gulped. "I needed to think, too, so I decided to take Chloe down there to have a look. Or rather, she took me. She almost seemed to know the way. But then I was stupid," he continued. "I knew it wasn't safe to try to get across to the other side of the stream. The wooden bridge broke, and I was stuck. I tried to get Chloe to go and find help, but she wouldn't leave me until the others turned up."

When he'd finished, there was a pause. Neil felt a large raindrop hit him on the nose, and Jake gave a bark as the wind suddenly picked up.

Charlie broke the silence. "Can we go home now?" she asked in a small, cold voice.

"I think we'd all be better off at home," said Sergeant Moorhead. "Looks like that storm's finally about to break."

Late the next morning, after a much-needed sleep, Neil and Emily walked Jake and Jasmine up to Railway Cottages to see how Mrs. Atkinson was.

"I'm so stiff today," said Emily as they set off.

"Me, too," agreed Neil. "Dad's the only one who's not suffering. His back seems to be completely cured! To be honest, I'm not really looking forward to finishing the walk today!"

They found Mrs. Atkinson sitting on a cushion in the front garden of Railway Cottages with a heavily bandaged ankle stretched out in front of her. With some difficulty, she was pulling weeds from a flower bed and dropping them into a wheelbarrow. Jasmine stepped delicately over the old woman's legs and pushed her face affectionately into Mrs. Atkinson's.

"Come to help with the gardening, have you, Jasmine?" said Mrs. Atkinson patiently, reaching up to stroke the Labrador's neck. "Aren't you a dear?"

"How did it go at the hospital last night?" asked Neil.

"Well, it was a long wait," said Mrs. Atkinson, "but the good news is, there's nothing broken. Just a really bad sprain."

Jasmine wandered off around the garden, then in through the open front door of Railway Cottages.

"Hey, Jas, come out of there!" shouted Emily.

"Let her be. She's all right," said Mrs. Atkinson. "It's nice to see she feels at home. She was wonderful company on the walk. I'll miss her not being around today."

"Well," said Neil slowly, "that's really why we've come, apart from finding out how you are. We wondered whether you might like Jasmine to stay with you?"

"Have a vacation here, you mean? To help you out? I don't know how you Parkers manage with so many dogs to look after."

"If you like," said Neil, smiling. "But if you still get along well in a week or so, perhaps you'd want to keep her. We'd need to tell the Guide Dogs for the Blind Association where she's living, and they'd probably come and visit you to see that Jas is OK, but I'm sure they'd be satisfied when they saw what a good home she had."

Mrs. Atkinson's face lit up. Jasmine walked back out of the house, and placed one paw carefully on Mrs. Atkinson's good leg.

"I think that's a magnificent idea. What kind people you are!" she said. "She'll be welcome company after all this time. I've really missed having a dog, you know."

Jasmine gave a short bark of approval and licked her hand.

* * *

After lunch, Carole gave Neil and Emily a ride to see Charlie. Bob had worked out that, if all the walkers managed to collect their sponsorship money, they would have raised about two thousand pounds. Neil couldn't wait to tell Charlie the good news.

The Elliotts' house was a converted barn set back from Colshaw Road, looking out over a field of blue flax. When Neil, Emily, and Jake arrived, everyone was sitting on the patio. Charlie and Syd were talking in low voices, Tim was reading, and Mrs. Elliott gave the impression of being unable to settle on anything. One moment she was wandering off into the kitchen and moving dishes around. Then she was pacing up and down in the garden, looking anxiously at Tim and Charlie. As Neil and Emily arrived, she pulled them to one side.

"I'm really sorry about Tim's behavior, you two," she said, looking embarrassed. "I told him he should call you to thank you for all you've done."

Neil and Emily didn't know what to say. Neil mumbled that it had been nothing, really, and he and Emily quickly went over to join Charlie and Syd. Emily sat by Chloe on the grass. As she ran her fingers through the Labrador's short, sleek hair, Chloe rolled over to have her tummy tickled.

Charlie seemed subdued, although she cheered up a bit when Neil told her how much they'd raised for the Guide Dogs for the Blind Association. Syd was really excited.

"That's fantastic. It will help a lot toward the advanced training of a guide dog," she said. "It's almost as if you — and everyone who took part — helped pay for Charlie to have Chloe."

"That's awesome!" said Emily. "We get a framed photograph of a guide dog to keep, too. We'll have to have Chloe in the picture."

Chloe wagged her tail as Charlie stroked her absentmindedly.

"How's it going?" Neil asked Charlie.

"Not great!" she whispered, nodding in her brother's direction. "I don't feel quite as angry with him as I did yesterday. But he doesn't seem at all grateful that we dug him out of a hole. And Mom's being even more uptight 'cause she's so worried about him."

Syd nodded her head sympathetically.

"I can't believe it," added Charlie. "What's it going to take to convince him that life's not so bad?"

Neil wasn't sure whether Tim had heard his sister, but suddenly he flung his book onto the patio and shouted, "Why are you all looking at me? Why are you talking about me behind my back? I've had enough! I can't stand being with any of you anymore." Fighting back angry tears, he ran into the house. They heard the sound of doors slamming and then, through the passageway beside the barn, Neil saw Tim setting off down the road in the direction of Colshaw. Neil acted decisively.

"Come on, Jake," he said. "Here we go again. Let's go and get Tim."

"It won't do any good," warned Charlie as Neil headed off.

Tim hadn't gone very far. It was almost as if he hoped somebody would come after him. Neil found him a few hundred yards down the road, hanging over a field gate.

Neil felt angry at Tim's rudeness and ungratefulness. "Look, I understand you're upset, but don't you think you should give Charlie and your mom a chance?" he said quietly as he and Jake reached Tim.

Tim turned and faced him.

"You don't know what it's like." He scowled. "No one does!"

"What don't I know?" asked Neil. "What it's like to lose a dog I loved? But I *do* know — I really do." And he told Tim about Sam, Jake's father, who'd died so recently. When he'd finished, there was a silence. The wind rustled the trees and grass. Tim looked crestfallen, and Jake whined and put his paws up on Tim's legs.

"No one'll ever replace Cosmo," said Neil. "Just like Jake here could never be the same as Sam. But there's always something new — you've just got to look for it. Spend time with us at King Street. Perhaps you could even become a puppy-walker for the Guide Dogs Association. And maybe one day Cosmo will be able to come back. It's not hopeless, is it?"

"I guess not," Tim admitted reluctantly.

"I know it's hard, but you've got to make up with Charlie," Neil said.

Tim nodded and they began to walk slowly back toward the Elliotts' house. As they reached the gate, Neil asked, "How d'you feel? D'you think you can face everyone now?"

Tim swallowed hard. "Yes," he said. "I think so."

Mrs. Elliott was waiting for them anxiously. Tim gave his mom a hug and then, as Chloe padded over to add her welcome, he walked up to his sister and said, "I'm really sorry, Charlie."

As Neil, Emily, and Jake prepared to leave half an hour later, the Elliott household was a much happier one.

"I must say thank-you to you two," said Mrs. Elliott. "You've both been really good friends to Charlie and Tim. Thanks to you, and to your sponsored walk, we all feel much happier about being in Compton. I always thought I'd feel terribly lonely when Charlie goes to Oxford, but now . . . well, it doesn't seem so bad after all. Now I know Tim and I have friends we can rely on!"

Syd's cheery face appeared at Mrs. Elliott's shoulder. "Compton's great, isn't it?" She smiled. "Just tell your dad, Neil, that if he ever needs another helping hand at King Street Kennels, he should give me a call. Maybe it's time I moved on from Bolton."

Neil grinned back. "You'd better watch out, Syd. We just might take you up on that!"

Charlie appeared from inside the house with Chloe in her harness.

"We need a ride up the road, Mom," she said.

Neil and Emily looked puzzled.

"Well, we've got a walk to finish, don't we?" Charlie smiled.

From behind them, they suddenly heard Tim's voice. "Can I come, too?" he asked.

Charlie turned around, surprised, and Chloe pulled forward and gave Tim's hand an affectionate lick. "Yeah," Charlie said, smiling. "Of course you can. Two's good company, but six is a lot more fun!"